JESUS AND THE NEAR-DEATH EXPERIENCE

JESUS AND THE NEAR-DEATH EXPERIENCE

by

ROY L. HILL, PSY.D.

www.whitecrowbooks.com

ACKNOWLEDGEMENTS

I humbly recognize my wife, Loli Hill, for all her loving support throughout the writing process. I feel the deepest gratitude toward Sharon Milliman in allowing me to share her amazing interactions with Jesus. I revere the writings of the Apostle Thomas, authors of the Gospel of Phillip, and Julian of Norwich. I appreciate Andrea Hill and Jon Beecher in their roles for making this opportunity possible. I thank Beth Rubel for painting a beautiful picture of Jesus for my book cover. Most of all, I give unending gratitude to Jesus, the ascended Christ, who has saved me in all ways.

CONTENTS

INTRODUCTION

A friend felt compelled to invite me to a Bible study. I met his pastor and enjoyed the hour. A few days later, I dreamed about desperately trying to open a small, wooden box. My efforts were being thwarted, however, by some unseen force. Eventually I succeeded after a valiant effort but then came upon a young blond-haired man dressed in black. He was sitting on a bench looking at me sullenly. Intuitively, I knew that this was the individual fighting to keep me from opening the box and asked him, "What was in the box?"

The young man flatly answered, "Jesus was in the box."

"You can't keep Jesus in a box!" I exclaimed, then woke up.

I told my friend about the dream. He, in turn, relayed its contents to his pastor who reacted with wide-eyed surprise. Apparently, the pastor had just created a promotional church video on YouTube showing this exact spiritual theme. In the YouTube video, two individuals were sitting in a car. One of them was trying to keep God in a small box. The other objected,

"You can't keep God in a box!"

I mulled over the importance of the dream in my mind. Based on the blond man's futile struggle, I understood that Jesus is bigger than human ideology. The responsibilities and activities of the ascended Christ, eons prior to and after his earthly ministry, remain largely unknown. Even our knowledge of His life's ministry is confined to a handful of ancient texts. Christian theologians could make a cogent argument that the nature of Christ, the Son of the infinite God, largely exists outside human comprehension. Yet, the Christian Church has kept Jesus in a box stuffed with ideologies. The Protestant Reformation was a reaction to spiritual confinement five hundred years ago; newly literate people demanded accountability and changes in doctrine. As humanity continues to develop into the modern era, the species may be at the verge of entering a new kind of reformation. Indeed, the signs are increasing. For example, Western culture appears to be shifting away from the religious status quo, both in practice and doctrine. According to the Pew Research Center, segments of society, especially the youth, affiliate less with religious organizations as evidenced by a gradual drop in church attendance over the last 30 years. Many sociological factors have been posed to explain this decline. Although the root causes are likely multifaceted, I suspect that a new spiritual awakening is occurring in the world today. The near-death experience (NDE) may have played some role in this awakening; NDE accounts have been dismantling the rusty box. Specifically, people who have met Jesus in death offer updated news about the ascended Christ.

Hundreds of books have been written about Jesus during the last nineteen hundred years. To my knowledge, not one book has been written on NDE testimonies of the ascended Christ. One may ask, "Do NDE testimonies about Jesus matter?" I would counter with my own question, "If you believe in the divinity of Jesus, what could matter more?" Jesus did not ascend two thousand years ago to play harps in heaven. He has remained active in our spiritual lives. Perhaps He has become increasingly active now that humanity has entered a new age of technological and environmental challenges. The increased frequency of near-death experiences may attest to increased divine involvement. It may be to our species' benefit, even to our very survival, that populations start listening to direct messages provided by the ascended Christ and other spiritual beings. So, with strong conviction, I have written the first book about Jesus and the near-death experience. By doing so, I hope to convey key spiritual concepts so that humanity can better meet the challenges of a new, precarious age.

In a spirit of meekness, I do not proclaim myself a guru. Rather, my writing rests on the shoulders of giants. I primarily report the testimonies of ambassadors from heaven, those who returned from the spiritual realm after death. If I deserve any credit, it should be for my efforts to synthesize hundreds of NDE accounts about Jesus. In this manner, I have endeavored to reveal the main themes of divine communication. It is the brave people who shared their experiences that deserve high credit. However, God ultimately deserves the final credit as the true author of all.

Much of what I present may seem new. Some content may unnerve the traditional religious reader. Yet, not everything that seems fresh is really original. There are several ancient Christian writers who have been silenced, or ignored, by those who tried to stuff Jesus into a small box. I revitalize some of these controversial writers for one purpose: their messages correspond and support the testimonies of near-death experience accounts. Consequently, I frequently quote these ancient contributors alongside NDE accounts of the ascended Christ. The three texts I use most are *Showings*, from Julian of Norwich, the *Gospel of Thomas*, and the *Gospel of Phillip*. I also include more traditional sources, such as the four canonical gospels, and a few personal mystical experiences. I will briefly introduce each source in turn. But first, let me say more about my primary resource, individual near-death experience accounts.

NDE Accounts of Jesus

Near-death experiences are more common than many people realize. According to a 1982 Gallup and Proctor survey, 15% of Americans reported having an unusual experience when close to death.[1] If only three percent of Americans experienced a full blown NDE, then millions of citizens have peered beyond the earthly veil. The largest collection of written accounts can be accessed through the Near-death Experience Research Foundation website (NDERF).[2] Constructed by Dr. Jeffrey Long and his wife, Jody Long, over 4,000 anonymous NDE accounts, as of this writing, have been made available to the public free of cost. The NDERF website has been an invaluable resource for my published work; these ambassadors from heaven serve as my portal to the spiritual realm. In order to synthesize reports from beyond the threshold of this life, I have read almost every NDERF submission and incorporated repeating themes throughout this book.

Since physical death is universal, people who die and return mirror society: agnostics and clergy, Buddhists and Jews, janitors and surgeons, children and elderly, housewives and movie stars. Despite this broad disparity of backgrounds, reports of the ascended Christ appear remarkably consistent. Consequently, it was easy to synthesize and categorize related accounts into several broad categories. In this manner, the reliability between NDE reports of Jesus may speak to their validity.

Let me add one quick note on referencing NDE accounts in the book. I took the liberty of making minor grammatical corrections for readability. However, I made my best effort to preserve the original content of every NDERF submission.

Near-death experience accounts of Jesus are relatively common. According to NDERF research conducted by Jody Long, people who visit the spiritual realm encounter Jesus more than any other religious being.[3] Given this relatively high prevalence, accounts of the ascended Christ appear highly relevant to both Christianity and the near-death experience. In other words, the reintroduction of Jesus seems appropriate to modern times. The current work will approach many interesting and fresh topics. We will grapple with a number of core questions throughout the chapters: who is Christ; what does Christ say; how does Christ transform people; what is Christ's relationship with the church; how does Christ foster salvation? I suspect that many readers will find these new revelations by Christ to be a little surprising, if not wondrous. Furthermore, they may find practical application that can potentially facilitate personal spiritual transformation. As will be discussed throughout the book, many NDErs became deeply transformed by their interaction with the ascended Christ. One of the earliest NDE accounts of Christ was written by Julian of Norwich. I submit that Julian of Norwich's NDE, although ancient, remains relevant for the present age.

Julian of Norwich

Julian of Norwich produced one spiritual book, *Showings*, also known as *Revelations of Divine Love*, in 1393 CE.[4] Although she was not an author by occupation, Julian felt compelled to document her NDE. Of historical note, Julian of Norwich has the distinction of being the first female to author a book in the English language according to the United Nations Organization for Education, Science and Culture (UNESCO).[5] Due to the relative fog of the medieval period, not much is known about her life other than that she served as a parish anchoress. Specifically, she devoted her life anchored to the parish and secluded in prayer. Even Julian's proper name has been lost to history. She is simply known by the name of her parish home, the Church of St. Julian in Conisford England, at Norwich.[4]

Julian of Norwich lived during the high middle ages. The date of her writing places her as a contemporary with Geoffrey Chaucer, who authored the *Canterbury Tales*, a favorite reading assigned by high school English teachers. Despite the popularity of Chaucer, there is no comparing the literary prowess of these two writers. Julian of Norwich stands heads above her medieval contemporaries, even writing beyond important spiritual writers of her day. Edmund College theologian James Walsh, made this glowing assessment, "Julian's book is by far the most profound and difficult of all medieval English spiritual writings."[4] In my own opinion, *Showings* demonstrates a deeper complexity than most spiritual books written today.

Julian of Norwich has never been a household name. Her lack of notoriety may reflect the unusual content of her work. Her book, *Showings*, conveys deep theological concepts based on personal experiences, much of it considered unorthodox and mystical. I find it most impressive that her work survived the ebbs and flows of history. Wielding vast political and religious power, the medieval Catholic Church could have readily convicted Julian of Norwich of heresy and burned her at the stake. Perhaps she was saved by her relative obscurity. After all, few would study the book of an obscure anchoress, or any woman, in the high middle ages. Fortunately, times have changed. Julian of Norwich's book can easily be purchased online at all the large online bookstores. Thanks to ready access in the information age, my personal spiritual journey has been impacted by her soul exposition, especially in relation to my studies of near-death experiences.

Julian of Norwich may have been wrongly categorized as a medieval Christian mystic. From my point of view, she was simply conveying what she learned during a near-death experience. In the early chapters of *Showings*, Julian of Norwich wrote about her descent into death after her last rites were read by the parish priest:

> After this the upper part of my body began to die, until I could scarcely feel anything. My greatest pain was my shortness of breath and the ebbing of my life. Then truly I believed that I was at the point of death. And suddenly, at that moment all my pain was taken away from me.[4]

At this point of death, Julian of Norwich transcended physical bondage and was greeted by Jesus and images of the Passion. Throughout her eighty-six written chapters, Julian of Norwich revealed the divine truths shown to her by the ascended Christ. Relevant to the present work, her revelations closely coincide with contemporary near-death experience accounts. So closely, in fact, that I reference her writings frequently throughout my book. Similar referential themes include, but are not limited to: God is love; God's love is unconditional; all creation is infused with God's love; God is the source of our bliss; it is against God's nature to become angry; God does not judge; mercy is none other than continuous operation in love; sin has no substance; sin is our bliss when we triumph over our failings; pain is temporary; pain is necessary for spiritual growth; all people are united in God without division; all people have inherent value as heirs to the Kingdom; Christ was born to be emulated; Christ died for us because of God's love; Christ nurtures us like a mother; people are not condemned but share in universal salvation. Whereas some may consider her writings to be strangely mystical, I consider them core tenets of NDE revelation. I submit that God showed Julian of Norwich a direction for humanity to pursue in order to spiritually progress as a species. We need to understand that Christ operates in love, for love. Through the internalization and expression of this reality, the Spirit of God transforms the very center of our being.

Knowing Christ in the Center of our Being

The expression of Christianity was quite diverse at its inception. Various religious positions were expressed in terms of belief, writing, and practice. As the Christian movement became institutionalized, so did its doctrine: the Christian creed became increasingly narrow during the first three centuries following the crucifixion of Christ. From looking at numerous discarded texts, it seems that theology was banned for either being too Jewish or not Jewish enough. Perhaps the greatest threat were the Gnostic Christian writings, which tended to blend Jewish Christian beliefs with ideas borrowed from the Roman mystery religions.[6] Without official set doctrine, the fledgling Christian church became vulnerable to the insidious influence of gentile faiths already established in the empire.

Bishop Irenaeus of Lyon was particularly vehement about eradicating the influence of Gnosticism. Like others of his day, Irenaeus viewed gnostic texts to be inconsistent with the message of the four canonical gospels.[7] As the Christian doctrine became solidified in the late Roman Empire, the banning of these texts became official. Many books were burned, including all Christian epistles and gospels deemed heretical by the early Catholic institution. The final nails were pounded in the gnostic coffin when the New Testament was more or less finalized in 367 CE by Bishop Athanasius.[8] The 27 books selected remain Christian cannon to this day.

Until the mid-twentieth century, only fragments of these ancient gnostic texts survived the early Christian purging. Thus, religious scholars had been unable to objectively critique banned Christian writings. The situation dramatically changed in 1945. Two Egyptian farmers from the area of Nag Hammadi stumbled upon an old earthen jar embedded within the rocky cliffs lining the Nile River.[7] The jar, sealed in a large earthen pot meant to age wine, contained 53 ancient gnostic books written on papyri in the Coptic language.[9] Apparently, the local monks believed that the texts were worth saving from fanatic destruction. It is amazing, if not miraculous, that this large earthen jar survived the passing of the centuries unscathed.

The 53 gnostic texts have collectively become known as the Nag Hammadi scriptures. Curious about most religious viewpoints, I have read the more celebrated texts. Although their historical pertinence remains absolute, I personally believe that most ancient gnostic texts lack much divine inspiration. I understand why most of the texts were rejected by the early church.

The Nag Hammadi scriptures were written at different times by individuals who were scattered throughout the Roman Empire. Not surprisingly, these texts are not homogeneous. So, when I say most lack authority, I am not making a blanket assertion. From my standpoint, two Nag Hammadi texts resonate powerfully: the Gospel of Thomas and the Gospel of Phillip.

Both the Gospel of Thomas and the Gospel of Phillip are considered gnostic texts. I concede to their gnostic flavor, but do not categorize them within the movement of Gnosticism. The religious doctrine of Gnosticism can easily be confused with the broad term "gnosis." The former refers to a complex set of ancient Christian religious beliefs whereas the latter refers to spiritual transformation by knowing Christ within. Gnosis is a little like the idea of taking communion. By ingesting the nature of God, truth sets us free by experientially transforming the center of our being. From the gnosis point of view, wisdom requires openness. Openness, in turn, facilitates wisdom. Based on this broad understanding, the gospels of Thomas and Phillip are very gnostic works.

Gnostics believe that Christ has the power to transform and elevate our spiritual being. The canonical gospels are hardly exempt from gnostic influence. There are dozens of biblical verses that contain some gnostic elements. One of the more overtly gnostic verses is found in the biblical book of John: "Then you will know the truth, and the truth will set you free." (John 8:32, New International Version) Even today, Christians claim to be made anew by the power of Jesus; a Jewish man who died two thousand years ago. In other words, most Christians seek a personal relationship with God. Herein rests both a basic soul need and a gnostic practice. In this manner, the gospels of Thomas and Phillip do not fundamentally differ from the four canonical gospels. Rather, their respective authors only emphasize ways to establish a connected relationship with Christ through wisdom and openness. Here we come to the main point. Near-death experience reports often appear gnostic. In fact, the mutual support between these two gospels and hundreds of near-death experiences seems uncanny. Accordingly, I reference both gospels frequently throughout the book.

It is my hope to infuse more God-connectedness into the Christian faith through my writing. For some Christians, Christianity has become an intellectual exercise to ward off the fear of death. Allaying fear does not promote relationship. As we will address throughout this book, spiritual transformation goes beyond saying, "Jesus, I accept you in my heart." Rather, lasting change involves accepting Jesus into your heart every day through open prayer, Christ emulation, expressing love, seeking repose through the Spirit, and drinking in the mystery. The renowned scholar, Jacob Needleman, aptly wrote: "Both in our civilization and in our personal lives, the growth of knowledge far outstrips the growth of our being." [9]

Connection with God can only be achieved by inner transformation, not just by ritual or belief. In this manner, we are transformed more by the knowledge of being rather than just accumulating facts. Let's explore more about how these two ancient gnostic gospels relate to the knowing of our being, starting with the Gospel of Thomas.

The Gospel of Thomas

The Gospel of Thomas differs in tenor from the four canonical gospels (Mark, Matthew, Luke, John). The work is silent on the life and ministry of Jesus; not even his miracles are told. Rather, the Gospel of Thomas simply quotes 114 sayings by Jesus.[9] Over half these quotes are recognizable from the Bible, either given/taken verbatim or presented in close variation to accepted gospel scriptures. However, a sizable minority of verses are different. Not only are these new teachings broadly gnostic, but their meanings are somewhat shrouded by open-ended complexity. In other words, the teachings leave the reader asking, "What does this mean and how does it apply to me?" Therefore, successful understanding requires contemplation, inner examination, and perhaps some supportive direction. Fortunately, Jean LeLoup, the author of *The Gospel of Thomas: The Gnostic Wisdom of Jesus*, offers insightful comments on each verse. I have found his insights helpful in understanding many complex quotes.

Many Christians believe that the Gospel of Thomas is heretical. Unfortunately, their opinions are usually based on hearsay; few Christians have ever read the book. Just because one apostle became influenced by the teachings of Jesus somewhat differently from the other apostles doesn't negate his quotation selection. Personally, I find that the Gospel of Thomas conveys brilliant wisdom that resonates with the authority of Christ. I challenge the curious seeker to read the text and develop their conclusions.

The high correspondence between gospels lends a degree of credibility to the Gospel of Thomas. Interestingly, some scholars propose that the Gospel of Thomas originated as a proto-gospel. The proto-gospel model theorizes that the teachings of Jesus were first written down by the apostles. These proto-gospels provided the foundation of the four canonical gospels, a later integration of Jesus' life history, ministry, miracles, and teachings from a wide collection of oral and written sources. If this theory holds true, then the Gospel of Thomas may be the only surviving transcript of Jesus' original teachings.[9]

As mentioned in the last section, the Gospel of Thomas complements the testimonies of people who have shared near-death experiences. Such inter-reliability supports the notion that the historical Jesus and the ascended Christ speak in united voice, despite that voice being separated by millennia. The core theological areas that cross-validate include, but are not limited to, the following: everything in the universe is an expression of God; all people are equal in worth without division; the Kingdom of God is not a place but a state within and without; childlike openness to the Spirit leads to wisdom and spiritual growth; Jesus transforms us through a tended, refining fire; ego is an illusion which disconnects us from the Real; the path of the world, or ego, is akin to living in spiritual death; to renounce ego, we may first need to experience ego; to be focused on God we need to be "passerby" during life and avoid strong attachments to the world; being genuine in love is central to the Kingdom whereas religious ritual has little importance; the awakening that follows connectedness creates movement and repose, or a state of dignified peace when handling life difficulties.

The Gospel of Phillip

The Gospel of Phillip was another lost text found among the Hag Hammadi scriptures. The longest of the Nag Hammadi texts, the gospel addresses many diverse spiritual topics important to the spiritual interests of the author(s).[10] Dating back to 150-250 CE, the Gospel of Phillip was written long after Phillip was martyred, probably by Christian adherents bestowing homage to Phillip.[11] The texts may reflect the spiritual interests of the early church, particularly those adhering to a gnostic bent.

The Gospel of Phillip lacks a strict cohesive structure.[10] Despite the organizational shortcomings, the Gospel of Phillip is a remarkable work. I can only describe the wisdom conveyed as deeply profound. Although parts of the gospel resonate little with near-death experience, there are numerous sections that resonate highly with NDE testimonies. Like the Gospel of Thomas, these consistencies make the Gospel of Phillip quite relevant today. The sections that resonate most with the near-death experience include, but are not limited to, the following: all beings are united as sons and daughters of God without division; Christ was born to heal our wound of separation and bring us into unity through the Spirit; the Spirit aligns each person and brings them into unity and a state of repose; the Spirit of God rests within all creation; like a rainbow, Jesus transforms each soul with a unique presentation that best connects them to God; embracing the world leads to addiction and spiritual death; connection to God frees people from worldly bondage; when we experientially know the divine, we become like the divine; all persons have equal value as eternal beings of God; as heirs to the Kingdom, our value never wavers; we have nothing to fear.

Personal Revelation

In this book I have included personal experiences that I believe to be divinely inspired. However, I feel conflicted in my sharing. I try to see myself as a humble servant. Somewhat shy and self-effacing, I do not seek homage or any type of guru attention. I'd rather celebrate the spiritual experiences of others, especially those who share near-death experiences. Yet, I cannot deny that I have repeatedly received spiritual messages for the last two years. Moreover, some of those mystical messages enhance certain points in my spiritual writings. Perhaps these messages were never mine to choose, but rather God's messages meant to be shared.

I do not claim that God or Jesus wrote this book through me. More pointedly, I am not an empty vessel transcribing the infallible word of God. Yet, I do claim that I repeatedly receive direction through imagery, light, and dream. Usually I receive brief images of symbolism, usually conveyed in simplistic drawn form, accompanied by a flash of bright light. These usually occur while I am in the hypnagogic state, the meditative place between wakefulness and dream. My spiritual dreams can easily be differentiated from standard dreams by their vivid content, amazing organization, and deep symbolic meaning. They may also be accompanied by flashes of bright light, visitations from deceased beings, and followed by an immediate awakening. Ordinary dreams, conversely, are usually the byproduct of the brain consolidating memories. Thus, their content displays the residual, chaotic, fragments of life. If my standard dreams convey symbolic content, they typically manifest my personal needs and fears. In this manner, images flow through the night; choppy, loose and surreal.

I know that my spiritual images and dreams are divine communications. For this bold assertion, I offer no proof or evidence beyond the inherent authority of my writing. Given my scientific background, I understand and honor people's skepticism, especially since my audacious claims are not supported by empirical evidence. Indeed, I would not have believed my own writings three years ago. Thus, I will not put forth any persuasive arguments against the skeptics; readers can take whatever value they see in my mystical experiences. For readers who choose to dismiss them entirely, I only hope that they find something worthy to mull over in my writing. So with a bit of indulgence on the reader's part, let me share a little more about my mystical experiences.

Whenever I have a spiritual question, or experience an area of confusion, I ask for spiritual guidance. More often than not, I receive an answer through image, light, and dream. For example, I initially debated whether to include the Gospel of Thomas as a reference. Although I immediately recognized the book's value, I was reluctant to treat these ancient gnostic texts like scripture. I asked God what I should do. I received an answer that night from an image.

An image was inserted in my mind as I woke up from sleep. The image, lasting maybe a third of a second, was of twelve blue circles organized in three rows of four. Of interest, each circle comprised three connecting blue feathers. I immediately understood that each circle symbolized one apostle. As to the meaning of the feathers, I was completely stumped. With a bit of Internet research, I learned that early Christians once forged three feathers into signet rings. The ancient meaning of these three individual feathers represented the virtues of *charity, hope*, and *faith*.[12] The color blue, especially in the Eastern Orthodox sect, often represented the heavenly love of *truth*. With this information, the meaning of the image could now be deciphered. The twelve circles represent the twelve apostles. The blue color represents that each apostle conveyed truth regarding Christ. In accordance with ancient practice, I suspect that these converts passed down the words of Jesus with precision. In doing so, the apostles imparted three important truths: charity toward the oppressed; hope in salvation, and faith in Jesus.

Feeling relief that my question had been answered, I moved boldly forward in my writing. Not only did I include Thomas, but referenced other apostle traditions as well. In this book, I have focused on the Gospels of Thomas, Phillip, Mark, Matthew, Luke and John.

Canonical Gospels

The four biblical gospels, Mark, Matthew, Luke and John, are considered the written gold standard for the Christian faith. Not only do they contain the richest teachings of Jesus, they are the most authoritative. Trusting in their authority, I reference the canonical gospels frequently throughout the book. The basis of my trust has been founded on the word itself. Call it grounded faith or wishful thinking, these teachings of Jesus resonate as truth for many people. Can I prove that Jesus actually spoke the words found in the gospels? Unfortunately, I must rely on my faith in the Jesus message. Like the Gospel of Phillip, the four canonical gospels were written decades after Jesus was crucified and the apostles martyred. Although their names are unknown to history, the authors of the gospels were likely students of the original apostles. Specifically, the Gospel of Mark was written in 70 A.D.

Mark was followed by Matthew and Luke in 80 A.D. John may have been written from 90 to 100 A.D.[7] Lastly, Philip may have been written around 150-250 CE.[11] Only the Gospel of Thomas may have been originally authored by an apostle, although this is still subject to debate.

The traditionalist may question my frequent use of the Gospel of Thomas and the Gospel of Phillip. It is not that I revere them more highly than the biblical gospels. Rather, I see each gospel as an enrichment of the broader Christian perspective—an integral part of the whole. In other words, each apostle contributed his own understanding of Christ when teaching the Word; each one's unique emphasis was colored by his own interests, disposition, and morals. Yet the general core values (charity, hope, and faith) remained consistent. The advantage of diversity is that one gospel may resonate more strongly with a certain type of seeker than another. Perhaps it was for this reason that Jesus selected twelve apostles instead of one. I reference the gospels of Thomas and Phillip frequently because they correspond nicely with NDE testimony. I suspect many readers will have the same epiphany as they read further into the book. It may be no accident that the Nag Hammadi scriptures were miraculously found just seventy years ago. This date corresponds with the dawn of widespread NDE reports, starting with George Ritchie. Could it be that these ancient texts came to light, literally and figuratively, on the cusp of a worldwide spiritual revolution? Time will tell.

The Purpose

Spiritual discovery underlies the purpose behind my writing *Jesus and the Near-death Experience*. The message of Jesus did not cease two thousand years ago. Jesus, the ascended Christ, has more to impart as humanity develops. For readers exclusively comfortable with traditional presentations of Christ: this book may not be for you. I have no desire to be a stumbling block for others. For readers ready to be challenged, to wrestle with ideas beyond their comfort level: be ready to marvel. In the Gospel of Thomas, Jesus explained the discovery process thusly:

> Whoever searches must continue to search until they find. When they find, they will be disturbed; and being disturbed they will marvel and reign over All.[9]

Near-death experiences, by their inherent nature, are testimonies that lead us to marvel. NDE experiences represent God-sized experiences that lead us down the unknown road. I hope that every reader will be disturbed in a way that leads to marveling. In order to choose the path of expansion, however, the reader cannot keep Jesus in a box. To connect with God, in divine knowledge, the searcher must be open to endless possibilities. For God is endless, in all ways, as a being of infinite creation. By learning the nature of God, we begin to discover our purpose. In that discovery, we begin to value ourselves and connect with the Father. By connecting with the Father, we discover our own mission. Finally, through connection and learning, we gain inner peace and wisdom.

CHAPTER ONE

DREAM AND VISION

What could be a better divine gift than direct communication from Jesus? I find it perplexing that some Christians dismiss mysticism, even claiming it to be the work of the devil, when the gospels describe mystical interactions with the ascended Christ by the apostles. Why should afterlife communications with Jesus end two thousand years ago? After all, no one can explain exactly how the ascended Christ communicates through people today, whether by subtle or overt means. Since humans know very little about God, or the ascended Christ, almost everything about Christianity is mystical. On what authority do religious experts limit God? How can some claim Jesus lives within the human heart, on the one hand, and dismiss testimonies of direct divine involvement, on the other? I have been cautioned that my dreams and brief visions may be the work of the devil. I have rejected those warnings. The content of my messages, as I see them, cannot be from the devil because they are love-based. More pointedly, they help me spiritually grow toward the good. Accusations from certain Christian corners remind me of how the Pharisees accused Jesus of using the power of Satan to cast out demons. Jesus answered them assertively:

> Any kingdom at war with itself is doomed. A city or home divided against itself is doomed. And if Satan is casting out Satan, he is fighting against himself. His own kingdom will not survive. (Mark 12: 25-26)

Only God can decide how my prayers are answered, not any human being. Thus, I will continue to embrace an open dialogue with the divine through dream and vision, so long as God chooses to communicate to me in this fashion. In fact, my decision to write a book about Jesus began with a dream and a vision. Perhaps it might be fitting to begin this book with a personal divine communication.

The Questioning

After finishing my first book, *Psychology and the Near-death Experiences: Searching for God*, the idea of writing about the ascended Christ began to appeal to me. As a rough outline began forming in my mind, I dusted off a number of books I had collected about Jesus over the years. I was looking through *Jesus Through the Centuries,* by Jaroslav Pelikan,[1] when I felt a twinge of anxiety. The book referenced so many amazing New Testament scholars. I soon recognized that there were hundreds of scholars writing about Jesus over the last twenty centuries. I began to feel a bit underqualified. With so many contributors, did I offer something special for the public? Well, my knowledge of the Bible was above par given my personal readings and undergraduate coursework as a Religious Studies minor. Unfortunately, this hardly qualified me as a New Testament expert. Alternatively, writing about Jesus within the context of the near-death experience was both original and bold. No one, to my knowledge, had yet tackled the task. So, I wondered whether I was meant to write a book about Jesus and the near-death experience. I reminded myself that Jesus selected ordinary people to serve as His apostles, skipping over the prestigious experts of the day. Perhaps there was an advantage in writing something fresh without being boxed in by preconceived doctrine. Still, how could I be sure? I put down the book and gave forward a quick prayer for guidance. That night I had a spiritual dream followed by a vision.

The Dream

My dream began like most dreams, disjointed and surreal. Accompanied by several companions, I was hustling through a dark landscape of trees, gnarled roots, and thick underbrush. There was little time to lose, I understood immediately, to escape the roaming bandits who meant us violence. I knew the bandits to be part of a large, heartless mob that ruled the earth, spiritually lost, preying on a few surviving devout people oriented toward God. Our little spiritual band made it to a cave and joined a larger group. I knew that we would all be leaving soon to find new refuge under the veil of semi-darkness. I believed the situation to be hopeless. Surely I would be discovered and killed by my pursuers. Only reliance on God sustained me.

The scene abruptly changed. Suddenly I found myself standing on a fishing boat. I was floating across a large, deep lake, making my way toward a stark church on the far shore. I suspected that this church was some kind of sanctuary from the violence that had earlier pursued me. It was a bright, sunny day and the water was calm. Unlike the prior foreboding scenes, I perceived peace and safety. By God's hand, I had escaped my doom. The scene shifted again, for the last time, as I found myself standing in the sanctuary of a medium-sized church.

The Vision

The church appeared to be of 19th century Midwestern architecture, except that the sanctuary had been built on the second floor. Although the design was familiar, the physical state was in decrepit disrepair. The small church was not a beautiful testament to the divine, but rather a barren shell of its past glory. The sanctuary was fully stripped, gutted, and missing its roof—protection from the hostile elements. Also absent were the religious symbols, statues, religious murals, radiant stained glass, and rigid pews. I was reminded of black and white pictures of German churches bombed by the Allies in World War II. Like those bombed-out shells, the sun poured into the sanctuary through the roofless ceiling and glassless windows. It would have been completely opened to the elements save for the drab brown, brick walls. Despite its austereness, the sanctuary was filled with many people, including men and women of different races and backgrounds. Everyone was lined up tightly in rows, patiently waiting for something important to happen. Yet, no one in the room, except for me, seemed anxious or curious about what was to come. It was at the start of this scene that I realized my dream was more than a dream.

How do I know that my dream was more than a dream? First, there was a lucid quality to the experience. I became acutely aware of my surroundings and my thoughts—even becoming aware that I was experiencing an altered dream-like state. Although I was aware of myself, I stood impassively apart as a third-party observer. I sensed that I was taking everything in without the mediation of ego. It wasn't that I was so much detached from transpiring events, but more that I embraced my new reality without judgment. For these reasons, I speculate that my soul was in the driver's seat of the experience. Second, the quality of the experience changed. Unlike the jumbled activities preceding the sanctuary scene, the dream coalesced into an organized flow of highly symbolic, sequential events. In other words, a meaningful plot unfolded in my dream within real time. Finally, the entire plot was vividly imprinted onto my mind. Consequently, I did not have any difficulty recalling content when I woke up. I might claim that I remembered everything, except that I have the odd sense that my soul was also receiving information and experiencing feelings my brain never registered. What I do know, with certainty, is that I usually do not dream with such lucidity. So, what do I make of this flowing dream filled with symbolic meaning? What do I make of the knowledge downloaded into my mind? My dream was, to my firm belief, more than a dream. My consciousness was somehow transported from a place of spiritual dream into a spiritual place of vision. So from that perspective, let's return to the unfolding plot of my vision.

As I scanned the lines, I suddenly knew that many in the sanctuary were religious in belief. I also knew, in my mind, that every person living outside the church was dead. Glancing out of the window, I witnessed a bleak, reddish-brown landscape purged of life. Not wanting to vacate the safety of the sanctuary, I joined the cause of the living and stood in line. The occupants of the church did not have to wait long for something important to happen. Nurses soon entered the sanctuary and began giving them shots. Specifically, they would come behind every person and inject them with serum using a large syringe. The medicine took immediate effect by inducing a grand mal seizure; causing the recipient to fall, convulse, waken, and stumble. However, the seizures did not cause death.

Interestingly, I recognized one of the recipients of the injection. He was an acquaintance from work who professed to be a strong, fundamentalist Christian fully dedicated to evangelization. He also fell to the ground and convulsed. Somewhat perplexing, he did not protest against the procedure. In fact, there was no unrest from anyone. Every person seemed to be oblivious to the painful after-effects of the drug. Moreover, everyone waited patiently to receive the serum by their own free will. Why they would do this suddenly became clear in my mind: the medicine inoculated people from whatever killed life beyond the church walls. In other words, people were lining up, waiting to be saved.

Just as I thought the injection process would continue without variation, a peculiar deviation in procedure occurred. One person in line received a shot in the neck without the needle in the syringe. He did not convulse without the serum, but neither did he die. Apparently, he was saved by some other means. It became my turn in due course. I looked over my shoulder to see a tall woman dressed in a vintage 1950's white nurse uniform, hat and all, with a large syringe in hand. Her face was completely blotted out by a gray fuzzy smudge, similar to a disguised face seen in a television crime show. I noticed my syringe also lacked a needle. I then received an injection without the serum; one of the few inoculated without subsequent pain. The nurse moved forward and gave an injection to a woman in front of me in line. She received the serum and convulsed. And so the process continued, down each line, until everyone was serviced. At the point of completion, everyone fled the church in a rush. I somehow understood that they would become scattered across the world to serve God. I, on the other hand, remained alone in the church.

I began to walk toward a gap in the church wall. I wanted to join those leaving the church in order to accomplish whatever world mission awaited me. Walking a few feet from the edge, I heard a commanding voice in my mind announce, "You are Jesus." I would best characterize my swift emotional response as being one of distaste. Such a proposition appeared blasphemous from my spiritual understanding. Interestingly, my revulsion was the first strong negative emotional reaction that I remembered during the vision. "No!" I replied in my mind, "I am not Jesus." As I took another step toward the edge, the bottom of the church crumbled beneath me. Rather than falling, I remained floating in mid-air. My attention was diverted to the gray clouds parting above. I noticed rays of bright, white light stream downward in an otherwise leaden sky. At that point, Jesus descended.

I felt surprise to see Jesus rapidly descend toward me. Jesus did not appear as I might have expected. I always pictured him as a tall Semitic man with olive skin, a long thin nose, and pronounced eyebrows. The Shroud of Turin probably best represents my mental template. Yet, the physical presentation of Jesus I witnessed clearly came from the European Catholic tradition. Jesus appeared as a friendly Italian dignitary in likeness, with a slight close-lipped smile, neatly trimmed beard, and a set of perfectly proportioned Roman facial features. But unlike the typical Catholic depiction, the descending Jesus was not wearing a robe or sash. As I saw Him only from the waist up, Jesus was actually wearing a white cotton t-shirt with a rainbow imprinted on the front. Not only did his physical appearance seem like an odd juxtaposition to me, but so did his behavior, or lack thereof. Jesus remained unmoving, like a plastic doll, as he descended. When he was only a couple of meters away, the plastic, physical presentation disappeared. A vibrant, white light supplanted the traditional image. I knew that this light had energy, movement, and power. Then it entered me. Still floating in mid-air, I made three full rotations. During each rotation, I heard a commanding voice singsong in my mind, "Jesus is heaven – heaven is Jesus. Jesus is heaven – heaven is Jesus. Jesus is heaven – heaven is Jesus." At that point I woke up into the darkness of early morning with my legs and feet tingling with energy.

Reflections

Various questions loomed large after waking from my dream and vision. After the tingling of my legs subsided, interpreting the contents of my vision became an immediate priority. With serious examination and consultation with receptive friends, my understanding of symbolic elements to the vision quickly fell into place, one by one, like pieces to a complex jigsaw puzzle. Quickly it dawned on me that my vision was an answer to the previous day's question: should I write a book about Jesus and the near-death experience? The short answer was, "yes." The longer answer related to the sequence and content of my vision: the vision was meant to serve as a broad template, or directive, for my writing. Before I could transcribe abstractions into text, I needed first to understand the dream and vision. This task would require a fair bit of reflection. The fruits of my reflections are described in this section.

Dreams can easily be over-interpreted. Due to the jumbled nature of the dream I had prior to my vision, I hesitate to go too deep into the symbolism. However, some general conclusions can be made at face value. My dream sequence started with apprehension; I was maneuvering through a dark, spiritually lost world. My companions and I were not part of an armed resistant movement, like heroes revered in action movies, but pacifists hiding in constant fear. I am reminded of early Christians concealing themselves beneath catacombs during the days of the Roman Empire.

I persevered by trusting in God. Would I be unfaltering in real life? I can only hope that I would act so nobly. The dark setting ended abruptly and changed to a scene of serenity. This portion of the dream was a reminder that all tribulations and persecutions are temporary. Returning to my early Christian comparison, most apostles were executed by the Romans. Their demise seems terrible from a human perspective. Yet, all that seems tragic to us, in fact, is well. People who have near-death experiences often report that people make far too much fuss about death. Some lives become consumed with grief, depression, and anxiety. Yet, the overwhelming majority of people who experience death prefer the bliss of heaven. In fact, most argue strongly against returning to their lives on earth. But those who do return know that death is natural and that every soul returns home to the Source in time.

The vision, as I now recognize, was uniquely designed for me; content was selectively downloaded in my mind, suitable to my spiritual experience and understanding. In this manner, interpretation came fairly readily. For this reason, I will strive to interpret my vision more deeply than my preceding dream. My vision began with my standing in a stripped-down church sanctuary. I believe that the dilapidated church represents the state of religion in the world today. Note that I refer to religion in the broadest sense. Although the sanctuary walls had Christian overtones, I believe that the setting was an artifact of my personal religious background. I understood, in my mind, that the vision applies to all religious systems. The parallels apply more to the idea of spiritual sickness than to economic collapse. In fact, I would submit that wealthy religious appearances can be a façade. Specifically, the ornate cathedrals and temples of the world glorify human status rather than glorify God. The church image cut away the pretense and exposed the underlying state of dereliction. Specifically, the larger fruits of God's Kingdom had been eroded by human pride, dogma, conflict, wealth, and other forms of non-Godly, human interference.

Despite the general malnourishment of Spirit in the derelict church, the foundation of religious practice was still built on the bedrock of divine purpose and truth. My vision of a solid church illustrated that point. The steady floor beneath my feet signified faith in God. The drab walls, rising toward heaven, represented the protective force of God's love. Indeed, love appears to be central to most religious teaching, even if the bricks had become scraped and tarnished due to human failings. The presentation of religion in my vision reminded me of a vineyard withered by drought. Although meandering vines remain firmly rooted, the fruit of the season become shriveled due to needed water and nourishment. Likewise, spiritual transformation will continue to shrivel without the sustaining nurturance of Spirit and love. Without change, the masses will only grow hungrier.

Tarnished walls were not the biggest concern, as I saw it. After all, the sanctuary was missing a roof. Roofless religion places the faithful in a vulnerable position to the harsher elements: the violence of lightning, the pelting of hail, and the coldness of winter. Doctrine has an answer for everything, except during tragedy. Pat answers do not give solace to the victimized, lost and grieving; those who have been abandoned to their core. Conversely, the Kingdom of God, as a state of being, protects the suffering through Spirit and love. This will be a central topic throughout the book. Unfortunately, joining the Spirit through love is not easy. Only a minority of people have dedicated their lives to transform a sickening world. Looking out beyond the church, into the wasteland, I saw just how sick the world had become.

The world beyond the sanctuary walls was devoid of God; a spiritual wasteland depicted by reddish-brown dirt. There were no dying bodies, white-washed bones, or other remnants of human activity in my field of vision. Only the black stalk of a burnt-out tree-trunk suggested the presence of previous life. The wasteland did not necessarily depict physical death, or even the final death of souls. Rather, I knew that the scene represented spiritual death; the tree of life had withered. Spiritual death refers to disconnection from the Source within; separation from all that is good and eternal. We are never actually separated in Unity. But we may choose an illusion of separation that can be painful. Without light, darkness reigns in those lives defined by greed, division, and destruction. I wondered whether the vision of the sanctuary, despite its poor health, signaled that religion kept people tethered to God. Although I did not receive any clear divine direction on this matter, I personally believe that religion remains vital to sustaining humanity, despite its serious shortcomings.

Although not every purpose was revealed, several elements of my vision were made clear. I understood spontaneously that the people lining the sanctuary were injected with religious doctrine. Doctrine was the serum that saved people, but not without great harm. Reflecting on the metaphor more deeply, I concluded that religious doctrine teaches morality, faith, and love to varying degrees. These spiritual anchors may be credited with saving the people in the church from spiritual death. It is no surprise, then, that they lined up eagerly in the sanctuary to be saved. Unknown to them, however, the inoculation had been tainted with human influences. These influences had not been received from God; therefore they were short-sighted, at best, and self-serving, at worst. Due to the inconsistencies with the Kingdom, the mixed batch caused pain to the unwitting recipients. Oblivious to the source of their spiritual pain, the recipients stumbled in a confused fog, wondering why they felt sore and fatigued. I believe that this vision has a pointed application to the church today. As explored further in the book, perhaps many of the faithful are unaware of the damage inflicted by embracing inflexible religious doctrines.

A few people, including myself, received the shot without being injected with the serum. It was my sense that they were saved by an invisible antidote. This antidote did not have any physical substance. Only one invisible power can breathe spiritual life into people: the Holy Spirit. Through the transforming power of the Holy Spirit, these non-indoctrinated individuals built a solid relationship with God based on love, openness, and faith. It is my opinion that those who become secure in their relationship with God do not need to feel threatened by differences in ideology.

Once everyone in the sanctuary had been inoculated, the crowd collectively scattered across the four corners of the earth to save the world from spiritual death. Sharing in their enthusiasm, I wanted to join the missionary effort but was immediately interrupted by the commanding words, "You are Jesus." My initial aversion stemmed from my traditional Christian upbringing. Even during this altered state, I accepted the orthodox view, which teaches that Jesus, the Son of God, lived perfectly in spirit and deed. In contrast, my behavior has never been perfect. I wondered, "How can anyone say this!?" But after some later reflection, it dawned on me that my immediate response may have been too reactive. I remembered that people who have near-death experiences talk about God in terms of a unity. Within the umbrella of unity, perhaps I was more like Jesus than I thought.

When the floor crumbled beneath my feet, I became separated above the foundations of human belief. I was no longer grounded on this earth, limited by the trappings of dogma, but was simply a soul ready to receive the infinite nature of God through Christ. I was liberated. As the clouds parted, my full attention became centered on the descending Jesus. The representation of Jesus, as noted earlier, came as a surprise. The portrayal appeared manufactured, presenting in traditional Catholic form. Along these lines, Jesus initially seemed unmoving in his physical appearance, somewhat like a plastic doll sent down from a roof on a string. A couple of weeks following my vision, I began to learn the reason for this type of Jesus appearance.

An NDEr reported that she recognized Jesus from her NDE in a portrait. In this painting, Jesus was standing next to Maria Faustina Kawalska, a Catholic saint. Searching through Bing, I found the portrait. For the interested reader, the painting is titled, "Canonization: April 30, 2000." As described, a nun was standing next to a portrait of Jesus (a portrait within a portrait). To my amazement, I also recognized Jesus from my own vision. Both presentations depicted a man with refined Italian features. However, there were some minor contrasts. Jesus was smiling more in my vision, whereas His expression was more piercing in the painting. Although colors played a prominent function in both appearances, I saw a rainbow, whereas the saint saw a stream of blue, white, and red colored light beaming from the heart of Jesus. Of course, the white cotton shirt in my vision was a more obvious discrepancy from the traditional white robe worn in the portrait. Still, the person was one and the same. So, I wondered, what was I to make of this amazing connection between a saint's portrait and my own vision?

The answer came after I stumbled across a flyer for a memorial service held at Saint Maria Faustina Kawalska Chapel. As I had never heard about this obscure Polish saint before, I realized that these two incidences could not be coincidental. Quickly I purchased St. Kawalska's defining book, *Diaries,* to delve into the mystery of her message.[2] I soon discovered that the 700-page book served as a testament to the saint's mystical, daily discussions with Jesus. I was disappointed, however, that the contents were not the weighty spiritual revelations that I hoped to read. Although I was impressed by some of her spiritual insights, I was disconcerted by the saint's focus on sin, repentance, and constant work toward atonement. These religious themes resonated much more with Catholicism than the NDE. I came to understand that the Catholic image of Jesus symbolized an institutionalized characterization of Jesus. The message of the vision implied that I needed to present a broader, universal, and more personal depiction of Jesus throughout my writing. The image on the shirt instructed me to describe Christ like a rainbow. I did so, faithfully, in chapter three and throughout the book.

In the last part of my vision, the manifestation of Jesus disappeared only to be replaced by pure white, vibrant energy. I rotated three times when the light entered me while thrice hearing the singsong words,

"Jesus is heaven – heaven is Jesus." Intuitively I understood the depiction of unity with God and creation; the very attributes of Christ were the same as the substance of heaven. Not only were they the same, but the identity of creation, and every being within, is united in Jesus. This becomes very difficult for humans, as individuals, to comprehend. We will try to decipher this mystery throughout the book. To whet the reader's curiosity, when we realize who we really are, united in God, then we discover that we share the inheritance of the Kingdom; we exist eternally within a single, perfect whole.

The Calling

It became clear to me, with some reflection, that my vision was an answer to my previous night's prayer. Although I am not degreed as a New Testament scholar, I knew that I was meant to write about Jesus. Consequently, I put self-doubts aside and attended to my work. I believe that my vision was a revelation, a gift, and a blessing. Most of all, it was a calling to serve in a broader spiritual transformation that I believe is occurring on earth. In the following months, the need to heed this call motivated me to study about Jesus and expand my conceptual horizons. The more I read and learned, the more I recognized the themes I had experienced in my vision. With the basic structure set, various pieces of information fit nicely into place. Of all the topics examined in this book, perhaps the concept of unity operates as my cornerstone. For this reason, let us first explore the unity of Christ in the next chapter.

CHAPTER TWO

THE DIVINE UNITY OF JESUS

Who is Jesus? I cannot fathom a larger question. Most theologians tackle the question using the rules set by the traditional Christian church. Others have veered off the safe path. Frequent veering has been a more recent phenomenon as demonstrated by numerous modern writers such as Rob Bell, Michael Morwood, Andrew Harvey and Robert Funk. Personally, I applaud honest attempts to explore spiritual possibilities. But what of the near-death experience? Hundreds of people, just from the NDERF website alone, claim they have met Jesus during their near-death experiences. Given the popularity of modern theologians, why aren't people asking about Jesus from those who have actually met Jesus? After all, NDErs report having asked Jesus questions, received direct answers, and become infused with divine knowledge. In this sense, NDErs are modern-day witnesses to Christ. With so many people making very similar reports, I believe their testimonies should be taken seriously. I generally accept their accounts as honest, as I do most near-death experiences. Their validity does not just rest on my opinion, but on various lines of evidence. For the curious reader, I highly recommend reading *Evidence of the Afterlife*, written by Jeffrey Long, MD.[1]

The numbers of people who dismiss near-death experiences outright appears to be shrinking steadily. People are starting to notice the many compelling first-hand experiences of the afterlife, as indicated by the recent success of NDE books and movies. Despite the growing popularity of the topic in general, no one has systematically analyzed what people are saying about Jesus when they return from death. My goal has been to fill this spiritual void by combing through near-death experiences on the NDERF website. So what have I discovered? Generally, I have found that the person of Jesus in the NDE accounts appears remarkably consistent with biblical accounts of His character and message. Some NDErs learn valuable lessons to take back to earth involving individual purpose, the suitable role of religion, and the need for expanded social concern. Others encounter Jesus as a liberator and a savior. Still others benefit from Jesus as a teacher of divine authority. Practically every NDEr who encounters Jesus, with few exceptions, becomes strongly transformed by His unconditional love infusing their souls.

Many of these topics echo the themes found in the New Testament. In my mind, inter-reliability co-validates the New Testament and the NDE. That is not to discount a certain level of addition, variation, and minor discrepancies between the Bible and the NDE. Personally, I have not become disillusioned over such minor deviations. Given our limited understanding of an infinite God, I would expect a broader, shifted understanding of Jesus as a byproduct of divine revelation. Based on my readings, NDE accounts rarely represent blatant inconsistencies, but rather different slants of Christ's teaching from the infinite context of heaven rather than from a narrower context of earth. There are certainly enough new avenues to explore to last a lifetime; this book may denote the dawn of a new inquiry about Jesus. For example, NDErs generally confirm that Jesus is the Son of God. This may validate the Christian viewpoint, yet in an expanded way: the Son of God has broader meanings and applications within the context of spiritual unity. It is the purpose of this chapter to explore these meanings and applications. In the first section, we will begin discussing the unified identity between Jesus and creation. In the second section, we will look at ourselves as part of the family of God. Finally, in the third section, we will discuss our mission to become Christ-like. Let us begin by expanding our view of Jesus.

Jesus as the Unity of All Things

Following his NDE, Alan reported learning that Jesus is the unity of all things. (NDERF #1760) God has traditionally been referred to as the Heavenly Father, whereas Jesus has been referred to as the Son of God.

This delineation seems easy to grasp, at first glance. It would be easy to compare the heavenly Father and Son with an earthly father and son. However, the attempt to assign human attributes to God reminds me of Michelangelo's painting of the Sistine Chapel; God is depicted as a masculine, white-bearded man sporting pronounced biceps. Understanding God by human analogy represents humanity's feeble, finite attempt to grasp the infinite. Unfortunately, humans lack the intellectual prowess and referential understanding of the divine to succeed in obtaining divine understanding. To understand divine concepts, we must try to grasp the infinite by thinking about the "big picture" more abstractly. This may be especially the case in viewing Jesus as the Son of God. In fact, Jesus called himself the Son of Man more than he did the Son of God. The dual identity of Son of God and Son of Man seems contradictory. How can God, omnipotent creator of the universe, co-exist as man, a measly biological being? Many Christian theologians have attempted to reconcile such contradictions by deliberating on the nature of Christ. There have been endless theories and debates about the Trinity without any final resolution. I refer the reader to *The Quest for the Trinity*, by Stephen R. Holmes, for an appreciation of the topic's complexity.[2] Can one cut through the morass with a greater degree of certainty? It turns out that the question of the dual nature of Christ is central to advancing our knowledge of Jesus, God, and ourselves. Fortunately, people who return from death may be providing the beginning of an answer. To understand duality, one first must understand the concept of unity.

According to many NDErs, there appears to be no separation between God and man. Their assertion may seem senseless based on the preponderance of appalling human behavior. The religious pessimist may ask the opposite question: "Is it possible for people to run any further away from God?" Although this argument may seem to have legitimacy, NDErs still report that there is no separation between man and God. One NDEr wrote, "We are God and God is us." (Carla, NDERF #3493) Despite the fallible nature of humanity, this concept is not new. Hindus and Buddhists have long professed that our true self is part of the One. Even many Christians agree that Jesus lives within the heart of each person. Indeed, perhaps the most profound understanding of divine unity is that God is everywhere. In other words, the full meaning of unity implies that we are completely of God, living as an integral element of the Source. Furthermore, the One resides within us.

How can any person, no matter how saintly, be one with God? I certainly don't have Godlike power, intelligence, or perfection. As a limited, fallible mortal, I recognize that the more I learn, the more I realize my ignorance. I may feel secure under the roof of home, but I am really at the mercy of time and the varied destructive forces of nature. I am also powerless against larger economic and environmental problems that impact my life, just as I am powerless to stop the cruelty of others. I make mistakes in relationships by hurting the people I love. Starting to feel a little bit tired with age, I relentlessly march toward my eventual death. If what is reported has validity, then clearly unity relates to some part of me existing apart from my declining body. Based on NDE reports, this indeed appears to be the case. The remaining section explores the meaning of unity between God and soul.

As the One, God exhibits universal consciousness throughout an infinite universe. Quantum physicists have theorized, and measured, what happens when subatomic particles "come" into existence. Subatomic particles, the unfathomable tiny building blocks of everything, are transformed from a state of energy into mass through conscious observation.[3] To a small degree, our consciousness seems to impact the very structure of the universe. To a large degree, the consciousness of God may manifest and sustain the entire universe. Meaning, God instantaneously transformed a universe made of solid energy, by means of a big bang, into the eventual structure of the universe we see today. An orderly, life-sustaining, eternal universe is the result of God's essence. As described by Julian of Norwich: "God is everything which is good, as I see, and the goodness which everything has is God."[4]

This expression of God's conscious creation, although miraculous, does not follow the traditional concept of "miracles." Rather, God's will becomes manifest via a structured organization that we can measure. For me, intuitively it makes sense that God's intelligence created an integrated set of physical laws that can barely be described by the language of math. Perfect laws must be constructed by a lawmaker, just as a beautiful painting must be constructed by an artist. Flawless structure does not derive from a non-conscious void. By this logic, the laws that govern the universe must have originated from the creative mind of God, who has manifested our universe for about the last fourteen billion years. I submit that everything, down to the smallest subatomic particle, is continuously manifested and infused with God. How does this relate to Jesus? If Jesus is truly the Son of God, then His will, by extension, should be integral to the manifestation of the universe.

Indeed, Jesus discussed His infusion of God-conscious energy into the universe within the Gospel of Thomas:

> Jesus said, "I am the light that is over them all. I am the All; the All has come forth from me, the All has attained unto me. Cleave a piece of wood, I am there. Raise up a stone, and you shall find me there." (Verse 77) [5]

I do not believe that Jesus claimed that His Spirit inhabits, or possesses, non-living objects. Jesus was not an animist. Rather, Jesus seems to be claiming that He was united with these objects, as with all things, because they were created by divine consciousness and creative will. Specifically, God is everywhere and everything. Everything also includes our own human consciousness. But unlike the constantly rearranged particles constructing the physical world, our soul essence remains permanent and pure. As a piece of God-consciousness, it was formed from a blank state, only later to be fashioned by individual experience and choice. Yet, the divine roots of the soul are eternal. For the soul, there is no separation at all from God. Unfortunately, people perceive mostly separation because of our biological limitations and material frame of reference. Julian of Norwich wrote about unity of soul after her near-death experience seven hundred years ago:

> Man's soul is made by God, and in the same moment joined to God... When God was to make man's body, he took the slime of the earth, which is matter mixed and gathered from all bodily things. But to the making of man's soul he would accept nothing (physical) at all, but made it. And so is created nature rightfully united to the maker, who is substantial uncreated nature that is God. And so it is that there may and will be nothing at all between God and man's soul. And in this endless love man's soul is kept whole. [4]

Julian of Norwich speaks powerfully about non-physical creation of souls. Think about the ramifications. If there is no separation between you and God, then God experiences everything you perceive, feel, and think. God even experiences your reading of this sentence. But let's not stop with the individual. Every soul, throughout space and time, likewise contributes to God's collective awareness. Richard, speaking to spiritual beings in heaven, asked to see God. The beings replied:

How can you see that which you are yourself a part of? We are all expressions of God. When you see with your eyes, you see through the eyes of God and he experiences reality through yours. When you speak to God, you speak to yourself. We are one and the same. There is no division or separation. (Richard, NDERF #578)

I would like to note that some NDErs do report meeting the person of God. Paradoxically, God appears to exist both as a collective entity and as an individual. Regardless of form, why would God choose to create individuals, like you and me, from the Self? Put more simply, what is the basic meaning behind our existence? As Julian of Norwich touched upon in the last quotation, love was the motivation. She further elaborates:

I was taught that love is our Lord's meaning. And I saw very certainly in this and in everything that before God made us He loved us, which love was never abated and never will be. And in this love he has done all his works.[4]

Let us explore God's motivation to create from love. Even God cannot love when there is no one *to* love. God created sentient life, and the supporting universe, in order to deeply share in all possibilities of existence. Being omnipotent, God might have imagined all facets of creation without expending the effort at continuous creation. Although all possibilities would have been known, God could not have *experienced* co-created reality by imagination alone. The desire to generate individuality was not motivated by curiosity, since there are no surprises in knowing everything, but rather to share existence out of love; to breathe life from the Self in order to create, share, nurture, renew, and do everything else love entails. We can think of our individual existence as a type of mitosis, or splitting from the Source, as a byproduct of God's love force. Although we are of God-consciousness, individual consciousness and personal will were added as a gift. From this gift, we infuse the universe with dynamic possibilities by our own free will. Our very individuality endows the universe with added meaning. Most importantly, we eventually yearn to return God's love and complete the circle of unity in reciprocal love. Because everything is unified, by loving God we also learn to love ourselves.

In saying "we," I am referring to a vast ocean of life peppered across galaxies and, perhaps, universes layered across multi-dimensional space.

The topic of sentient life beyond earth has been revealed to a number of NDErs. I have yet to read one NDERF submission that claimed human beings existed alone throughout the vast reaches of the cosmos. Those who broach the subject agree that the human species denotes one tiny part of God's infinite creation. We represent one sand grain on an endless beach; a single sentient species coexisting with many other sentient species within a diverse, universe-sized, spiritual singularity. Amazingly, the size of the singularity has no limit. How small-minded of humans to think of ourselves as truly separate and unique. Human beings perceive separateness only due to the illusion of individuality on earth, estranged by dimensional space, human biology, spiritual immaturity, and free reign of choice. But at the very soul of the matter we are eternally part of God's conscious energy, manifested from the Source into an infinite expression of diversity. Jesus says as much in the Gospel of Thomas: "If they say to you, 'Whence have you come?' Tell them, 'We have come from the Light, the place where the Light came into being through Itself alone.'" (Verse 50)[5]

If, ultimately, we all come from the Light, then our true identity is one with God. The illusion of individuality allows for ill-advised, unrestrained freedom; choosing selfishly motivates life paths of ego, greed, and exploitation. The spiritually ignorant feel entitled because they see only division between the self and others. But there is no truth in gauging ourselves to be better or worse than others. Even though some souls are more spiritually advanced than others, we are all equal as parts of the Whole. This seems counterintuitive because people assign personal value to wealth, accomplishments, fame, beauty, and adherence to various cultural codes. In the divine realm, however, such delineations have little meaning to the soul's eternal development and growth. Let me use myself as an example. I have made many mistakes living as a human named Roy Hill. So what? These are only lessons for my soul, necessarily trapped in a biological brain expressing animal needs. If I choose spiritual growth over the eons, by my own free will, I will eventually lose my ignorance and connect with the divine. People judge people based on their short earthly development, living in symbiosis with a human body. Unlike we mere humans, however, God sees time as a block and does not judge any particular moment. As Julian of Norwich emphasized several times throughout her writings: "For just as the blessed Trinity created all things from nothing, just so will the same blessed Trinity make everything well which is not well."[4]

We never die, given that our progression is infinite. Problems that plague us now will be conquered over time as we help each other grow. Through our mutual spiritual advancement, all that is not well will be made well. If everyone truly internalized this premise of collective growth, perhaps we would treat others, and even ourselves, with an inherent, deserved respect. After all, we are all royalty of the Most High. Note that Jesus didn't judge others by making cultural delineations. He never claimed that the Jew was better than the Samaritan or the holy scribe was better than the prostitute. He never coerced anyone to follow him by issuing threats of violence. Jesus only invited people to choose the Kingdom of God by showing them the Kingdom of God. Reading further into the Gospel of Thomas, Jesus said:

> I am He who is from that which is equal; to me was given of the things of the Father. Therefore I say, when it is equal it will be filled with Light, but when it is divided it will be filled with darkness. (Verse 61)[5]

Although darkness exists as a choice of being, division is really an illusion. In reality, everyone is equal because we are part of the Light, the Source of everything. Nothing substantial has ever been created by the darkness. To the degree that we reject the Light, we will create our own temporary darkness due to the illusion of division. Personally, I grieve for those who reject the Light rather than hate them. Although the lost fail to love, they are still a part of God. Unfortunately, they misused God's gifts of individual consciousness and free will. They turn their backs against that which is equal; blinding themselves away from truth, love, and unity. Rather, they embrace selfish division.

Jesus not only speaks of divine unity, but exemplifies divine unity. Susan, during her NDE, witnessed Christ's divine love expanding into everyone, everywhere:

> The whole environment felt and appeared as though the body of consciousness of Christ was alive in each person making up a whole that was expanding beyond the universe. Love was so peacefully exuding from within each presence. (Susan H., NDERF #2543)

Susan's experience may strike a chord with Christians who teach that the love of Jesus lives within each accepting heart. Perhaps more difficult to accept, every human soul is likewise boundless. In other words, we cannot be separate from each other if we all are a part of

God. Denise, during her near-death experience, was shown an inclusive unity while visiting heaven:

> I felt the presence of something immense and eternal standing next to my right. It informed me that the people I was seeing were all those who had ever lived. Yet, here they were alive. It told me that all of them were me! Not only that, but I was each of them! I understood this presence was "God." And then God made it clear that all these people and I were God and that He was us. (Denise V., NDERF #3221)

What an amazing submission. If everyone is me, and I am everyone, then almost everything we believe about ourselves, and each other, is wrong. First, we are not merely animals briefly living isolated in our thoughts. Instead, we are magnificent, spiritual beings interconnected with one another. Second, we maintain an eternal group identity integrated with the Source: we are all sons and daughters of God.

Sons and Daughters of God

If we are joined to God, without separation, then we can claim our divine heritage. In relation to unity, the term "Son of God" does not apply just to Jesus. Even Jesus implied as much. After giving the matter some thought, I find that several biblical scriptures make sense to me now. For instance, no one had ever been able to explain for me the verse Psalm 82:6. The author wrote, "You are gods; you are sons of the Most High." One might overlook this obscure passage, except that Jesus repeated the very same scripture in John 10:31-34:

> Once again the Jewish leaders picked up stones to kill him. Jesus said, "At my Father's direction I have done many things to help the people. For which one of these good deeds are you killing me?"
>
> They replied, "Not for any good work, but for blasphemy, because you, a mere man, have made yourself God."
>
> Jesus replied, "It is written in your own law that God said to certain leaders of the people, 'I say, you are gods!'"

Again, "we are gods" because, like Jesus, we are joined with God as sons and daughters of the Source. We come from royal lineage. In a similar vein, Jesus expressed this same unity when He declared: "The King will say, I tell you the truth, when you did it to one of the least of these my brothers and sisters, you were doing it to me." (Matthew 25:40)

Perhaps Jesus was not talking in metaphor or hyperbole, as many theologians suggest. From a perspective of unity, what we do unto each other we literally do unto God. Moreover, since we all are part of the Whole, what we do unto others we also do unto ourselves. We can only realize our true self by growing toward the divine. We can only grow toward the divine if we stop hurting ourselves by wounding others. Truly, people act in ignorance when they intentionally harm fellow sons and daughters of God.

Unity is a common theme conveyed in near-death experiences. It was not necessary to comb through thousands of NDERF submissions before finding a few sources; almost all NDERF submissions convey at least one message of interconnectedness. This widespread conveyance is not accidental. I suspect that God intentionally emphasizes unity at this juncture of human spiritual and technological development. With the inherent stresses of overpopulation and globalization, God beseeches everyone to cease preying on one other and treat people as brothers and sisters in Christ. In effect, God implores us to love one another by emphasizing this kind of message, "Stop hurting yourselves! You are One!" When I doubted my qualifications for writing about Jesus, God did not simply reply with a "yes" or "no" answer. Through vision, I was directed to write about Jesus within the context of unity. There could not have been a more powerful message than when the Light of Jesus entered my body, rotated it three times, and thrice repeated, "Jesus is heaven, heaven is Jesus." An earlier scene awakened me to another aspect of unity: I heard a voice announce that I was Jesus. I strongly rejected the proclamation believing it to be the voice of heresy. Who was I, a weak sinner, to be compared with the Son of God?! Yet, if we are all united in God consciousness, then perhaps I could be called Jesus. Christine received the same message during her NDE. She wrote:

> I knew that I had felt Christ. I felt the crucifixion and I knew without any doubt that I had experienced exactly what Jesus experienced on the cross. I felt completely one with Him, meaning I actually WAS Him. (Christine, NDERF #1292)

Betty Eadie, in her New York Times best-selling book *Embraced by the Light*, described blending into the brilliant, gold light that was Jesus. She wrote:

> It's hard to tell where one light ends and the other begins; they just become one light. Although his light was much brighter than my own, I was aware that my light, too, illuminated us. And as our lights merged, I felt as if I had stepped into his countenance, and I felt an utter explosion of love.[7]

Not only do we share a unified experience with Jesus, but we also share in a mission to become closer to God. Although I lack the spiritual maturity of Jesus, I share, like many others, His mission to bring God's Kingdom on earth. Like Jesus, my soul is a part of God's infinite being. I am a son of God, just as we are all are sons and daughters of God. In like fashion, we are brothers and sisters to each other. We are also brothers and sisters to Christ and in Christ. It is difficult to wrap the human mind around this endless concept of unity. Douglas conveyed his difficulty understanding unity prior to his NDE. He writes:

> So even at that time I had an elementary understanding of 'Him in Us', but it was far short of comprehending 'Us in Him.' (NDERF #1113)

During his NDE, Douglas learned that our unified identity with Christ flows in a two-way direction: us in Him and Him in us. Jesus understood His bidirectional connection with the Father in the same way. For Jesus said, "The Father is in me, and I am in the Father." (John 10:30) If we are unified in Jesus, then by extension we are also unified in the Father. Again, circles of unity are endless.

There is a conduit of power between soul and the Source. Perceiving disconnection, human beings struggle, seeing the magnificent spiritual being within; the quiet soul unified with the omnipotent power in the universe. Jesus communicated that we can utilize God's omnipotent power, even as humans, by making the body one with our true nature, the Spirit. Only by recognizing our divine self can we merge the two and understand that we are both sons and daughters of God and the sons and daughters of man. In the gospel of Mark, Jesus responds to a man who asked him to "do something if you can." Jesus replied, "What do you mean, 'if I can'?" Jesus asked. "Anything is possible if a person believes." (Mark 9:23)

In the Gospel of Thomas, Jesus said: "When you make the two one, you shall become sons of man, and when you say, 'Mountain be moved,' it shall be moved." (Verse 106)[5]

In response to the challenge made by Jesus, I would say, "Easier said than done." I have yet to see anyone move a mountain. The illusion of separation is too strong while human faith is too weak. Moreover, human beings lack spiritual maturity to surrender ego and orientate their entire being toward God. Although we may be sons and daughters of God, we lack the power of Jesus. Through His connection with the Father, Jesus can make mountains move, if needed.

To the degree that I have accepted that "I am Jesus" in core essence, I can begin to realize some of the divine power of God within. Obviously, I don't claim that I am the person of Jesus nor the living messiah. I claim only that we all share a common divine heritage. Not to boast, I can speak of obtaining a small measure of success. I have applied myself to increase interconnection through openness in faith, faith in understanding, and understanding in humbleness. Perhaps partly for these reasons, I have received divine messages through dream, brief visions, and images of light. Although I still cannot move mountains, my own experiences have brought a radically new place of understanding. I no longer *believe* in God by faith. I now *know* God through experience. I see the Jesus within me. But to nurture better my true divine nature, as a son of God, I need to become more Christ-like.

Becoming Christ-like

What does it mean to be Christ-like? The short answer is learning to be more like God; to live in accordance with our true divine nature. But this answer begs another question, "why Christ?" Jesus was unique because He embodied the unity of God while living as a human. Because Jesus remained unified with the Source, He drew up from the well and drank of the Spirit. Put more concretely, Jesus lived in concordance with God's unified will and taught accordingly. It was not an accident that Jesus was unique. Although unity assumes equality within the All, spiritual beings function at different levels of capability. This is not a question of value, for everyone is equally treasured. Rather, spiritual beings are afforded different levels of authority based on their spiritual development. According to witnesses returning from death, Jesus presents with the highest level of developmental authority. Vivian, from her NDE, writes about Jesus being honored by the angels:

> I was in a very long, dark tunnel moving very rapidly toward a very large, bright light that radiated love. I could hear beautiful, high pitched wind chimes, and I could hear angels singing; legions of angels. They were singing the Doxology. The light was Christ, and I was fully aware of that at the time. (Vivian, NDERF# 430)

Similarly, Eric describes the divine hierarchy in this fashion:

> I would almost describe the experience as having three degrees of light. The light that surrounded me and emanated from the Angels was the first degree of light. The light that filled me from Jesus was the second degree of light. And the ball of light I saw in the distance was the third degree. Each degree of light was greater and brighter than the previous one. (Eric A., NDERF #3326)

In these and similar submissions, Jesus presents uniquely in spiritual development and authority. Jesus not only has a special purpose in heaven, but He had a special mission on earth. Christ's humanity was necessary because the human race lacked the spiritual maturity and knowledge to progress independently toward God. We needed divine assistance to move beyond polytheism, anthropomorphic myths, and animal/human sacrifice. We needed a better way to handle ambition than to subjugate and enslave. We also needed a better way to manage conflict than to maim and kill. Because we were languishing in our own ignorance, God's ambassador, Jesus, was sent from heaven to demonstrate the Kingdom of God through love and service. In other words, Jesus modeled what it meant to be the ideal human as envisioned by God. He was born to be emulated.

Humans were meant to love one another. Jesus was born on earth to model the possibilities of human love. He did so by pouring out compassion for the poor, respecting the lowly and the lost, serving anyone who welcomed his attendance, advocating for the downtrodden and oppressed, forgiving the sinner, revealing the oppressive nature of power and ego, suffering evil with passive obedience, and sacrificing his own human life in service for humanity. Jesus came, and died, so that we could learn to love; to follow His footsteps in service. Which brings up a larger question: what might be our grade, as a species, in our being like Jesus? I fear that humanity's marks would be abysmally low. First, people killed Him. Although many now worship Jesus in most Western countries, few put on His worn-down sandals and continually walk in Christ-like service. Likewise, few regularly practice forgiveness, sacrifice, pacifism, and non-materialistic spiritualism. Perhaps Christians tend to spend too little time trying to be like Jesus. Only by emulating the love of Jesus do we live in spiritual vibrancy.

What would the state of the world be like if humanity had emulated Jesus during the last two thousand years? By walking in His footsteps, I believe humanity would become more tolerant, cooperative, and socially responsible. Teaching my thirteen-year-old son world history, I am dismayed by the sustained record of war, ethnic cleansing, oppression, and other indicators of spiritual stagnation. What a primitive species Homo sapiens has turned out to be—so slow to learn. When will we realize that anger, exploitation, and intolerance do not triumph in the Kingdom of God? What an opportunity God gifted humanity, through Jesus, to move the human species toward the divine. How tragic that humanity has largely rejected that gift. Fortunately, messages from Jesus, the ambassador, were not completely lost. A select minority from all over the world has emulated Jesus, even if the Christ message derives from other spiritual sources. If they hadn't, humanity would probably be in a worse condition than it is today.

I realize that I speak harshly against humanity. I do not write out of anger, but merely out of observation. As Julian of Norwich said, "All that is not well will be well." This means that the reader need not despair. Divine love is unconditional; God never gives up on humanity. God understands that a certain degree of our wretchedness lies beyond our control. Our souls are wedded to a primitive biological brain assailed with strong emotions and base biological needs. Coupled with limited intelligence, human perfection will always be an ideal out of reach. Accordingly, I am not suggesting that anyone can perfectly emulate the spiritual life of Jesus. I only propose that we can act better than our past would suggest. It is not too late to emulate the love of Jesus and pursue a wiser global course. If we reject the wiser path, God will continue working with people to be more Christ-like. If there is any central message to this book, it is that Jesus busies Himself showing us the Kingdom then, now, and always. We only need to put our best foot forward to walk in Christ's footsteps.

I aspire to be Christ-like and help bring forward the Kingdom of God. Success requires a certain degree of confidence, even boldness.

I can do my part by being true to my soul nature. Everyone else has the opportunity to succeed for the same reason. To be like Jesus, who encompasses the unity of heaven, I need to speak with authority and fearlessness about revealed truth. For me, revealed truth often derives from the Bible and the near-death experience. Moreover, I also need boldly to proclaim personal revelation. I hope that does not sound grandiose. I actually proclaim connection out of humility, for I need to be humble and recognize my spiritual immaturity and fallibility. Do I know every truth behind each near-death experience? Certainly this is not the case. Do I know, at every level, the complete meaning of all God has revealed to me through dream, light, and image? I wish it were so, but no. Do I live a perfect, mistake-free life? I fall quite short. In actuality, it is still hard for me see the Jesus essence within because I pale in comparison. After all, I lack the spiritual maturity to come close to accomplishing what Jesus did in a few short years. Perhaps in a million years from now I will act significantly more concordantly with my true divine nature. Although I am of God, I am also Roy Hill the human. Still, I will try my best to live Christ-like.

I sometimes wonder how much, or how little, I have become Christ-like. This probably matters little to God, however, who views time as a block to be observed forward, backward, and all at once. Thus, my current state of development doesn't really matter within the eternal picture. Perhaps it would be healthier to focus on the gradual march toward Christ rather than obtaining immediate flawlessness. After all, my successes and mistakes will be revealed during a life review after I die. Not only will I fully evaluate growth in mission, but I will put this life behind me, simply as a series of lessons, when my soul merges into the ocean of Spirit who is the Source. All that is not well will then be well.

Perhaps too much emphasis has been placed on right and wrong by religion whereas too little attention has been placed on orientation toward Spirit. Clearly, these two ideas are not mutually exclusive. A person consistently living in concert with the Spirit will naturally choose Christ-like behavior. Unfortunately, people mired in shame tend to lose sight of the Spirit. Shame, unlike guilt, is tied to feeling worthless and impotent. Consequently, shame demands attention toward the self, not toward others, or God. Consequently, people who don't like themselves perpetuate maladaptive behaviors; their spiritual and moral growth becomes stagnated. Correcting with love facilitates growth, whereas shaming out of anger facilitates stagnation. As will be explored in chapter four, portions of Christianity have a long history of shaming people. The church, and people in general, need to look at human faults differently. Mistakes are part of the process of becoming Christ-like. Even the lost individual will hopefully realize, eventually, that the selfish path leads to unhappiness. Describing her NDE, Cami eloquently describes our divine mission to learn from mistakes while being human. She writes:

> We exist as life itself, as divinity itself, and we ARE the face of God in this world, every single messed-up one of us, every single rock and tree. We are God. We are Divine. At the same time, we're inherently limited and blemished as humans...
>
> We are each Divinity's opportunity to experience and create a unique face of life, to allow it to shine right through our inevitable, insufferable flaws. And when that particular life form is done, we recycle back into the ocean; a wave that dances and melts back in, to reform and experience anew, moving our way higher and higher up the spiral of lessons. Blessed be those who are cracked, for the cracks are where the light shines through. The veil just makes us think we have darkness inside. (Cami R., NDERF # 2901)

Although we make mistakes, we can focus on the Light of Jesus shining within. Christians correctly say that Christ lives within us. Perhaps Christians, as a whole, would do better to center their lives in this teaching. People lose sight of the divine within because of the veil of separation. They choose darkness by suppressing their true nature. In reality, God will always be within us. Pamela learned about the permanency of God within, during her near-death experience. She writes:

> God knows what we want before we even ask because He lives in us. God's many mansions are each and every one of us. That God says He will be with us until the end of the age, again, is because he lives in us. (Pamela D., NDERF# 1995)

I believe most souls yearn to return to the Source. Unfortunately, many seem completely unaware of the true divine within. They only count their imperfections. Jesus truly understood both His Godhood and His humanity. Jesus lived both realities, for us, so that the Kingdom may be emulated through Him. Accordingly, we can also live both realities, human and divine. We will approach the divine to the level we become Christ-like. When this life's lessons are complete, we will all become transformed when we pass over after our last breath.

Transformation

Transformation occurs when the soul discards the human body. Our magnificent soul rises above the reducing power of the brain when we die. Jesus also discarded both body and brain when He ascended. Although He remained the same in spiritual nature, Jesus regained divine power and authority. One might argue that Jesus had divine power and authority walking on earth. That would be true, but only to a degree. Yes, Jesus healed by tapping into the power of God. Jesus also conveyed an elevated wisdom by tapping into the will of God. But could Jesus calculate differential equations? Did he have a handle on aerospace engineering? I am guessing that Jesus was most adept at religious law and carpentry. My point: Jesus was reduced in similar ways to us. He lived fully as man. Yet, Jesus regained all the knowledge and power of heaven after He died on the cross. Jesus no longer lived a dual existence because the Son of Man role had been fulfilled. He simply returned to being the Son of God.

Many theologians ponder over the dual nature of Jesus the Son of Man and Son of God. However, few have pondered the singular nature of the ascended Jesus. Most would shrug and ask, "Who knows what it is like to be God?" Well, hundreds of people who have returned from death have reported meeting Jesus. No NDEr, to my reading, has claimed to fully know the Jesus face of God. Even so, many describe various facets about Jesus that can be explored and expounded. We will delve into this fascinating topic throughout the rest of this book. Specifically, we will tackle the nature of the ascended Christ. Moreover, we will explore how Jesus relates to us. We will begin the next chapter by examining the infinite, yet personal, nature of Jesus through the image of a rainbow.

CHAPTER THREE

THE RAINBOW OF JESUS

S unday school stories kindled my childhood imagination. There were many religious superheroes to entertain my young mind, such as Noah corralling animals all over the planet, David slaying the giant Goliath with a slingshot, and Delilah cutting off Sampson's magical hair. The more I learned science, the less fantastical stories of the Bible seemed possible. Wanting to be true to my religion, what was I to believe? Some people who ask such questions work toward reconciling religion and reason. They do so by exploring new perspectives. Unfortunately, rational explanations and symbolic interpretations of the Bible are often chastised by some Christians. For these faithful, the Bible is the inerrant Word of God. I try to brush off such criticism and remain open to new possibilities in my Christian faith. Although biblical stories still have value and truth in my life, my view of Jesus does not solely depend on strict doctrinal interpretations of the Bible. For me, reading the Bible is a fluid opportunity to learn; a vehicle meant to deepen my relationship with God. Perhaps a metaphor would help. I have found that my reliance on doctrine is like eating a juicy steak every day. The savory meat tastes great at first, but becomes timeworn after a few weeks or months. In other words, personal relationships are dynamic whereas doctrines are static. I tend to believe that we need less emphasis on doctrine and more emphasis on our personal, ever-evolving relationship with God.

It seems to me that some have a human need to quarantine the message of Jesus into a small, tidy, box. They like to spruce up their little box of doctrine with the promise of love, changed lives, and eternal salvation. Although this pretty box begs to be opened, it is nevertheless a box. The box serves to select a few qualities of God and divvy them into small packets of rigid understanding. Some people prefer a simple, reliable faith that can be passed down through the generations. By compressing Jesus, the human mind defends against ambiguity and mystery. By offering certainty, clear-cut theology can easily be accepted by almost everyone in a religious group. Likewise, challenges to faith that may otherwise cause anxiety and doubt can be defended or avoided altogether.

Creating God in our own image is nothing new. It is human nature to desire structure and certainty in our lives, particularly relating to spiritual matters. For many, the validation of religious beliefs becomes the bedrock of their faith. However, there are far more ideas about Jesus than there are church denominations. One may then logically conclude that Jesus transcends any one belief system. Despite the organized efforts to the contrary, Jesus cannot be stuffed into a box. Let's look at the reasons why.

There appears to be a great hubris in glorifying human intelligence. Just because humans are the smartest species on earth doesn't mean we can know everything. Put bluntly, a finite species, regardless of their scientific and religious development, cannot comprehend the eternal and infinite nature of God. How many Bibles would it take to describe and explain completely an infinite God? Might the number be very large, say a trillion? I propose that a trillion Bibles could not begin to capture the full complexity of the divine. Infinity, by definition, is a number that can never be reached. Given obvious human limitations, it seems arrogant to propose that God can fully be described by a handful of ancient books. Even the fundamentalist believer may admit, if pressed, that there are gaps in their personal knowledge about God. Unfortunately, insincere humility becomes exposed by contrary action. Too often the fundamentalist exclusively promotes his or her limited understanding of God while strongly attacking any divergent or broader exploration.

Again, personal relationships are dynamic whereas doctrines are static. Perhaps it is no wonder that humanity behaves little better now than during the time of Jesus. Yet, God tries to guide us into a larger state of spiritual awakening by means of ever-evolving revelation.

Self-perpetuating Christian doctrine, however, seems to teach that God stopped teaching and guiding humanity two thousand years ago. How can that be the case if Jesus relates to us on a personal level? I believe that God speaks to us today through gentle nudges, insights, other people, dreams, and even visions. The near-death experience also serves as an increasingly important source of revelation from God. If static religiosity shuts down new revelation by coercing the faithful against "heresy," then human efforts to evolve toward God will continue to be squashed.

The Rainbow Analogy

If I could improve on my argument, and somehow make it more compelling, I doubt it would make any impact on a fundamentalist believer. Those who desperately need certainty will never be swayed, regardless of their religious doctrine. I suspect that some people fear mystery and cannot relate to a limitless God. For some, the fear may be based on the need to believe in something rooted and unyielding; people need to have an anchor in their lives. To be fair, most people don't experience the divine in a direct, observable way, so naturally they lean on widely-accepted belief systems to sustain their hopes. Without this anchor, a mysterious Jesus might seem unapproachable. One could ask, "How can I relate to something I can't understand?" Fortunately, these fears are unfounded. Any perception of disconnection with the divine is created by people, not God. I will try to explain why God is quite approachable. The first step is to understand how God relates to both the smallest individual and the entire universe at the same time. I will do so by using the metaphor of the rainbow.

When I experienced a vision of Jesus descending from the heavens, I was drawn to the rainbow depicted across His white shirt. This may seem an odd image to many. However, I am certain, from experience, that God does not gift imagery arbitrarily, even when it seems highly unusual. I surmised that the image conveyed a beautiful, blended message of diversity and unity. How can these seemingly opposite states coexist? To integrate these opposing ideas, we need to look at the attributes of white light and the light of a rainbow. White light contains all the wavelengths of light, or all colors mixed together. Now, all these wavelengths, or colors within white, can be separated if directed through a prism. This process occurs when sunlight shines through rain droplets. Once these wavelengths have been separated, they fall in a continuous array of light based on increasing frequency. This array, or spectrum, appears to you and me as a rainbow. Put more simply, a rainbow represents the seamless smearing of white light into vivid beautiful colors.

The reverse process is also possible. Mixing all the wavelengths, or individual colors, produces the color white. According to the writer of the Gospel of Philip, Jesus used this very analogy to explain Himself through the ancient process of dyeing cloth. The text reads:

> The Lord went into the dye works of Levi (Mathew). He took seventy-two different colors and threw them into the vat. He took them out all white. And He said, "Even so has the Son of Man come as a dyer." (Verse 54)[1]

As any artist knows, gray is produced when colored paints are mixed together due to the absorption qualities of paint. Levi's dyes, apparently, lacked such impurities because they were white rather than gray. In this passage, Jesus presents Himself as the summation of everything. By extension, God can be viewed as the singularity of all creation over all time. Yet, God can also be represented by the expression of all separate, interconnected parts of creation. These individual parts would include, but not be limited to, souls like you and me. The writer of the Gospel of Philip further wrote: "The Truth is one and many, so as to teach us the innumerable One of Love." (Verse 12)[1]

Perhaps it is no coincidence that vivid colors punctuate the spiritual realm. For example, spiritual beings, in their natural form, present as colorful beings of energy. Many NDErs report that these colors, or vibrational frequencies, characterize the predominant attributes of each spiritual being. Each color signifies, through complex synesthesia (crossing of senses), the exact traits of each unique individual. The separate frequencies of trillions of spiritual beings create a rainbow-type appearance in heaven.

Perhaps it is no coincidence that white light pervades much of the background in the spiritual realm. If Jesus is heaven, then God is also heaven. God is the Alpha and Omega, the One and everything, and the summation of all possibilities. According to many NDE accounts, God appears as a white energy infiltrating every spiritual landscape. Perhaps this is the reason why NDErs say it is never night in heaven. Jesus also represents all possibilities. Yet, all the possibilities have been separated, for our understanding and growth, like a rainbow. Howard Storm learned, from his NDE, that Jesus is the revelation of the unknowable God.[2] In other words, Jesus serves as a mediator between God and humanity. More pointedly, Jesus serves as a mediator between the infinite and the finite. In Colossians 1:15, the Apostle Paul wrote, "Christ is the visible image of the invisible God." In the Gospel of Thomas, Jesus explains how the invisible light of the Father becomes embodied through Him:

> Jesus said, "When images become visible to people, the light that is in them is hidden. In the icon of the Light of the Father (the embodiment of God by Jesus), it will be manifest (evident) and the icon veiled (completely covered) by the light." (Verse 83)[3]

Jesus appears to be saying that God is hidden in the material realm. Yet, the Light became evident in the world through enveloping Christ. Perhaps the light of God became most visible in the form of a rainbow. In the book of Ezekiel, approximately 590 years prior to the birth of Jesus,[4] the writer described a vision of the Lord in this way:

> Like the appearance of the bow that is in the cloud on the day of rain, so was the appearance of the brightness all around. Such was the appearance of the likeness of the glory of the Lord. (Ezekiel 1:28)

Leonard, during his NDE, observed a similar rainbow image while looking upon Jesus. He wrote:

> What stuck out to me was His eyes... Picture microscopic rays of sunlight, but instead of rays being white or yellow they were all the colors of the rainbow. (Leonard R., NDERF #2552)

In her astounding book, *Clouds of Heaven*, Sharon Kay Casey described Jesus during her near-death experience in this fashion:

> The spirit of Jesus and that of the Holy Spirit had merged with His spirit. Now there is what looks like galaxies spinning within Him. His skin is like a rainbow with an illuminating shimmer of the whitest white. His form is that of a great arch.[5]

By exploring the rainbow diversity within unity, we can now answer the question, "How do we relate to a mysterious and unknowable Christ?" At a deeper level, we can ask, "How does the finite understand the infinite?" The rainbow represents all possible variables through God's omniscient knowledge and omnipotent power. As the rainbow, Jesus relates to each tiny frequency by becoming united with every tiny corner in the universe. What does that mean for you and me? It means that Jesus understands our every emotion, thought, challenge, and lost situation. Jesus does not just exist as a two thousand year old memory. Rather, Jesus knows us at the deepest, most personal level throughout time. Consequently, it is not necessary for any of us to fully know Jesus, or pretend to have all the answers. God meets us right where we are through our accessibility to Jesus. In the book of John, Jesus said:

> I am the good shepherd; I know my own sheep, and they know me, just as my father knows me and I know the father. (John 10:14)

When Jesus says He knows us, he means that he completely grasps each person, just like the Father and Son fully grasp each other in unity. In turn, humans can also know simple aspects of Jesus. For instance, we can know Jesus as our protector and guide, our good shepherd. According to the Gospel of Philip, Jesus reveals Himself according to each individual person's level of understanding. The author wrote:

> Jesus did not reveal himself as he is in reality, but according to the capacity of those who wanted to see Him. He is the Unique for all. Yet, to the great he appeared great, to the small he appeared small, to the angels as an angel, to human beings as a man. (Verse 26)[1]

Howard Storm, during his near-death experience, asked Jesus whether he was born to different worlds. Jesus answered that he had been born to every world throughout time and space.[2] He presented to each species in a way they could best understand. In other words, Jesus became the right rainbow for countless species. The universe teams with diversity, from the biggest galaxy to the smallest microscopic organisms. Even human beings express a diverse set of attributes. Although there are over seven billion people on earth, each person presents with a different defining combination that includes, but is not limited to, variances in genetics, personality, brain structure, personal history, and culture. Consequently, each person carries a different collection of psychological and spiritual needs: the confused need wisdom; the grieving need to be comforted; the guilty need forgiveness; the abused need compassion; the lost need motivation; the skeptic needs faith. In physical life, we may seek out a diverse array of people that meet different needs. Jesus can assume all spiritual roles because He has a rainbow of knowledge, wisdom, and experience. There is not a thought or feeling that Jesus cannot know or understand. Moreover, Jesus knows and understands our thoughts and feelings from a perspective of love. He fully understands and cares about your circumstances, now and forever, whether it is fear, joy, physical pain, or monster tribulations.

Jesus could grow as tall as a skyscraper and boom out orders and proclamations. Always true to His divine nature, Jesus rather presents as a humble, loving servant to humanity. His divine nature was as true in life as it has been observed during near-death experiences. As God's rainbow, Jesus meets each person in a manner that he or she can understand. In this manner, we learn to love in love. Throughout the book, we will explore various modalities in which Jesus relates to people. In this chapter, we will examine how Jesus relates to us like family. Let us start by exploring a surprising role for Jesus: our Father.

Jesus as Father

In Christianity, God has been typically viewed as the Father whereas Jesus has been viewed as the Son. The Son identity has deep biblical roots as Jesus frequently described himself as the Son of Man and occasionally as the Son of God. However, the Son identity may not apply to the ascended Christ in every instance. The delineation between Jesus and God became less sharp after Christ ascended and returned to the Source after physical death. Jesus is heaven and heaven is Jesus, just as God is heaven and heaven is God. As a human being, I cannot pretend to know the intricate relationships and hierarchies within the divine realm. However, I can share that some people who experience Christ during near-death experiences relate to Him as a father figure. From reading their testimonies, it seems that most do not concern themselves with the theological nature of the Trinity. They do, however, share the emotional impact of experiencing Jesus as a father figure. Ellen, during her NDE, was one such person who experienced the fatherly spectrum of the ascended Christ. She relates her interaction in this way:

> The voice said he was Jesus and my father... I felt a tremendous sense of paternal love, which I found odd afterwards because I was brought up in a single parent family having never had a father...

Then the voice who called himself Jesus asked me, "Well, how do you think you did?" I paused and giggled and said, "Much like my school report, really; I could have done better." The voice said, "So, what do you want to do?" (Ellen K., NDERF #615)

Jesus probably presented to Ellen as a father figure during her NDE because she needed paternal guidance. It is unclear what she meant by the term "paternal love," as experiential definitions vary widely. Given that Ellen was raised in a single-parent household, perhaps she experienced a newfound sense of stability and security being with Jesus. As a good father guides, Jesus challenged Ellen to review her life choices to consider better options. Unlike some human fathers prone to impatience and anger, the ascended Christ expressed neither temper nor judgment. Jesus respected Ellen enough to preserve her right to make her own choices, for better or for worse. Moreover, there was no expectation that she had to meet Jesus's approval.

If I am to emulate Jesus, how would I measure my success as a father? Like most parents, I respond to repeated child misconduct with frustration, and open defiance with a bit of anger. Although I am not the perfect father, I try to be a good father. When I lose my patience, I soon give my son a hug and say, "Okay, tomorrow is a new day. Please try to do better." But whereas I endeavor to forgive quickly, the ascended Jesus has no need to forgive out of hurt or anger. Rather, Jesus genuinely demonstrates unconditional love from start to finish.

Christians don't always perceive Jesus showing unconditional love. There is biblical precedence for Jesus expressing righteous anger. Indeed, Jesus became incensed at the religious elite, calling them vipers, and smashed the vendor tables at the temple. In my opinion, Jesus presented as the ideal human to be emulated. However, even the ideal human behaves quite differently than the ascended Christ united with God. Even Jesus noted His human limitations in the gospel of Mark: And Jesus said to him, "Why do you call me good. No one is good except God alone." (Mark 10:18)

Further into Mark, we read that Jesus, as a human, feared a painful death: "He went on a little farther and fell face down on the ground. He prayed that, if it were possible, the awful hour awaiting Him might pass Him by." (Mark 14:35)

Jesus may have lived the ideal human life, but the human species has inherent limitations. What would it mean if I owned the ideal dog? For me, the ideal dog would be quiet, friendly, and not dig holes in the yard. However, the ideal dog does not generalize entirely to the ideal human. Likewise, the ideal human, limited by biology, does not entirely mirror an unlimited God.

The human Jesus did not act exactly like the ascended Christ does today. After all, the ascended Christ is not constrained by linear time, human education, limited brain ability, and general biology. The writer of the Gospel of Philip wrote the following about Jesus' crucifixion, "The Teacher rose beyond death. He became what He was before the separation." (Verse 72)[1] It seems odd to me that Christians tend to worship Jesus with the human incarnation in mind. For me, it makes sense to honor the ascended Jesus in addition to the human Jesus. In the last NDERF submission, the ascended Jesus loved Ellen unconditionally, not two thousand years ago, but right now.

In the next NDERF submission, a woman named Theresa felt undeserving of Christ's unconditional love when she crossed over into the spiritual realm. Sensing failure in human life, Theresa approached Jesus feeling guilty. Let's see how Jesus, the perfect father, related to her:

> In the next instant, Jesus Christ himself reached down and picked me up. It was so much like the feeling I had felt when I was oh so small and so scared of a fire truck and my daddy had picked me up. I held him so close around his neck. I wanted to do the same, yet I felt so undeserving.
>
> As Jesus held me and I looked into his eyes; I will never forget how wonderful and awesome his eyes were! The first thing I asked him was, "Do you hate me because I am a drug addict?"
>
> I will never forget what He said to me, "No! I only want you to know that I love you."
>
> There were other things said and then he started to set me down. I said, "Please don't leave me." And He said, "I will never give you more than you can handle." Then I was back in my body. (Theresa O., NDERF #1911)

Some people abuse drugs to blot-out overwhelming problems in life. Artificial highs, in essence, provide an escape route for the individual running in fear. This scenario may apply to Theresa. Although Theresa felt unworthy, Jesus picked up the beaten, scared, young woman and embraced her. She was safe in daddy Jesus's iron arms. It appears that Theresa knew that everything bad was actually going to be alright. All that was not well was going to be well because Jesus loved Theresa perfectly despite her faults. In sum, Theresa felt like a little girl again who was deeply cared for in a secure atmosphere. Moreover, she would be given another chance.

Just before being returned to her body, Jesus informed Theresa that He would not give her more than she could handle. A competent human father assigns his children responsibilities (chores, school work, and extra-curricular activities) based on his or her level of maturity. Yet, even a perceptive father can underestimate or overestimate a child's readiness. Jesus does not make these mistakes because He knows everyone fully, just as he knew Theresa down to each hair on her head. Prior to her NDE, Theresa lacked the confidence to tackle life problems, so she tried to escape them by using drugs. Jesus assured Theresa that her mission, although difficult, was achievable, despite her past performance. Jesus' message may not be relevant to just Theresa, but to everyone struggling through the tough schoolyard of earth. None of us are given assignments that we cannot accomplish with perseverance and prayer. Although our success may be partial and imperfect, we can handle it with God's guidance.

There are children of various ages who pass over and meet Jesus. As a rainbow, Jesus meets the developmental needs of each child. For a young child, Jesus may manifest as a playful daddy. The following ten-year-old girl wrote:

> I was taken to a field where I skipped stones on the lake with Jesus. We also swam in the water and had a water fight. We swam with dolphins. Later Jesus let me fly with an eagle.

> It was fun. (Denise, NDERF #1045)

In the next NDERF submission, God's unconditional love profoundly transformed a fourteen year-old girl. Tragically, this child was abused and neglected by her own family. She was taught, like most abused children, that she lacked basic rights because she was inherently defective and worthless. Jesus transcended the child's fear and self-loathing by becoming the ideal father she never knew on earth. Namely, He repeatedly validated the child and showered her with affection. In this manner, Jesus' paternal love was simple, continuous, and intimate. She wrote:

I said, "I wish I was special, like the people in the Bible." Jesus replied, "You are." I asked, "Really, I am?" He answered, "Yes, you are." I then said, "I wish God loved me like the people in the Bible." Jesus said, "He does!" I asked, "He does?" He answered, "Yes, He does!"

There is no living person to ever exist that could match the beauty of Jesus Christ. He was perfect in every sense of the way. He like ran to me and I to Him. He embraced me and held me so close. I melted into Him and was hooked to His side there on out. We just got lost in each other's loving gaze for a long while, it seemed. He asked me what I would like to do, stay there or go back to earth. I answered, "I don't know what I am supposed to do there (on Earth). He told me, "Love and have fun." I asked, "That's it?"

Smiling at me so kind and full of love, He seemed to say it like He was proud of me. I was thinking to myself, 'well, no one likes me there.' He said, "Yes they do." I asked, "They do?" – thinking, 'well, they have a funny way of showing it.' He said, "I love you!" I asked, "You do?" He held me close, holding my hands in front of Him, close to His chest. He said, "Yes, I do." (Sarah, NDERF #2523)

Throughout her lengthy NDE experience, Jesus consistently validated the young girl with every response. Specifically, Father Jesus redefined reality for a girl who believed in the lies of her family. Father Jesus cut through their lies and righted her path. Moreover, He communicated pride and acceptance of her being. Note that Jesus consistently validated her through simple words of love. I can't think of anything more impactful than a father hugging a child, holding hands, and saying "I love you." Jesus' message was exactly what this isolated and insecure girl needed. But for others, a different presentation may be more powerful. Whereas some people relate to Jesus as a perfect father figure, others relate to Jesus as a perfect mother figure. In the next section, we will explore the maternal frequency of the Jesus rainbow.

Jesus as Mother

NDErs have occasionally sensed a female presence emanating from Jesus. I have yet to read an NDE submission, however, that reported Jesus manifesting in the shape of a female in heaven. I suspect Jesus manifests as a man to oblige human expectation. After all, Jesus was born a boy and died a man. Perhaps for this reason, the masculine template was readily upheld for the last two thousand years through the paternalistic lens of Christianity. Indeed, it would be accurate to view Jesus as having masculine attributes, like a son or father. Despite having masculine traits, the true essence of Jesus is neither male nor female. Assigning a sex to God only serves a human need. Namely, we try to know the unknowable Spirit by describing relatable physical properties that have no parallels to the spiritual realm.

I once experienced a dream of walking down a banquet isle between beautiful, young people who had lived about a hundred years ago. In the dream, a telepathic message remarked that the beings were androgynous. I did not fully understand what this meant. A greater awareness developed after reading the following verse from the Gospel of Thomas:

> Jesus said, "When you make the two into One, when you make the inner like the outer and the high like the low; when you make male and female into a single One, so that the male is not male and the female is not female…then you will enter into the Kingdom." (Verse 22)[3]

Jesus breaks down all division, including the inner-outer, high-low, and masculine-feminine. For division is illusionary in heaven; we are unified with the All. Unlike all people trapped in a divisive world, Jesus was connected to God's realm while living on earth. Likewise, the ascended Christ exists as the rainbow of God. Refracting the All, Jesus can exemplify feminine frequencies of the rainbow as equally as male frequencies.

Although some NDErs hint at the feminine qualities of Jesus, none provide as much detail as Julian of Norwich. Julian of Norwich had a very long, complex near-death experience over six hundred years ago. Her experience deeply involved Jesus as a source of deep revelation. Julian of Norwich related to Jesus as both a Brother and a Mother. The fact that she related to Jesus as a Mother was quite remarkable given the paternalistic culture of medieval Europe. Probably risking her life, Julian of Norwich reported that Jesus works as a Mother in the context of the Trinity. She wrote:

> From this it follows that truly God is our Father, so truly is God our Mother. Our Father wills, our Mother works, and the good Lord the Holy Spirit confirms.[6]

Julian of Norwich appears to report that Mother Jesus executes the will of God through His work. How does Jesus, as a mother figure, work in our lives? According to Julian of Norwich, Jesus works for humanity as a source of sustenance, nurturance, and sacrifice. In regard to sustenance, Jesus sustains a soul's spiritual life and health. Julian of Norwich described the process using a mother/infant analogy:

> The mother can give her child to suck of her milk, but our precious Mother Jesus can feed us with Himself, and does, most courteously and most tenderly.[6]

As God's children, the mothering quality of Jesus feeds us when we are spiritually hungry, clothes us when we feel vulnerable with layered love, and provides us shelter when we are tossed around by the storms in life. It is important to note that Jesus, like any good mother, does not foster dependency. Pushing us toward greater independence, Jesus does not always wipe clean our vulnerabilities or silence the breaching storm. But if we run to Mother Jesus during troubled times, Jesus will sustain us during each tribulation with gentle guidance and a greater peace inside. Such peace comforts us in the knowledge that, as eternal beings, life challenges are only temporary. When we open ourselves in faith, our spirit begins to understand that difficult lessons are just spiritual blessings to help us become closer to God. As we grow in faith, Jesus endows us with His motherly strength, endurance, and guidance through mutual closeness. By rejecting Mother Jesus, we tend to close ourselves in doubt while despairing in the darkness of circumstances.

In a real sense, humans are like little children running to Mother Jesus whenever we suffer a scrape or bruise. According to Julian of Norwich, Jesus doesn't mind our childlike response. He actually welcomes it. She wrote:

> We act as children toward Jesus as mother; we run to Him when we act like a hurt child...But our courteous Mother does not wish us to flee away. For nothing would be less pleasing to Him.[6]

Jesus welcomes childlike responses because He fully appreciates what it means to be a spiritual infant. Just as a patient mother recognizes that crawling precedes walking, Jesus recognizes that human dependency precedes a balanced relationship with the divine. In other words, Jesus appreciates why people turn to God in times of desperation instead of minding God in every season. Jesus wants our love, but does not need our love. As a patient Mother, Jesus nurtures us every step of the way in our journey of growth, whether we live as a spiritual infant, toddler, child, or adolescent. Julian of Norwich further wrote:

> For in our Mother Christ we profit and increase, and in mercy He reforms and restores us and in the power of His Passion, His death and His Resurrection, He unites us to our substance.[6]

What did Julian of Norwich mean by writing that Jesus unites us to our substance? I believe she referred to all spiritual beings becoming united with God, as discussed in the last chapter. Restoration through unity is a very powerful concept. From my perspective, she speaks of an ongoing interaction between Jesus and humanity. We are slowly, but constantly, reformed through a circular growth process. This circular process includes facing adversity, making mistakes, learning from mistakes, restoring through grace, and ultimately enhancing the spirit through reformation. Only by experiencing many upward cycles do we ever so slowly become united with our true nature, becoming concordant with the essence of God within. All the while, Jesus modifies His relationship with each person to meet individual developmental needs. Although our relationship with Jesus becomes more in-sync over time, Jesus remains steadfast in His patience and love during this long, perhaps eternal, process. Again, Julian of Norwich likens the patience of Jesus to a mother raising a child:

> And always as the child grows in age and stature, she acts differently, but she does not change her love...This work, with everything which is lovely and good, our Lord performs.[6]

As quoted earlier, Julian of Norwich speaks of a restoration through the power of the resurrection. Orthodox Christianity teaches that Jesus died in sacrifice for our sins. Although I accept the general principle, I personally struggle with the notion that personal salvation hinges on the sacrifice of Jesus, with hell being the unequivocal destination for the unbeliever. It seems to me that Christ died for everyone, no matter their religious upbringing. The topic of salvation will be discussed in depth in Chapter Nine. I realize that many Christian readers disagree. Perhaps most Christians can agree, at least on this point, that Jesus died for us to hasten the Kingdom of God on earth. According to the gospels, Jesus foresaw His death well in advance, yet never wavered in His mission to serve, teach, and sacrifice. Sacrifice may be the ultimate expression of love. Moreover, sacrifice can be viewed as feminine in nature. Although the masculine sacrifices during acts of heroism, the feminine sacrifices daily for the young and helpless. Perhaps human mothers provide the most consistent example by sacrificing for their children during childbirth, sickness, or tragedy. Likewise, Mother Jesus sacrifices His energy to attend to our discomforts and tribulations, all in an effort to help us grow up spiritually within a backdrop of love.

Jesus can sacrifice because He can empathize with the human condition. Jesus can empathize with every tragedy because He has suffered worse, either on the cross or during other experiences living eternally in a big universe. In this manner, Jesus also exemplifies the darker colors of the rainbow spectrum, the frequencies of pain and suffering. On this matter, Julian of Norwich wrote:

> But our true Mother Jesus, He alone bears us for joy and for endless life, blessed may He be. So He carries us within Him in love and travail, until the full time when he wanted to suffer the sharpest thorns and the cruel pains that ever were or will be.[6]

The Passion, above all, demonstrates God's deep love for all humanity, not only two thousand years ago, but forever. During her NDE, Julian of Norwich asked Jesus whether He would have been willing to sacrifice His life more than once. The answer she received from Jesus was that he would sacrifice Himself for humanity more times than beyond understanding. She continued by writing:

> And when he had died or would die so often, he would count it all as nothing for love, for everything seems only little to him in comparison with his love. For although the sweet humanity of Christ could suffer only once, his goodness can never cease offering it. Every day he is ready to do the same, if that might be.[6]

As our divine Mother, Jesus would sacrifice His life for us, His children, over and over again. The idea of Jesus being a mother figure grinds against the traditional patriarchal view of Jesus. Unfortunately, the patriarchal view limits God to the masculine and ignores the feminine nature of creation. Without the feminine, creation could not be nurtured or sustained. Humans need the feminine to nurture and sustain us, regardless of a person's sex. It is partly for this reason Jesus serves humanity as a rainbow; His work is fulfilling everything which is lovely and good. Up to this point, we have touched on Jesus relating to us as a Father and a Mother. Jesus also relates to us on another important frequency, namely as our Brother.

Jesus as Brother

Christians have long greeted one another as brothers and sisters in Christ. The term transcends the usual greeting of acquaintance or even friendship. It refers to a deeper relationship connection, one of permanence and shared familial identity. It seems likely that Christians first borrowed the practice from Jesus. In the Gospel of Matthew, a messenger informed Jesus that His mother and brothers were waiting to speak to Him outside. Instead of acquiescing to custom, Jesus replied: "Who is my mother? Who are my brothers?" Then he pointed to his disciples and said, "These are my mother and brothers. Anyone who does the will of my Father in heaven is my brother and sister, and mother." (Matthew 12:47-50)

Jesus defied everyone's expectations because he transcended the culture of his day. Rather than acquiescing to human authority, His actions were rooted in following the One authority. Human traditional rules, varying between societies, usually have little bearing on God's Truth. Yet, most people seem oblivious to this illusion. Not so with Jesus. He contradicted everything that a god represented in ancient society. For example, the Greek and Roman gods were fickle in emotion and fallible in deed, despite their super powers over nature. They were, in essence, figurative extensions of human kings and emperors. Like their lower, human counterparts, they typically removed themselves from everyday riff raff; the human minions were of little consequence within their hierarchy. Sometimes feeling magnanimous, they might throw morsels of sustenance in exchange for sacrifice and worship. Sometimes feeling indignant, they might punish human insolence and disobedience by toying with nature.

If Jesus followed the human expectations of a god, would He not reward and punish our worship through rain and drought? Would He not separate the divine by calling us "subject" or "mortal"? Yet, Jesus defied all ancient understanding of divinity. Shunning all human hierarchies of power, Jesus was humbly born human and raised as a poor carpenter's son. More importantly, He wanted people to call Him brother. The request would be seen as radical; what kind of God calls mortals brother? This request suggested a stronger connection with family than worship. The term brother can have many affiliated meanings, such as loyalty, permanency, mentoring, camaraderie, service, and sacrifice.

Although Jesus challenged all human notions of power, the NDE reports of Jesus often echo the brother descriptions of the Bible. Namely, each person is a brother to Christ because we are sons and daughters of the Father. Julie, meeting Jesus, wrote:

> I felt like I was the most precious, most loved, most beloved person in existence. I asked, "Just what is your relationship to me?" Jesus said, "I am your brother." Next I asked, "I know that's what the Bible says, so it's true then?" Jesus said, "Yes, I am your brother. We have the same blood running through our veins. I will never leave you or forsake you. I will always be there for you. Never, ever forget who you are." (NDERF #3228)

Julie correctly points out that the Bible claims we are brothers and sisters of the Father. In the book of Romans, Paul wrote:

> For God knew his people in advance, and he chose them to become like his Son, so that his Son would be the firstborn, with many brothers and sisters. (Romans 8:29)

God knew his children in advance and will know them forever more. It is not just a matter of relationship, but shared being. As brothers and sisters to Christ, we are of the same divine essence in Spirit. Jesus used the metaphor of blood to convey this message to Julie; royal blood flows through the lineage of the Father. Although our soul essence is unified, we do not share the same level of spiritual development or connection to the Source. Most souls assigned to school earth may be likened to a family of kindergarten students. Jesus, on the other hand, came to earth as an adult, older Brother. Consciously united with the Father in thought and purpose, Jesus was uniquely qualified to guide His younger siblings by paving a spiritual path through service and sacrifice. It is no accident that the cornerstone of Christianity rests on Jesus dying in sacrifice for us on the cross. As a human, Jesus taught humanity how to walk in accordance with the One by Word and deed. As the ascended Christ, Jesus continues to serve in both familiar and fresh ways.

I think back to being raised with an older brother. He taught me how to relate to peers and make friends, navigate the challenges of high school, ask girls out for a date, and prepare for college. He never asked me to return the favor. Rather, he mentored knowing that a strong brother-brother relationship was well worth the selfless effort. After all, our relationship was rooted in a common past and secured by mutual family goals. In greater fashion, our eternal past and futures are intertwined with our elder brother, Jesus. For our earthly lives, Jesus mentors us how to love, navigate the challenges of school earth, achieve intimacy through fruits of the Spirit, and prepare for elevated work after death. The older brother analogy, however, only works so far. I rely less on my brother now that we are both adults; we each have our own families and responsibilities. Jesus, conversely, will never cease to mentor each one of us. Loyal for eternity, Jesus will neither abandon His younger siblings, despite our rebellion, nor forsake us during our hours of need. Yet, Jesus does not seek compensation for His service and sacrifice. He only encourages our openness. Don, during his NDE, reported the following conversation with Jesus, the servant:

> I asked, "What am I going to do in heaven?" I was setting on some steps. I then asked, "Is it going to be my job to shine these steps?" He said, "No, Donald. The reason I made them of gold was so they would not have to be shined. I'm your brother and I want to serve you. I went away to build this place for you." (Don, NDERF #2431)

Donald's expectations of Jesus appear rooted in the human psychology of power and fairness. He assumed that Christ would be his master, an expectation harkening back to the ancients worshipping arrogant gods. Again, Jesus defies such human expectations. He reached out to Donald as a Brother-Servant. In God's Kingdom, those who are last will be first, and those who are first will be last. In this way, the ascended Jesus will continue to serve us in love, now and forever, as a model of divine perfection.

Jesus meets each individual at the heart of their need, be it Father, Mother, Brother, or any other spectrum of the rainbow. For *anyone* who needs to see Him as Brother, Jesus will genuinely become a brother. The next NDE account was submitted by Shalom, a physician and a Messianic Jew, who was the great grandson of the Chief Rabbi of Moscow. He wrote:

> I immediately walked over to him and asked, "Are You the Being, called Jesus?" With a warm soft, sense of love & laughter, he replied back, "I am called by many names, however because of your background you can call me Big Brother, and I will call you, My Little Prince of Peace"... He then went on to indicate, that I could either stay with Him or return to earth. However, if I did not return, many people would miss their connections in order to complete their missions and purposes in life. Reluctantly, but with a deeper understanding of My Mission, "To help Healers, Heal, so they can be of service to GOD and ALL his children", I chose to return to help ALL of my assigned brothers and sisters, on our planet. (Shalom G., NDERF #448)

Jesus mentored a Jewish man as a Brother in healing. Interestingly, Jesus did not call this Jew a "Christ Killer," but a "Prince of Peace." I can see, in my mind, a certain type of Christian wag his or her finger at Shalom and shout, "See there, unbeliever; there stands Jesus in Holy splendor. I told you so!" Yet, at no time during this submission did Jesus suggest that Shalom convert to Christianity. Rather, Jesus respectfully accommodated his non-Christian beliefs by calling himself, "Big Brother." Jesus was more interested in facilitating Shalom's mission as a healer than flashing His "Son of God" credentials. In similar fashion, Jesus probably cares more about our accomplishing our mission to love than our proselytizing. If we are to be Christ-like, we need to strive toward unity rather than division. Perhaps a great way to become Christ-like is to be brothers and sisters to each other. Motivated by our unified heritage, we can teach and be taught to love each other within the huge family of God.

Jesus as Son of God

There are many historical opinions about the identity of Jesus. Some people believe He is just a good man. Others view Him as the Son of God. A number of NDErs have proposed that Jesus came to earth as an enlightened being, much like Buddha, to help guide humanity. Although this book partly supports this NDE premise, I submit that Jesus represents something more. As a rainbow, He encompasses many more spectrums than we can know or imagine. Just because we are within Jesus and Jesus is within us, that does not mean we share the same exact mission or history. Indeed, I have a different history, character, maturity, authority, and life directive from that of Jesus.

The biblical gospels claim that Jesus is the Son of God. Some NDE adherents challenge this position by asking, "How can Jesus exist as both the Son of God and still be connected to everyone in Unity?" In seeking truth in both positions, one needs to consider divine dualities. As a man, Jesus was both fully human and divine at the same time. But, as the ascended Christ, Jesus shares a singularity with God while exhibiting personality based on His own unique cosmic history. Consider the following possibility. Although everyone shares in God's Unity, the ascended Christ manifests God's infinite authority and expression with little, or no, limitation. Most other spiritual beings, on the other hand, are limited in God's infinite authority and expression depending on their level of spiritual development. Do NDE reports support my theory? Indeed, a fair number of NDErs recognize the biblical authority of Jesus when they interact with the ascended Christ in heaven. In her book *Embraced by the Light*, Betty Eadie recognized Jesus during her NDE:

> There was no questioning who he was. I knew that he was my Savior, and friend, and God. He was Jesus Christ, who had always loved me, even when I thought he hated me. He was life itself, love itself, and his love gave me a fullness of joy, even overflowing. I knew that I had known him from the beginning, from long before my earth life, because my spirit recognized him.[7]

Although many NDErs recognize the biblical authority of Jesus, others just describe the unity that Jesus shares with all beings. Due to this complexity, I have been struggling to answer the central question of Christ's identity for over a year. I prayed to God, "How can I write a book about Jesus without knowing His true identity?" A partial answer was revealed to me after I experienced a vision of the ascended Christ.

I believe that Jesus appeared to me about an hour after I requested to meet Him in prayer. Surprisingly, He did not present in human form, as He does for many. Rather, the ascended Christ presented in a more expansive configuration. As I mulled over the day's events in bed, my thoughts became diverted by waves of soft golden light rolling in my mind. Lined patterns emerged on gold sheets beneath the waves. It was as if I were looking at several layers of leaves, all deeply demarked by parallel and branching veins. I didn't sense any end to the scene. It was as if I were experiencing an expansive, yet partial, churning image of cosmic infinity.

I have frequently witnessed images and light—usually in a state between wakefulness and sleep—ever since I began writing about the NDE two years ago. However, the rolling light was unlike my usual showings of discreet flashes or short images. Specifically, the gold light was sustained and everywhere. In fact, I was able to marvel at the patterns for several minutes in a state of full wakefulness. One image, however, did flash within the light: I saw a drop of blood fall from a human wrist. Seeing a snippet of the crucifixion, I recognized immediately my night visitor to be Jesus.

The light infused image eventually faded but quickly returned. The second image quickly changed when a "leaf" section zoomed inward, much as if it had been magnified by a powerful microscope. In retrospect, I felt like a biologist watching tiny organisms swim around in a drop of swamp water. But, instead of looking at microorganisms, I witnessed hundreds of gold, short lines that looked like meteors suspended in a dark night sky. I understood, in my mind, that each little streak represented a person's life. Remarkably, I also knew that each life had been infused and molded by Jesus. There were hundreds, if not thousands, of these tiny streaks in my magnified field of vision. It is hard to guess how many lives might be represented in the entire leaf pattern. I would not be surprised if the number exceeded trillions. Whatever the sum, the showing was far beyond my comprehension.

The light faded and returned a third time. The third image quickly moved away like a raincloud after a thunderstorm. But, instead of rich blue skies, an inky blackness filled my mind. The only structures in the void were brief images of snarling dog teeth. The void lasted only a couple of seconds before the golden cloud returned and covered the abyss. As soon as the void was covered by gold light the entire vision vanished. I lay there quietly, in my bed, sensing an odd vibration course through my body. As I began to reflect on these three images of Jesus, I had the most amazing epiphany. I understood that I was not looking at a more advanced son of God, but rather the Son of God.

Although not a word was uttered, the three-part vision revealed the basic nature of the ascended Christ. I was comforted that the vision's message supported the biblical account of Jesus. Certainly, any lesser view would concern Christians all around the world. After all, there's a number of biblical verses that assert Jesus as the Son of God. Of these, John 5:19 resonates highly with my vision. It reads:

> I tell you the truth, the Son can do nothing by himself, only what he sees his Father doing, because whatever the Father does, the Son also does.

The Son cannot do anything by Himself because His will is in full concordance with the Father. Although we are all equal in God's Unity, we do not equally express God's divine nature. For God gifts people with self-determination. In other words, we grow and return to our heritage as sons and daughters of God over vast stretches of time, albeit some faster than others. This is all part of the Good, for God enjoys creation through diversity of existence, self-discovery, and growth.

As the Son of God, the ascended Christ does not grow in His heritage toward the Source. His heritage has already been fulfilled; the Son fully expresses the mind and will of the Father. In other words, the ascended Christ is perfect. Living in full concordance with God, Jesus realizes every facet of His inheritance. Like a prince who shares dominion over a kingdom, Jesus shares dominion over Creation with the Father. That does not mean we are barred from the same inheritance, for we are also granted freedom and vast power in the spiritual realm connected to God's tapestry. But unlike the ascended Christ, our mission authority is limited to our level of spiritual "child" development. Because we lack perfection, we do not share full dominion over creation.

In my vision, the scope of the ascended Christ appeared endless within waves of gold; the ascended Christ exists in every action, every moment, everywhere. With infinite channels of awareness, He knows our every thought and impulse, every worry and hope. In this manner, the ascended Christ creates a stunning conscious universe by working with everyone collectively. Such an infinite process is difficult for the finite human brain to fathom. We can catch only a glimpse of this infinity through metaphor. For instance, we can imagine a beautiful shooting star pattern in an endless sea of gold. Or, we can visualize a rainbow capturing all that has happened, all that is occurring, and all future possibilities. If that doesn't work, then we can imagine God as an ocean. You, I, and other spiritual beings are drops in the ocean. Some of the more mature spiritual beings may even be buckets of ocean water. Jesus is the ocean from shore to shore. As drops in the ocean, we will reconnect to the Source when we die as sons and daughters of God.

However, we will not call ourselves the Son of God, for that is reserved for a very special being of mystery, the ascended Christ.

The Breaking of Barriers

Categorizing Jesus may seem a bit like stereotyping. Admittedly, applying human descriptors to Jesus, like father-mother-and son, fails to convey His full divinity. Analogies may be useful, nevertheless, to provide human reference to describe the unknowable. In other words, categorizing Jesus provides humanity with a finite description of the infinite divine. Perhaps the best we can hope to do is to capture the essence of Jesus. Certain terms were commonly used to describe Jesus in the Bible. The purpose of this chapter is to expand that singular, masculine-based descriptor and encourage people to see Jesus in new ways. Thus, one is not required to view Jesus as a Brother, or even as a Father or Mother. For instance, some may rather view Jesus as a Teacher, Protector, or Savior. Although any group of descriptors may be insufficient to describe Jesus, it may be sufficient for the seeker to understand Jesus in limited ways. Whatever section(s) of the rainbow spectrum we seek, Jesus will be there for us, at the right frequency, to fit our spiritual needs perfectly. That is not to say, however, that the divine spectrum includes hate or immorality. The common thread that ties all the rainbow colors together is love. In the next chapter, we will explore just how much Jesus loves us all.

CHAPTER FOUR

REDEEMED BY JESUS

How do we measure the value of being human? There are many opinions about human nature, a discussion that often leads to more questions than answers. Are we good? Are we bad? Are we a mixture of both? Most people want to view themselves as good. By extension, I gather that many hope that their life journey will someday be celebrated by God. It seems logical, then, that humanity would evaluate itself through rose-colored lenses. However, positive self-assessment does not encompass much real estate of religious doctrine, particularly from the Christian tradition. If Christians were to paint a character portrait of a human, most colors would fall in the darker shades. The blacks and dark blues would predominate because of original and accumulated sin. Original sin, as any versed Christian would confirm, began with Adam eating the forbidden fruit. Adam, and his temptress Eve, were forever expelled from the perfect garden only to be banished to a spiritual world of sin and death. There was no turning back after Adam and Eve shared the fleshy apple. Inheriting their fall, every person since Adam and Eve deserves God's wrath and punishment.

According to the book of Genesis, humanity eventually fell into such an excessive state of corruption and evil that God flooded the world in order to start over with the progeny of Noah. So it was written that all the innocent animals, save two of each species, were sacrificed to achieve a clean slate. Was rejuvenation worth a divine act of planetary carnage? One might argue that God should have started again at the DNA level. After all, a simple reboot didn't seem to improve the programming. Post Noah history is filled with wars, genocides, slavery, and many other atrocities. Although many use the Bible and history to paint a somber picture, others prefer to paint in lighter shades. Obvious human faults aside, optimists point to examples of human charity, forgiveness, and sacrifice. Some even argue that humans have inherent value because they have the capacity for good, despite having such a messy record.

It is the aim of this chapter to wrestle with the complexity of human value. We will first look at Christian theology over time, starting with medieval Catholicism and then moving on to Protestantism. Next, we will compare and contrast religious opinion with the teachings of Jesus through the near-death experience and within the New Testament.

A Legacy of Spiritual Damage

With the brutal actions of people on full display, century after century, it became easy for the medieval Catholic Church to emphasize the dark nature of humanity. Exploiting wretchedness became a "big business" for the old hierarchy. One may argue that the antiquated Catholic Church preyed on the obvious human flaws by selling indulgences. In doing so, they set a tone of spiritual negativism throughout medieval Europe.

The Catholic Church, the predominant Christian organization since Jesus, sold indulgences for about four centuries. For those unfamiliar with the term, the religious practice of selling indulgences involved a priest petitioning God to forgive sins. Unfortunately for the impoverished masses, the priest would only act as an intercessory between man and God for a fee. The sinner was often compelled to pay the church through spiritual blackmail: the faithful were told that God would torture Christians in purgatory if they didn't pay up. The higher the payment, the fewer days a person had to spend in the refining fires of purgatory after death for original and accumulated sin. The selling of indulgences came in several marketing schemes. The sinner could pay for deceased loved ones to decrease their time in purgatory. If wealthy, a rich person could pay the poor to do the suffering for them. The poor did so by fasting, fighting in the crusades, making pilgrimages, and flagellating themselves.[1]

The long-standing practice of selling indulgences became official during the Council of Trent (1545-1563). It was written, "The pious are purified by a temporary punishment so that an entrance may be opened for them into the eternal country in which nothing stained can enter."[1] Because of the wretched nature of humanity, refinement necessitated a lengthy and torturous suffering for many sinners. Only until all sin had been atoned would a person be saved from the worst, traumatic agony. Very few were exempt. Alice Turner, the author of *History of Hell*, explained, "Almost everyone, it was soon widely assumed, would go to purgatory, the exception being saints, martyrs, and the incorrigible wicked."[1] She continues, "Purgatory gave the Church, so powerful in every aspect of medieval life, new powers that existed beyond the grave."[1] In addition to filling church coffers, the religious culture shaped the populous more by fear than love. It was not enough for the good Christian to suffer in this life. With this belief, the arrival of death must have been terrifying event for most Christians.

For centuries, aspects of Catholic theology portrayed a wrathful, unmerciful, and unforgiving God. From this perspective, God's relation to humanity can be likened to a tallyman, counting every sinful thought and deed in order to punish in exacting measure. God would only be merciful through Church bribery. Despite teaching purgatory, the faithful were taught that God somehow loved them. In turn, it was their duty to love God with all their might. Imagine if you lived during these fearful times, worshiping a God that would torture you for the original sin you inherited. How would you feel about yourself? How would you feel about God? Personally speaking, I would view myself as pathetic and unworthy. I would only relate to God out of fear of judgment. Additionally, the acidic nature of fear would dissolve any positive emotion I had toward God.

Let's take our imagination about the past one step further. If you lived five hundred years ago, would you develop your own spiritual conclusions separate from church teachings? There is an off chance you might. After all, people are not robots. History demonstrates that some people disagreed with the church, just as some independent thinkers react against various levels of religious authority today. The protestant reformation, for example, was based on a growing discontent with indulgences and other church practices of the time. I, personally, believe that God's love worked in people's lives even during these dark times. Meaning, God's love is more powerful than any human institution. A dogma of fear and inquisition cannot withstand the test of reason or the power of love. That being said, many people were spiritually scarred by fearing a wrathful God. To the degree that this scarring occurred, the love of the sinner toward the creator would have been harmed. If you lived during those times, would you bother sending up prayers of thanksgiving and joy? It seems more likely that you would send up prayers like a hungry beggar looking for a morsel of forgiveness. This is not the first or last time the religious elite twisted God's truth for their own purposes. There are pockets of religious adherents, across various religious institutions and denominations, who misuse religion today in order to gain control, power, and profit. I am reminded of how Jesus accused the religious leaders of his day:

> How terrible it will be for you teachers of religious law and you Pharisees. Hypocrites! For you won't let others enter the Kingdom of Heaven, and you won't go in yourselves. (Matthew 23:13)

The greatest abuses of the Catholic Church have long been buried in history. Personally, I am very encouraged that the current pope, Frances, has recently embraced a strong doctrine of love. Although indulgences have long been discontinued, history always reverberates down through the tapestry of time. Although the Catholic doctrine has made great efforts to no longer shame the faithful, particularly during the last hundred years, one may question whether it can entirely be divorced from centuries of belief and practice. The Catholic Church still emphasizes confessions and acts of penance through a priest. Penance involves people paying for their sins through acts of "satisfactions".[2] The Catholic Church continues to endorse officially the belief in purgatory to purge sins, even if some Catholics now view purgatory as a spiritual metaphor.[2] Excommunication continues to be practiced when members express heretical beliefs or seemingly unforgivable behaviors.[2] Do these practices produce shame? As a non-Catholic, I am not in the best position to judge. Perhaps members of the Catholic Church are best suited to evaluate their own faith.

I want to emphasize, particularly to the Catholic reader, that it is not my intent to attack the Catholic Church as an institution. I value the Catholic path to discover God. As an outsider, it seems apparent that most priests try to bring the Kingdom of God in people's lives. Catholic members pray with sincerity, worship in love, and give generously to the poor. My aim is to encourage a dialogue about specific religious practices that might disconnect people from God. I became acutely aware of this shaming side of religious culture after reading *Diary*, a 700 page ongoing discussion between Jesus and Saint Marie Faustina Kowalska. As discussed earlier, my interest in the Polish saint peaked after I had a vision of Jesus much as He was depicted on the saint's canonization portrait. I expected an enlightened mystical discussion, but was rather bombarded with themes of personal guilt, penance, and the desire for personal suffering. The following dialogue with Jesus provides a sample of her writing:

> Jesus asked me, "Who are you?"
> I answered, "I am your servant, Lord."
> "You are guilty of one day of fire in purgatory."
> I wanted to throw myself immediately into the flames of purgatory.[3]

I am unclear as to why St. Kowalska was guilty of one day of purgatory by answering that she was a servant of Christ. I am even more perplexed why she was so eager to accept this punishment and suffer. From a general Christian perspective, Jesus modeled holy suffering by dying on the cross for our sins. If Jesus suffered to serve others, one could argue that we should do the same. But suffering for the sake of suffering, in my mind, only amounts to masochism. I don't believe that is how God intended people to love Jesus.

Nowhere is it written in the Bible or NDE accounts that Jesus shames people. God wants to build up people in love, not belittle them or tear them down in wrath. Unfortunately, these teachings not only impact Catholic believers, but also reverberate across the tapestry of human experience over time. After all, people's attitudes and beliefs can be infectious in a way that is passed down through the generations, not only through religion, but through every walk of life.

The Protestant Reformation

It doesn't take an ancient biblical scholar to notice inconsistencies between medieval church doctrine and biblical scripture. For example, the apostle Paul repeatedly taught that all Christians are justified by faith. Accordingly, most Christians believe that God forgives the repentant and faithful sinner. Let us examine a passage from a letter Paul sent to the early church in Rome:

God showed his great love for us by sending Christ to die for us while we were still sinners. And since we have been made right in God's sight by the blood of Christ, he will certainly save us from God's judgment. (Romans 5:8-9)

Indulgences, conversely, are based on the premise that God judges all sin. A growing number of literate people during the renaissance disapproved of such non-biblical assertions. Criticisms were stifled, however, because the punishment for disagreement, or heresy, was usually death.

Despite the prospect of an untimely demise, a few people bravely challenged church authority. The boiling-over of discontent eventually culminated in the Protestant Reformation. Martin Luther was the first notable trailblazer for change after he pinned his famous 95 theses on the Wittenberg church door in 1517 A.D. The document spelled out 95 arguments against the practices of indulgences.[4] Let's look at three pivotal points:

#24: It must therefore be the case that the major part of the people are deceived by that indiscriminate and high-sounding promise of relief from penalty.

#27: There is no divine authority for preaching that the soul flies out of purgatory immediately after the money clinks in the bottom of the chest.

#36: Any Christian whatsoever, who is truly repentant, enjoys plenary (full) remission from penalty and guilt, and this is given him without letters of indulgence.

All three points stab at the heart of indulgences. Luther's 95 theses primed a revolution of religious change. However, Luther's proposed challenges were targeted at a few theological points. It is important to note that Martin Luther did not disagree with the Catholic Church regarding the pervasive and serious nature of sin. Still partly aligned with the Church responsible for his educative upbringing, Luther believed that people are inherently sinful to the point of wretchedness. So wretched, in fact, that he believed that people deserved eternal hellfire damnation. His divergence with the Catholic Church related to the biblical concept of grace: God forgives all human wretchedness by the blood and sacrifice of Jesus Christ, even if undeserved. Let's take a look at two related points from Martin Luther when he presented at a religious conference, the Heidelberg Disputation[5]:

> #3. The works of man may always be attractive and seemingly good. It appears nevertheless that they are mortal sins.

> #7. The works of men are all the more deadly when they are done without fear, and with the pure and evil assurance.

Looking back at point number three, Martin Luther strongly asserts that even seemingly good behavior represents sins worthy of death and punishment. Regarding point seven, Luther asserts that people should fear God's wrath, despite being saved by grace. He elaborates:

> #11. Presumption cannot be avoided, nor can there be true hope, unless the condemning judgment is feared in every work.

Why would Martin Luther advocate fear when God's grace protects all repentant Christians? How can one live in a state of grace and fear at the same time? Perhaps Luther associates a fear of God with an awe-driven respect for God. For Luther, not recognizing the spiritual gulf between human wretchedness and divine perfection would be sacrilegious. Luther underscores the point further by emphasizing human unworthiness in all our efforts:

> #13. "Free-will" after all is nothing but a word, and as long as it is doing what is within it, it is committing deadly sin.

For Martin Luther, original sin became embedded in the human soul during the fall of Adam. Because sin has become engrained and pervasive in the human soul, seemingly good deeds have their real basis in immoral thought, selfish motive, and in misdirected action. Even individual will, the very core of self-direction, exists as a mortal sin whenever incongruent with the will of God. Martin Luther believed that humans have no inherent positive value apart from God.

Many credit Martin Luther with a great service by challenging indulgences and developing a biblically-based theology. Most Protestant churches share Luther's theology of grace. One might suggest that even the Catholic Church has increasingly moved in this direction. This shift, in my opinion, navigates the Christian faith toward a healthier space. Salvation liberates Christians from needless fear of purgatory or hellfire damnation. My concern with Luther's theology, and contemporary fundamentalist positions, revolves around the belief that God sternly judges people even though they are saved.

By placing conditions on love, the judgmental Christian creates a measuring stick to evaluate oneself, and others, against God's perfect nature. The ramifications impact everyday life due to the pervasive nature of sin. Few, if any, can measure up to any strict, arbitrary religious standard. Shame and fear are the consequences for the religiously-judged believer. These negative emotional states create an artificial separation from God. May not a disobedient child, fearing a spanking, hide from his or her parents? In similar manner, may not fear lead one to cower away from God in self-disgust? Psychologists have long observed the detrimental psychological effects of perpetual self-devaluation. Such distorted thinking goes hand-in-hand with low self-esteem, self-absorption, and depression.[6] From looking at the self with narrow blinders, it is difficult for the shamed believer to see him or herself as special. Perhaps more important, it is difficult for the shamed believer to accept that he or she is special to God. Rather, the devalued religious individual may believe that he or she should atone for their sins through divine punishment. Yet, Jesus did not come to earth to judge or punish people. Jesus starkly pointed out the difference between religious judgment and divine judgment to religious leaders, the Pharisees. In John 8:15, Jesus told the religious elite, "You judge me with all your human limitations, but I am not judging anyone." Not only did Jesus not judge anyone's sin, but He conveyed that humanity was special to God despite sin. According to Mathew 10:30-31, Jesus said:

> Are not two sparrows sold for a cent? And yet not one of them will fall to the ground apart from your Father. But the very hairs of your head are all numbered. So do not fear; you are more valuable than many sparrows.

Although the gospels attest to human specialness, the ascended Christ repeatedly emphasizes the extraordinary value of human beings during near-death experiences. If we are not measured by sin, then what can be said about sin and the human condition? People returning from death indicate that the traditional views of sin should be redefined: God does not see our seemingly "good" deeds as mortal sins.

God does not view our seemingly "bad" deeds as mortal sins. Further-more, God does not even view our "bad" deeds as deserving punishment. Rather, NDErs overwhelmingly report that God loves everyone unconditionally without judgment, regardless of human imperfections.

There is no separation between you and the different faces of the One God, not even a hairline fracture. How can such a fallible species be interconnected with God? The truth, I believe, comes from under-standing a greater spiritual complexity. Fortunately, people who have had near-death experiences explain the process. Let's now try to un-tangle this complexity by turning our attention to what Jesus commu-nicates to people during their near-death experiences.

Jesus Loves Me This I Know

Most Protestant Christian readers know the song, *Jesus Loves Me This I Know*. I learned this song as a small child during my first year of Sunday school. Perhaps Christians enjoy a healthier spiritual perspective when their theology becomes based on those simple lyrics. There were other gems I learned from those early years. For example, I was instructed to memorize the Bible verse John 3:16. I can still write it down by mem-ory, "For God so loved the world that He gave his only begotten Son, that whoever believes in Him should not perish, but have eternal life." I also cherish the next verse, "For God did not send His son to condemn the world, but to save it." Of all the thousands of verses in the Bible, John 3:16 remains one of the most popular because it resonates deeply with people of Christian faith. Why? It speaks to humanity's greatest hope. In a few simple words, the apostle John declares that God loves everyone beyond human understanding. Sin does not have to be an unmovable barrier between creator and creation. The verse may also resonate at a deeper, subconscious, soul level. I propose that the soul yearns to rejoin with the all-powerful, all-present love of God. In other words, subconsciously we miss the divine. It is a verse that promises eternal reconnection with the One.

Let us now revisit the question on how much God values people. As recently explored, religious answers vary. Direct near-death experience observations, on the other hand, are remarkably consistent. Accord-ing to thousands of NDE accounts, God values every person immeas-urably and equally. The following writer learned about human worth from the unified perspective of God and Jesus:

Rays of light seemed to encompass me, and I felt that I was picked up and cradled in these big arms. I was engulfed in the most amazing sense of compassion and love I had ever felt. I had never felt anything like this before. I knew that I was being held in Christ's embrace. All I could see was this warm, golden light; I couldn't actually see Christ or the Father. God spoke to me in this beautiful, masculine voice, not with words but telepathically. It was amazing. God said to me, "I'm here for you, my child. I love you completely. You are my child, and I am your Father."

Right then it was conveyed to me that God loved every cell of my body, every molecule, and I felt his love as though I was immersed in this tremendous ocean of love and complete acceptance and forgiveness. God said to me, "I love you, and I have always loved you. There is nothing you could possibly say or do to separate you from my love. You are perfect and will always be perfect." (John, NDERF #3628)

In this spiritual exchange, God conveyed that perfect, divine love has its foundation on full acceptance and forgiveness. In particular, God declared to John, "There is nothing you could possibly say or do to separate you from my love. You are perfect and will always be perfect." Speaking in absolute terms, God defines perfect love as unconditional. In the quest to understand human value, it is important to wrestle with this declaration. It is not enough to understand unconditional love as a definition; we only need a dictionary for that. The struggle begins when we apply the definition of unconditional love to our lives. There are two primary mental barriers to experientially understanding the word 'unconditional.' First, unconditional love has no common reference to human love. Human love, by its imperfect nature, is inherently conditional. Although some may demonstrate an occasional act of altruism, unconditional love cannot be sustained. To illustrate, I have yet to see a marriage that does not have a set of expectations or conditions of continuance. Put more succinctly, no human being can fathom God's unconditional love beyond the abstract. This is why people keep adding conditions to God's perfect love. Secondly, shame works as a barrier to understanding unconditional love. I will share my own fallibility. Even though intellectually I grasp the concept of God's unconditional love, something within me still does not want to disappoint God. Unless I really monitor my attitude and feelings, I worry about how God sees me when I make mistakes. Perhaps you, the reader, may also relate to this anxiety.

It is human nature to feel shame. Unfortunately, Catholicism is not the only religion that exploits such human vulnerabilities. I remember receiving a black sheep sticker on the "sheep-board" every time I missed Sunday school at our local Baptist church. To coerce kids to attend church more frequently, leaders of the children's ministry shamed them by judging their weekly attendance. I largely ignored the practice. Although I occasionally feel shame, I am not a particularly shame-ridden person. Unfortunately, the consequences are more extreme for others who are susceptible to condemnation from self and others. Some falsely believe that God has abandoned them in life because of their sin. They believe that they somehow crossed an unmovable line that exceeds the limits of God's love and forgiveness. What a tragedy! I can't think of anything more heartbreaking than when a person turns their back to loving, outstretched arms. Through the near-death experience, God repeatedly tells us to embrace the divine: God asserts that you are loved to the same degree of perfections, no matter what you have done. This may be an appropriate time to pause and reflect. I find the concept of unconditional love quite liberating. There is no act or thought that can take me from the love of my heavenly Father. Christians claim that we are made perfect through the sacrificial love of Jesus; our sinful nature becomes as white as snow. If we are truly pure, then perhaps shame-ridden Christians should work harder to fully accept God's unconditional love, without shame, to better reconnect with Jesus.

There are more ramifications to the expression of unconditional love. Reexamining the NDERF submission from John, I found it interesting that he wrote, "I was immersed in this tremendous ocean of love and complete acceptance and forgiveness." Remember, Martin Luther's rift from the Catholic Church was primarily based on a disagreement about the nature of grace. Although Luther put his life on the line asserting his beliefs, he understood only half of the gift. Although he acknowledged forgiveness, he seemed to overlook God's complete acceptance of our natural human state. After all, Martin Luther greatly feared God. His legacy holds true for many Christians today. But if we are truly made pure as snow, then there should be no reason to fear God at all. Yet, some people still believe that God relates to people like a stern parent rather than a fully-accepting parent.

Let's take a look at a few hot-button moral religious issues going on right now in society. Does God love homosexuals, or does God punish them with AIDS? Does God love Muslims, or does God punish the infidel with war and pestilence? Some readily answer, "God smites." NDEs report that God loves. If God smites people for major sins, then might not God punish everyone for minor sins? Some would readily answer, "Yes, God punishes me whenever I am disobedient. This is how God makes me a better Christian." For some, tough love necessarily involves punishment. In other words, inflicting pain out of anger may be seen as an aspect of perfect love; God's correcting rod for disobedient children. As reported through the near-death experience accounts, perfect love and punishment are incompatible. In reality, punishment is not necessary because there are plenty of reinforcement contingencies, or correcting elements, in the natural environment that leads to learning and growth. In the material realm, selfish choices will eventually result in undesirable outcomes whereas loving choices will eventually result in positive outcomes.

For those who scoff and point toward examples of worldly injustice, I understand that "karma" can be very untidy. Although positive or negative consequences may not always seem immediate, there are unseen psychological and spiritual consequences to our actions. In this manner, life often catches up to most self-serving people eventually. For example, those who gain wealth by exploitation may suffer personal alienation and spiritual disconnection despite keeping their material possessions. After all, what society claims to be desirable usually does not lead to happiness or spiritual connection. It should also be noted that people bring their natures into the spiritual realm, even if personal accountability can partially be avoided while living on earth. According to many NDE accounts, those who mature in love during physical life will exist at a higher spiritual level than those who stagnate or digress. The natural order should not be confused as a system of rewards or punishments, however, but rather a natural extension of personal growth. God loves us all equally, whatever path we choose. As many pastors preach, Jesus meets us where we are at. This is true now and forever. Thus, there will always be second chances. Jesus loves me, this I know. Because unconditional love lacks conditions, there is no reason to let fear create a blockage between ourselves and God.

Everything was made in Love for You

After reading about thousands of near-death experiences, I have yet to read of an NDEr tremble before God in fear. Neither was anyone encouraged to kneel, prostrate, grovel, or otherwise humbly beg for forgiveness. These are human notions of God deeply embedded in church doctrine. Julian of Norwich learned a similar lesson during her lengthy conversations with Jesus. A product of 14th century Catholicism, Julian of Norwich contritely spoke to Jesus with reverent fear during her NDE in 1373 A.D. However, her level of self-depreciation lessened as Jesus revealed a completely foreign reality from the religious ethos that pervaded medieval Europe. Given her strict religious life, living within a Catholic Abbey, one can appreciate Julian of Norwich's astonishment when Jesus taught her that God accepted everyone. This radical message has been echoed over and over again throughout the near-death experience literature. In her book *Showings*, Julian of Norwich wrote:

> This, then, was my astonishment, that I saw our Lord God showing no blame to us than if we were as pure and as holy as the angels are in heaven.[7]

Did Jesus actually tell Julian of Norwich that humans were on par with the angels? Certainly, this assertion flew in the face of her prior personal experience. Living in the middle ages, she must have known or understood the violence of dark times: religious intolerance, ongoing ethnic hatred, exploitation, and wars. Yet, I believe Julian of Norwich was being quite literal in her conveyance, even to the point of risking execution by the Church for heresy. A woman named Laura experienced a similar transforming jolt while conversing with Jesus during her near-death experience. She wrote:

> My life flashed before me. A life review was in order. When it was over, my head hung in shame – for he had seen it. I was not happy about many of my actions! But then in awe, I turned to Him asking, "How could you still love me so completely after witnessing my many sins?"
>
> "You are a Child of God," He said. "And God is love. I see you purely as love." There was no judgment, only love coming from Him. In order for me to understand this, however, I needed to forgive myself and realize that I was part of divine love... He said, "Everything was made in love for you!" (Laura, NDERF #2995)

Laura's NDE provides a key in understanding God's relationship with humanity. God relates to people like a father relates to young children.

Does a caring, tolerant parent angrily punish a toddler for reaching toward a frosted cupcake? Typically, the parent does not. Instead, the parent realizes the limitations of the child based on his or her level of developmental maturation. For instance, the parent knows that the young child has not yet learned how to delay immediate gratification. If an imperfect human parent can accept a child's impulsiveness without anger, imagine how God realizes our developmental limitations without anger. Would not God, omnipotent in all things, demonstrate unconditional love through perfect knowledge and patience? Indeed, thousands of NDErs affirm the unconditionally-accepting nature of God. Let's dig deeper to understand why.

Have you ever wondered why we live a short while on earth rather than eternally in heaven? Souls are merged with biological organisms for a special purpose: we are sent to earth to complete one or more important missions. We cannot learn all these lessons due to the soul's natural state in heaven. In the spiritual realm, all spiritual beings are interconnected with God and others in a vast unity. There is no confusion, ambiguity, mistakes, interpersonal conflict, suffering, or death. In essence, we are purified because our being is entwined with the essence of God. Although spiritual beings can learn about a wider existence through readily available information, or universal knowledge, they cannot grow from a state of bliss while connected to the perfect Source. There is a qualitative difference between learning facts and learning by experience. Using a crude human analogy, one cannot become an expert tennis player by watching the game on television. Any aspiring Wimbledon player must practice many hours every day. Only through years of instruction, mentorship, and training might a novice player compete professionally. In like manner, God sends souls to difficult physical locales, like planet Earth, to evolve spiritually by learning through challenging soul exercises.

School earth becomes inherently difficult due to our disconnection from the divine unity. This disconnection, although in essence illusionary, becomes necessary so that spiritual beings can make decisions freely. Free-will is a special gift bestowed from God so that spiritual beings can develop with autonomy. God does not want to share existence with robots. Although we are gifted with free-will, we pay a price for our freedom. Mistakes inevitably occur whenever free-will is expressed in the material realm. Should we berate ourselves in an ongoing state of self-loathing? The perfect path lacks viability because it only leads to hopelessness and despair. After all, a flower does not bloom from a withering plant. Perhaps our lives would fully bloom if we approached mistakes from a developmental, growth perspective. The central question then becomes, "Are you learning from your mistakes today?" Think about the most meaningful lessons you have learned during your own life. For me, I have learned the most by making mistakes and conquering adversity. From a developmental growth standpoint, making mistakes, or "sinning," is part of the perfect plan for us all to move toward God over time. I realize I may be losing some readers concerned with this last statement. One may ask, "Is sinning not evil?" The answer is complicated.

To understand sin, it is important to realize that there is a difference between engaging in harmful behavior created out of limitation or ignorance and just being evil. People who generally desire exploitation and violence are acting with perpetual evil *intent*. When they die, lost people will bring their evil intent with them to the spiritual realm. Their souls will be separated from God due to this inconsistency. After all, how can they connect with the good if there is little good within? They would be too disruptive for the spiritual realm. However, God will not throw them into hell as punishment. Rather, they will choose hell by rejecting God by their own free-will. Yet, the human propensity for making daily mistakes does not equate with a psychopath's life-long intention to exploit, inflict pain, and wreck-havoc on society. Julian of Norwich had much to say on this topic, which will be reviewed in depth in chapter nine. For current purposes, she asserted, "Sin is necessary but all will be well, and all will be well, and every kind of thing will be well." (p. 225) Bridget, a non-religious NDEr, had a similar interaction with Jesus who revealed something about the nature of sin. She articulated God's expectation for human imperfection, thus:

> His light seemed to go dim for an "instant" and the beam disappeared. Then "He" said, "You are forgiven. You were flesh and with flesh is biology, and psychology, and instinct, and desire, and mechanism, and ego, and the serving thereof. To be flesh is to sin and that is the nature of being. There is no fault in being human." This made me relax like I have yet to feel since. (Bridget F., NDERF #1654)

Bridget relaxed beyond recollection after she learned that she was not responsible for her biological limitations. She did not have earthly punishments or purgatory hanging over her head. In this manner, she became liberated from her shame. Perhaps Bridget finally understood that living with freedom entails a large measure of messiness in thought and deed. Some people don't want free-will because the responsibility of freedom can be scary. Freedom can be even more frightening, however, for people who believe they failed God and subsequently live in a state of disgrace. But thousands of NDErs, like Bridget, know that God does not judge.

The Patient Conductor

Recently I have been able to relate to God as a patient conductor. Specifically, I experienced a transcendent dream about God one week after I started writing the present chapter. The dream transported me back to a time when I played the euphonium (a type of brass baritone) in the high school band. The band instructor was a rather impatient sort. He would frequently yell at students whenever they made mistakes. Unfortunately, his anger would escalate when a student repeated mistakes. It was not pleasant to watch him stomp his feet and throw his baton down like a child in tantrum. Occasionally, I took the brunt of his wrath whenever I missed my count. So, I dreamt that I was back in my old high school band room accompanied by tight rows of bandmates. The setting generally appeared as I remembered, except that the impatient band director had been replaced by a stranger. The new director was an older gentleman who presented with a poised, confident demeanor. He started the music with his baton and I began to play.

Notes and measures appeared in my mind telepathically. I noticed that the music was amazingly easy to play. Measures of whole notes and whole rests appeared in my mind in a 4/4 time signature. Despite the simplicity of the musical structure, I made several mistakes playing the first measure. The band director stopped the music, calmly instructed me how to play the music without making mistakes, and started the measure over. I messed-up again. "Unbelievable!" I thought in frustration. "Why can't I play this easy piece of music?" Amazingly, the band director did not share my own frustration or impatience. Rather, he simply stopped the music again and made corrective points with poise and calm. Never did he yell or demean me. He did not even shoot me an exasperated glance. He was perfectly patient. Eventually I played the first measure correctly and we proceeded on to the next. As one might guess, I muddled-up that measure as well. Eventually I started playing rows of music correctly after an indeterminate amount of time. Just as I gained confidence, the sign signature changed. The music now became harder. I asked the instructor, "Is this the right way to play the cadence: Dat...dat....dat.dat.dat?" He answered, "Yes." I then began to play the on-going piece in the new time signature. As before, I royally messed-up the first measure and had to do it over again. The band practice continued on in similar fashion, indefinitely.

I woke up in amazement. It felt that I experienced, first hand, the non-judgmental patience of God. I reflected excitedly on the content of my dream by relating it to my spiritual life. As to my first insight, I realized why I struggled to play easy music. I was a spiritual novice, a young trainee learning the fundamentals of love. This explained why I was stuck living on such a spiritually unsophisticated locale as earth. Although humbling, my novice trainee status didn't bother me much because the music continued on forever. This band director would never stop instructing me. It didn't matter how many times I butchered the music. With patient instruction, I knew that I would become an expert musician someday. I was perfect in my imperfection. As for my second insight, I perceived that the other bandmates seemed unfazed by the musical interruptions. I wondered why they were not frustrated by my inability to learn quickly. Then the answer materialized in my mind. The other bandmates were also being interrupted in a similar fashion. Yet, many seemed oblivious that they were playing in a vast orchestra. Deaf to the rich music being played around them, they thought they were playing solo. Some even lost awareness of both the director and the notes. As this second insight began to solidify, I realized that the long soul journey of the non-attentive would be more arduous than the attentive. But, in either case, everyone was learning to play in a vast orchestra at their own speed, whether they knew it or not. Specifically, each bandmate played a musical part within a section entwined with all other parts. Somehow, the end result was rich, beautiful music. This beauty, I realized, could be conceptualized as a gestalt. By gestalt, I mean that the integrated whole was greater than the sum of all individual parts. Likening my band session to the unfolding of the universe, I thought of trillions of spiritual beings creating a universe-sized song throughout eternity. Again, I was amazed.

There was one other insight from the dream I would like to share. Despite my slow pace in learning easy music, I felt that the band director honored my effort. Why would this be so? Julian of Norwich provided an eloquent answer to this question through the use of allegory. The allegory involves a story between a master and his servant. Obviously, the master represents God and the servant represents us. For the sake of brevity I included only some of the relevant text. She wrote:

> The servant stands before his Lord, respectfully, ready to do his Lord's will. The Lord looks on his servant very lovingly and sweetly and mildly. He sends him to a certain place to do his will (life on earth). Not only does the servant go, but he dashes off and runs at great speed, loving to do his Lord's will. And soon he falls into a dell and is greatly injured; and then he groans and moans and tosses about and writhes, but he cannot rise or help himself in any way. And of all of this, the greatest hurt which I saw him in was a lack of consolation, for he could not turn and face to look on his loving Lord, who was very close to him, in whom is all consolation...
>
> I was amazed that this servant could so meekly suffer all this woe; and I looked carefully to know if I could detect any fault in him, or if the Lord would impute to him any kind of blame; and truly none was seen, for the only cause of his falling was his good will and his great desire. And in spirit he was as prompt and as good as he was when he stood before his Lord, ready to do his will...
>
> Then this courteous Lord said this: See my beloved servant, what harm and injuries he has had and accepted in my service (the inevitable suffering tied to growth in physical existence) for my love, yes, and for his good will (personal growth through acts of free-will). Is it not reasonable that I should reward him for his fright and his fear, his hurt and his injuries and all his woe? And furthermore, is it not proper for me to give him a gift.[7]

What an amazing revelation. Within these short passages, Jesus revealed a radically divergent understanding of human worth from traditional Christian doctrine. Whereas the church emphasizes the tragedy of sin and the horrendous state of the human condition, Jesus emphasizes compassion for our painful condition living in the material realm. Moreover, Jesus respects our willingness to serve God on the tough grounds of school earth, or some other challenging school yard. In other words, God admires our bravery to work disconnected with the divine unity. Greatly impacted by the allegory, I have begun to apply these teachings to my life attitude and mission. I do not see myself as a mediocre individual relegated to live on a path of social convention. Instead of hiding in a state of self-doubt, I speak loudly by sharing through spoken and written word. Moving ahead in confidence with the direction of God, I am all the more motivated to play life's music correctly. I want to grow in harmony with God's cadence rather than stagnate by playing solo. With Jesus at my side, all will be well. I do not have to worry about making mistakes as long as I learn from them and try to do better. As my life comes to a close, I will be able to look back, despite my failings, with an attitude of celebration.

The Celebration of Us

The good is recognized more in heaven than on earth; there is no holding back the celebration of God's wonderful creation. Celebrating the return of an earth sojourner is no exception. As portrayed in Julian of Norwich's master and servant allegory, God honors all difficulties and suffering endured by souls living as humans on school earth. After all, how I grow greatly impacts others and how others grow greatly impacts me. In this manner, it is not just for our own benefit that we grow, but for the unity of heaven. How is growth recognized? Jesus does not just give us a pat on the back when we return. Heaven, itself, joins together in festive celebration. Here is an example of an NDEr, named Carlos, who returned home and was greeted by a rejoicing heavenly host:

> I "saw" Christ as the most indescribable, radiant, powerful, ever Divine Light Essence coming through an immense Golden Portal surrounded by infinity...
>
> The whole of Heaven was loudly celebrating and rejoicing with me on my arrival! I was back! I could "hear" heavenly bells, trumpets, angelic choirs, laughter and all kinds of happy, joyful sounds of infinite gladness for which we have no name here on earth because those things do not exist here.
>
> I felt the unspeakable, all encompassing, unconditional Love of God for me. It felt really "personal" and because of its unconditional character is almost incomprehensible. To the point where I thought: "All this Love for me? Who am I? I am just a boy who grew up in a middle-lower class family, in a regular neighborhood, went to a regular school. I have no accomplishments." (Carlos, NDERF #3601)

Carlos expressed wonder at the large, lavish welcoming presented in heaven on his behalf. Still existing in a transition state between the physical and spiritual life, he appeared confused by all the attention. Carlos did not understand, at that time, just how special he was to God. But that was to be expected given that he just departed a life defined by human frailties. I can relate to his confusion by identifying with the servant falling into the dell. Just as I try to get up on my own, I fall down again. Even though Carlos evaluated his life to be mediocre, God used a different gauge to measure his worth. Perhaps the difference boils down to a matter of perspective, or seeing the "big picture." Whereas we, as humans, tend to measure our worth through achievements or wealth living on earth, God measures our worth through our eternal being. Our eternal being is not defined by any one action, or even set of actions accumulated over the years. Rather, our eternal being signifies an accumulative existence stretching from the indeterminable past to an endless future as one of God's children. Jesus explained this concept to Julie, during her NDE, in this way:

> We then walked over next to the river then Jesus took both my hands turning my palms upward. While holding my hands he said, "I want you to remember something. You are of a royal lineage. You are a child of God, the Most High God. You live in the world, but are not of the world. Your rightful place is in heaven with the Father." I said, "Yes, I understand." (Julie H, NDERF #3228)

Julie learned that she needed to transcend the perspective of a short human life span. God, interconnected with all heaven, measures worth through the crystal lens of unconditional love. We are individually loved within the context of unified spirit; a unified progression built over trillions upon trillions of years. Who uses the right measuring gauge? Obviously, an all-knowing, eternal God has the correct perspective. Hard as it is for us to accept, God endows each of us with immeasurable value. God values us so much that we are always the center of divine love and attention. Julian of Norwich writes:

> And just as we were to be without end, so we were treasured and hidden in God, known and loved from without beginning.[7]

> We are his bliss, we are his reward, we are his honor, we are his crown. And this was a singular wonder and a most delectable contemplation, that we are his crown.[7]

Do loving parents lavish attention on their young child? Of course they do. Might not these parents perceive their smiling baby like a royal prince or princess? Seen in this context, the crown becomes a metaphor for the expression of complete, attentive love toward a helpless dependent. The following NDEr expounds on the unity metaphor of a crown:

> He then lifted me off the bed and propelled me at great speed such that reality became a sort of tunnel; at the same time the conversion of reality towards a single point was emphasized by the 'words', "The Union of All Things." This Union was in fact Jesus, though I saw no typical person, but felt the magnificence of mercy and kindness, and then stopped abruptly at the endpoint where an unbelievably beautiful but simple gold crown was fixed over my head, and at the same time I paused there for several seconds. I was bathed in jewels that could be described only as spiritual concentrations of pure kindness. (Alan F., NDERF #1760)

Doting parents crown their infant with kindness, despite all his/her little messes. In greater fashion, God loves and crowns us with pure kindness despite all our bigger messes.

As a side note, only a minority of NDErs report experiencing large celebrations, like Alan, during their near-death experiences. Just because reports of these experiences are sparse does not mean they are reserved just for a few special souls. I suspect that everyone will eventually experience an individualized type of celebration in heaven after they die. It is important to remember that scenes within near-death experiences are only snapshots into the spiritual realm. No person returning to earth experiences remembers the entire process of spiritual transition into death. People returning from death likely experience what they most need to learn and see at that point in their earthly life. Along these same lines, they are most likely to remember certain messages meant to be relayed back to humanity.

In the next celebration example, a man named Herbert struggled to value himself while living on earth. The heavenly host expressed a different assessment of Herbert. He wrote:

> The place was an endless field, full of grass and flowers of all colors, and trees that sang quiet songs, and they were all welcoming me. Me? "Who the hell am I that they would do this," I thought. "Why do they welcome me?"

I took a path that continued toward a place where bright lights shone, some kind of a structure, full of people, by the thousands. And they all cheered and welcomed me. I knew that I am not any kind of a hero or person of importance, but they were rejoicing in that I had come. Then, out of the bright lights came members of my family, many dear people that we had lost over time, my grandfather, aunts, uncles, cousins, and even those whom I only knew in pictures - and my childhood friends and their relatives. And they all came to greet and welcome me... (Herbert M., NDERF #322)

Herbert had difficulty grasping the lavish celebration he received in heaven and long searched for answers after his return to earth. The love of heaven seemed incredulous from Herbert's limited human view of himself. Hopefully, over time, Herbert will gain a greater grasp of the big picture of unity and infinity. As he moves forward in his quest for knowledge, he will at least know that he is loved by his extended family and the heavenly multitude. Hopefully, over time, many more of us will begin to grasp the "big picture" and join in the celebration that constitutes our fallible, human lives.

Responding to Love with Love

As we finish this chapter, the unconditional nature of God's love cannot be emphasized enough. Unconditional love signifies that we are always cherished even when we mess up very badly in life. Unconditional love also signifies that our value is celebrated by the entirety of heaven even when our lives seem mediocre to us. How are we supposed to respond to the highest echelon of love? Perhaps Jesus said it best. Jesus states that the greatest commandment is to "love your God with all your heart, all your soul, all your mind, and with all your strength. But of *equal* importance, you are to love your neighbor as yourself." (Mark 12:30) In this manner, we are all to respond to God's unified love with unified love toward others. Learning how to love through independent experience is how we grow as spiritual beings in the material realm. It is the meaning of life.

The commandment to love with all our heart becomes difficult to see clearly through the small, warped lens of strict religious doctrine. Only a personal relationship with God can unlock love in a tangible way, not unbendable laws or strict commandments. We must step beyond

76

mere belief to make love real through knowing God as a loving Father rather than as a stern master. According to Mathew 11:28, Jesus said:

> Come to me, all of you who are weary and carry heavy burdens, and I will give you rest. Take my yoke upon you. Let me teach you, because I am humble and gentle, and you will find rest for your souls. For my yoke fits perfectly, and the burden I give to you is light.

Jesus did not say, "My yoke only fits perfectly if you are perfect." After all, Jesus asserted that he came to earth for the sinner, not for the righteous. The yoke fits perfectly when we are intimately transformed through a loving personal relationship with Jesus. Generalizing our love to everyone we meet becomes easier with this transformation. What is the biggest obstacle to an intimate relationship with God? Beyond the pride of ego, the biggest obstacle is fear of judgment.

Fear, like anger, is a primitive emotion. Even reptiles and fish will engage in flight or fight responses when danger is perceived. The emotion of fear is incredibly strong because organisms depend on fear for survival. So strong, in fact, that it overpowers all positive emotions. Some people become paralyzed with fear when making difficult decisions. Either they are mired in guilt for past decisions or afraid of making new ones. Ironically, it may be their fear of God that keeps them from best achieving their mission to serve God. Simon Peter serves as a relevant example of someone who tried to reject his mission to serve God because of fear. Peter loathed himself when he met Jesus: he viewed himself unworthy of following Jesus because he believed that he was a wretched sinner. Let's take a look at the dialogue between Peter and Jesus found in Luke 5:8:

> When Simon Peter realized what had happened, he fell on his knees before Jesus and said, "Oh, Lord, please leave me. I'm too much of a sinner to be around you."

> Jesus replied to Simon, "Don't be afraid! From now on you'll be fishing for people!"

Initially, Peter couldn't even face Jesus. Transformed by unconditional acceptance, he put his fear aside and followed Jesus. Jesus demonstrated the same lesson to an NDEr named Odell who had a near-death experience at age eleven. Odell shares the following experience:

I almost fell all over myself trying to get away from Him. He was so pure and clean that I was not worthy of being in His presence, nor anywhere close to Him. I was too adulterated and contaminated with the impurities of this world. I was contaminated with the impure deeds of the things that I had done: lying, stealing, fighting, all of the negative things that a little 11 year-old boy had done. I was contaminated with all the mental impurities that I had done: hatred, distrust, sarcasm, resentment, fear, narcissism, and anger. Even though I wanted to stay there in His presence, I couldn't, because God's law forbids everything evil from heaven.

Jesus stretched His hand toward me and immediately, all my guilt fell away and I received the most overpowering feeling of love from Him. Although His lips did not move, He said "Fear not. Peace." ... (Odell H., NDERF #2583)

When Jesus stretched his hand, all of Odell's fear fell away. Fear's opposite, peace, suddenly enveloped him. How did this radical transformation occur so rapidly? Remember, fear is a powerful, primitive emotion. Peace can only surface when fear is removed. Like anger and peace, fear and peace cannot coexist at the same time. Fear was removed when Odell was transformed by the perfect love of Jesus. John 4:18 explains about the power of divine love, "Such love has no fear because perfect love expels all fear." Both Simon Peter and Odell were transformed by an intimate interaction with Jesus. Rather than sulking in the shadows muttering words of self-disgust, they put their sin behind them as past lessons learned. Then they moved forward with confidence to fulfill their mission in life. Take a look at Simon Peter. He, later, denied Jesus three times. Despite his huge failure, Peter held steady in his love for Jesus and later founded what became the Catholic Church.

I would love to witness a spiritual transformation on earth emulating the tenacity of Peter. But how many people hold back their relationship with God by saying, "I am too much of a sinner to be around you Lord." It is time to see Jesus from the lens of unconditional love, not from stern, angry deity. If love is truly unconditional, there can be no anger. Julian of Norwich learned this truth from revelations imparted by Jesus during her NDE. She writes:

We are sinners. ... And despite all this, I saw truly that our Lord was never angry, and never will be. Because he is God, he is good, he is truth, he is love, he is peace; and his power, his wisdom, his charity and his unity do not allow him to be angry.[7]

Julian of Norwich's words are incredibly powerful, especially given the broader religious culture of fearing God. I hope this chapter has impressed upon you, the reader, that there is nothing to fear. God loves you without any strings attached. God does not want to measure your worth by counting sins, judging your biological drives, showing disappointment, and punishing out of anger. God certainly does not want to throw you into eternal hell as an act of punishment. These teachings fly against the very nature of unconditional love. Because God is not angry, God's peace can envelop us with perfect love. After all, God's love is the force that connects all of creation. Julian of Norwich writes:

> I was answered in spiritual understanding, and it was said: What, do you wish to know your Lord's meaning in this thing? Know it well, love was his meaning. Who reveals it to you? Love. What did he reveal to you? Love. Why did he reveal it to you? For love. Remain in this, and you will know more of the same. But you will never know different, without end.[7]

What an amazing passage of text written over seven centuries ago. If the writings of Julian of Norwich are to be believed, then love captures the when, how, why, and what of God. Love exists as the eternal driving force of the universe. The more amazing aspect is the depth and scope of God's love. Some people believe that love exists merely as a biological feeling. In reality, bliss is only an emotional byproduct of love. Rather, love includes various other-centered acts that include, but are not limited to, genuine respect, unconditional regard, sincere caring, hard forgiveness, and self-sacrifice. Love demands people to step forward courageously to lift up others, even when loving tasks are demanding, difficult, or emotionally challenging. What remains so hard for us, God does automatically. Moreover, God loves us unconditionally all the time. In the next chapter, we will explore just how God relates to us in full, perfect love. Specifically, we will explore the myriad of ways that Jesus loves each individual.

CHAPTER FIVE

A FIRE TENDED BY JESUS

*T*he *Tragedy of Macbeth,* Shakespeare famously wrote, "Life's but a walking shadow, a poor player, that struts and frets his hour upon the stage, and then is heard no more; it is a tale told by an idiot, full of sound and fury, signifying nothing."[1] What does it mean to live a life that signifies nothing? More specifically, how do people live without a true life standard? At best, the aimless invent an internal moral compass to find their way. At worst, they lack any real compass beyond selfish need. Perhaps most operate between these extremes; their compass needle fluctuates. Many of these people abide by the law but frequently exploit cracks in the system for personal gain. For those who respect divine order, life is not a tale told by an idiot. Rather, all life is sacred. Unfortunately, divine living appears less sacred when it is drowned out by a hedonistic lifestyle filled with sound and fury. How do the faithful reconcile spirituality with a seemingly nonsensical world? By examining the near-death experiences, we learn that our lives have special meaning despite the chaos and the hurt. For those who feel overwhelmed by the selfishness of the world, it is important to focus on the eternal picture rather than mere decades of human life. Eternal existence is a process. As we will explore in this chapter, life is a series of refinements that allow us slowly to become perfect through our imperfection. Jesus can play a big role in this journey. In fact, Jesus lies at the heart of refinement for it was He who set the world ablaze.

Setting the World Ablaze

There is an organized progression to God's plan. Thinking about big picture ideas, I received two related images lying in bed while between wakefulness and sleep. In the first vision, tall yellow flames lapped upwards into the blackness. In the second vision, the flames were replaced by a dense cluster of green embers bursting forward and outward. What did these brief images symbolize? I quickly recognized that fire, although destructive, primarily works as a transformative and regenerative force. A forest fire, for instance, burns away dead forest litter so that new growth can germinate. Without a process of destructive renewal, the forest slowly sickens and dies. Perhaps my images parallel how God sustains the human soul through regeneration. Indeed, this hypothesis is supported by the Bible. In Luke 12:49, Jesus said, "I have come to bring fire to the earth." Now, Jesus did not literally threaten to burn planet earth in fiery destruction. Rather, Jesus was assigned a special mission to burn away the rotten spiritual refuse of our souls. The term "earth" refers to Jesus' interest in refining the entire human species. That notion may seem impossible, at first glance. How can one man soften the resistance of an entire planet? But with God anything is possible in time, especially when Word and Spirit are active. In this manner, Jesus boldly challenged the human status quo with divine Truth. As a testimony of this power, the Roman Empire converted to Christianity within several centuries after Jesus' crucifixion.

The human desire for power pervaded the ancient world. Jesus entered the human stage under Roman rule: a typical human society built on ego, status, power, and oppression. Armed only by Spirit and Word, Jesus upset the human normalcy. Interestingly, the initial target was not the Roman government itself, but the very religious establishment that claimed to represent the will of God. Jesus never reacted more strongly than against the religious elite who led people away from God in the name of God. In the Gospel of Thomas, Jesus told His disciples:

> The Pharisees and scribes have received the keys of knowledge and were hiding them. They did not go within, and those who wanted to go were prevented by them. (Verse 39)[2]

The religious leaders failed to embrace knowledge about God's true Kingdom. Moreover, they prevented others from discovering the Kingdom. Consequently, the only monotheistic religion in the ancient world was floundering. God responded by sending Jesus to save the world from spiritual stagnation. To achieve this goal, Jesus boldly attacked religious bureaucracy by stoking fires beneath the Pharisees and Sadducees: thwarting legalism by healing on the Sabbath, confronting financial corruption by overturning money tables at the temple, publicly denouncing religious coercion, undermining the moral authority of religious hypocrisy.

Throughout His ministry, Jesus taught that God's Kingdom was based on service; the self serves others rather than others serving the self. When asked about the greatest commandment, Jesus answered:

> You must love the Lord your God with all your heart, all your soul, and all your mind. This is the first and greatest commandment. A second is equally important: Love your neighbor as yourself. (Matthew 22: 37-39)

This commandment by Jesus, gaining high authority in Christendom, has become infused into the Western spiritual lexicon. Such was not the case in the ancient world where the attitude "might make right" fueled greedy empires. Although Jesus ignited the fire in first century Judea, the fire has continuously spread continuously over the earth and continues to refine humanity more than ever. In the Gospel of Thomas, Jesus said: "I have sown fire upon the world, and now I tend it to a blaze." (Verse 10)[2] The word "tend" adds depth to the Luke 12:49 verse. In a forest fire, the out of control inferno causes mass destruction, not only to the forest, but to the seedlings below. In a tended or prescribed fire, the dead brush is burned away, leaving the healthy trees and seedlings intact. As a testimony to the power of Jesus, the world is ablaze today with many tended fires. Meaning, God used Jesus to ignite the fire and Jesus tends it through other spiritual beings and people transformed by the Spirit. Unfortunately, we barely seem to notice the heat because the tended fire burns slowly within our souls.

Although the Spirit is transformative, it is subtle. Humans may not even notice God working powerfully behind the scenes. It is easy to ascribe change to environmental factors rather than spiritual causes. For example, people may attribute guilt as a brain function—a normal human reaction to moral teachings infused by parents, church, and society at large. Behavioral scientists wouldn't study guilt in any other way. As a psychologist, I accept that rewards and punishments, or conditioning, greatly impacts human behavior. Powerful environmental influences are constantly in play and cannot be avoided. Nor would we want to avoid outside influence, for our environment gives reason why spiritual beings are born on earth in the first place. Meaning, we learn most efficiently by experiencing the consequences of independent choices; our behavior is shaped constantly by rewards and punishments through trial and error. For example, if we move away from love toward a selfish stance then, ultimately, our relationships fail and we suffer. Conversely, if we move toward a stance of love, away from selfishness, ultimately our relationships succeed and we discover peace inside. In this manner, suffering decreases the probability of selfish behavior while peace increases the probability of loving behaviors.

Many spiritual people step beyond scientific objectivity and consider mystical operations of the Spirit. Working in tandem with biology and environment, the Spirit, through Jesus, refines our being like a prescribed burn. Specifically, piles of rotten refuse become ignited and slowly burn down to ash while leaving the living wood intact. After the pain, what is left may be refined, beautiful, and most usable. The fruits of the Spirit are diverse actions in love: respect, sacrifice, forgiveness, submission, and repose. Burned away are all the attributes of ego: power, arrogance, sadism, oppression, anger, and hate. By the fire of Christ we are refined. The unrefined individual says "As the one who matters the most, I am so special that I do not need God", whereas the refined individual says "I am special acting as an integral part of the One."

On a side note, a similar refinement process occurs when souls transition into heaven. Apparently, impurities must be burned away for a soul to rejoin God, Jesus, and the angels. NDErs consistently report that spiritual beings lose their pride and negative emotions; there are no quarrels in heaven. Unlike the arduous refining process on earth, purification is relatively immediate in the Spiritual realm. Loni wrote about a cleansing fire during her NDE:

> The fire hit me. It did not burn like fire here. It pierced through every atom of my being, pulling me apart to almost breaking. It was agony and cleansing, both. I knew, without a shred of doubt, that if even a shred more force were added to the fire, I would explode into non-being. At some point, I surrendered to it. I could see into my own energy weaving, for lack of a better term. In my head, I asked, "What are we? How are we judged?" In that same moment, He showed me the golden threads, interwoven, that made me, me. But that I did not exist alone. My golden energy threads extended throughout the universe, and they were not "mine" at all. We, humanity, are all woven together

and we are part of God's tapestry, of sorts. There really are no words that can adequately describe this. In between the golden threads, however, He leaves each of us empty spaces. The way He showed me is that we can fill up these empty spaces between the weave of threads with light or with darkness during our lives. We are made of God, but we are given free-will. He has only to glance at us to know how we spent that free-will. There is no way to hide any of it. And only His fire can clean up the dark spots. (Loni NDERF #3429)

As seen in this submission, refinement cleans up the dark spots so that the golden threads can shine unblemished. These golden spots are not just our own, but the essence of Spirit pouring into all of us. Steve wrote this about his NDE:

In a paradoxical sort of way you could say that anger, hatred, greed, jealousy as well as all other forms of human suffering were designed to exist in this world exclusively for our benefit because they do not exist back home. (NDERF #441)

All these negative drives and emotions, although disconnecting to the Source, also serve us. Through a spiral of lessons they motivate us to connect with the divine through spiritual growth. The process of spiritual growth is very slow; a process that has ramifications here on earth. Some people think that they can make poor choices without notice or impact. They are wrong. Every choice creates a recognizable spot within our soul that carries into life after death. For me, I would like to return to God with more light spots than dark. Partly for this reason, I choose to emulate Jesus to hasten my journey of transformation. Through this emulation, I hope to shower embers of the Spirit on to others.

The Spreading Embers

In the second part of my vision, hot green embers supplanted the fire. To me, these embers represented all people of the Spirit emanating from the fire as fire. Meaning, those unified with the Spirit propagate the Kingdom outward in message and deed. Christ-minded people, from diverse cultures and religions, have tended a fire of love throughout the centuries. When good soil becomes fertilized by the Word and watered by the Spirit, green growth germinates beneath the ash. With the widespread power of the Word and the Spirit at work, planetary renewal can occur. Let's look more closely at the process.

Fiery embers of love fly out and spark up little fires here and there. Sometimes wet wood resists the spark. At other times, the embers spark up small fires. On rare occasions, one spark may hit just the right place and cause a large forest fire. Unfortunately, the dead underbrush is wet with ego. Although the burning process seems painfully slow, I do believe it is steadily progressing. After all, why would God, knowing the future fully, create and invest in a hopeless situation? As Julian of Norwich stated, "Every kind of thing will be well."³ Perhaps one can think of the glacial pace of spiritual evolution as seasonal epochs. In Ecclesiastes 3:1, it is written, "There is a time for everything, and a season for every activity under the heavens." The ministry of Jesus marks the beginning transition between our winter and spring. We have been in very early spring ever since Jesus set the world ablaze two thousand years ago. In the Gospel of Phillip, it is written:

> Those who sow in winter reap in summer. Winter is this world, summer is the world of Openness. Let us sow in the world, so as to harvest in summer. To pray is not to prevent winter, but to allow summer. Winter is not a time of harvest, but of labor. (Verse 7)⁴

All seasons are perfect in human imperfection. In the grand scheme, there is nothing wrong with living through the growing pains of late winter and early spring. It may not always feel that way for human beings stuck on earth. No individual can prevent the winter, not even through our prayers for peace and the end of suffering. Rather, it is our collective mission to make the world a better place through diligent labor and perseverance. After all, the fire, started two thousand years ago, needs much more tending. Although spiritual transformation seems painfully slow, I believe a delayed spring is finally starting to sprout in earnest; buds are popping up everywhere. This book would not have been well-received only a few decades ago. Now, people are beginning to search for the God of Openness and expand their spiritual horizons in love. Eventually, green growth will spread throughout the world as our springtime matures. Hopefully, many souls will flower from our love sent now and into the future. In due time, even summer will arrive for the time of harvest. I partially credit the quiet influence of the near-death experience for the recent uptick in global spiritual transformation. A good related question to ask is, "How does the NDE transform people globally?" The answer is multifaceted. In one aspect, transformation comes from the power of our mission.

Tending the Fire through Individual Mission

Some people perceive their lives as pointless. I can understand their stance. After all, NDErs describe heaven as a place of love, interconnection, cooperation, knowledge, freedom, and bliss whereas earth is a place of struggle, conflict, sickness, and physical death. It seems that God's sending souls to earth would be wasteful, even a bit cruel, if it didn't serve a specific purpose. Fortunately, divine purpose is woven within the fabric of the universe. For humanity, the soul's fusion with body becomes a vehicle for personal growth. Perhaps it would be most accurate to compare life on earth to attending a challenging school. The following NDEr wrote:

> I was told that the earth is like a big school, a place where you can apply spiritual lessons learned and test yourself, under pressure, to see if you can actually "live" what you already know you should do. Basically, the earth is a place to walk the walk and literally live the way it should be done. (NDERF #2932)

Humanist psychologist Abraham Maslow created a psychological construct called self-actualization. He proposed that self-actualization occurs when a person reaches their full potential as a human being. He wrote:

> Self-actualization, since I have found it only in older people, tends to be seen as an ultimate or final state of affairs, a far goal, rather than a dynamic process, active throughout life, Being, rather than Becoming.[5]

Although I applaud Maslow's concept of a fixed human ideal, I have yet to observe a human being who has reached full potential. Even the most mature, self-aware person seems riddled with imperfections. Earth's most actualized may have achieved, at best, a rudimentary grade on the God scale. Still, the general idea of self-actualization may have some spiritual merit. NDErs consistently report that souls advance through eternity by realizing the true Self as a part of God; the unified divine found within and without. As Jesus said in the Gospel of Thomas:

The Kingdom is inside you and it is outside you. When you know yourself, then you will be known, and you will know that you are the child of the Living Father. (Verse 3)[2]

Although we are children of the Living Father, no one can ever become God, no matter the level of spiritual advancement, because God is infinite and perfect. Yet, perhaps we can achieve spiritual self-actualization, reaching our full potential in heaven, by becoming all-loving in our inner essence. The path toward self-mastery is no doubt very long and winding, reaching near eternity in time. Reaching this pinnacle requires much more than a lifetime of work due to the arduous nature of learning by experience.

Anyone who has sat through class knows that people can learn through observation and instruction. Although rote learning has merit, raw information cannot replace life experience, especially when it comes to learning how to love. Reflect on your own life. Do forgiveness, sacrifice, and unconditional respect come automatically? Even when we know love's attributes, we often fail to act accordingly. In my own life, I was taught love well as a child. Yet, I am just beginning to master the art of love, decades later, in a crawling fashion. For love attributes must be learned through a series of lessons, both positive and negative. In fact, it is the negative life lessons that often teach and refine us the most. To fully learn empathy, we need to fall down and know pain. To fully learn sacrifice, we need to go without and know suffering. To fully learn unconditional regard, we need to become an outcast and know rejection. To fully learn forgiveness, we need to make mistakes and know mercy. To fully learn humility, we need to deflate ego and know weakness.

Learning humility, or selflessness, may be the first step in learning love. After all, one cannot empathize, sacrifice, respect, or forgive others when ego dominates. The egotistical have no time to devote to others given their insatiable demand to fulfill the "me." Although ego may provide immediate pleasures for the spiritual novice, it will ultimately fail to provide lasting gratification. The astute spiritual wayfarer eventually discovers that humility through service, although difficult, is the key to finding happiness on school earth. In other words, they need to push ego aside before they can reach out in service and grow in earnest. Jesus explained the process within the Gospel of Thomas: "Whoever has become rich, may he become king; whoever has power, may he renounce it." (Verse 81) Jean-Yves

LeLoup, a Gospel of Thomas scholar, explained Verse 81 in this way, "We cannot renounce something that we do not truly possess. Before surrendering our ego, we must have an ego to surrender!"[2] In other words, before we know to choose the righteous path, we need to bite into the apple from the tree of knowledge.

The soul leaves a state of perfect spiritual unity to co-exist within a physical body. Limited by flesh and brain, the soul becomes temporarily isolated from divine connection while trapped in the material realm. In the Gospel of Thomas, Jesus asked, "When you were One, you created two. But now that you are two, what will you do?" (Verse 11)[2] Jesus' inquiry centers on God's gift of freedom to each being living on earth. God does not want to share existence with "mini-me" clones. Rather, God wants us to develop individuality through life experiences created by choices. As when a young adult first leaves the safety of home, he or she must partially disconnect from parental nurturance in order to be independent. With our new-found spiritual freedom, do we choose a materialistic path built on selfish pleasures? Or, do we choose a soul path built on loving service? The former is a path of the body while the latter is the path of unified Spirit. Our divine mission is eventually to choose a path of Spirit and grow toward God.

Most NDErs agree that each person has been given a special divine mission to learn how to love on school earth. Their mission may consist of one or two core assignments. Some may have even been blessed with several important assignments. The topic of mission is detailed in chapter six of my first book, *Psychology and the Near-death Experience: Searching for God.*[6] But, for current purposes, it is important to emphasize that our life mission(s) are critically important. How we choose to live human life impacts not only our personal growth, but the entire interconnected tapestry of creation. The following NDEr, named Atilla, likewise reported:

> But you have a mission. In this moment I saw all the people with their unique destinies as a great mosaic, and my destiny was intertwined in that mosaic. The harmony of all these destinies together was amazing. I knew that if my own destiny failed then the harmony of the whole would be destroyed. I knew that I had to fulfill my destiny. (Atilla, NDERF #1658)

The connection between mission and destiny speaks to the ultimate purpose of every conscious being. Mutual spiritual evolution creates balance whereas avoidance of responsibility upsets the harmony of the Whole. Perhaps people would take life more seriously if they understood the eternal picture, knowing that their every action influences the eternal unfolding of the divine mosaic. No one lives in isolation; spiritual growth is mutually interdependent. Others depend on our success of mission because we help each other grow toward the Source in a stepwise fashion throughout eternity. So important are individual missions, in fact, that God assists in a variety of ways. For instance, Jesus, the rainbow of heaven, has an important role in helping us succeed on our long, important journey. Initially, He modeled the Kingdom during His life ministry. But just as importantly, Jesus continues to transform the heart of each spiritual wayfarer, tending the refining fire one soul at a time. It is to our benefit to listen and accept the message, as our mission belongs to God.

Our Mission Belongs to God

Many assert their right to make individual choices within the law. The U.S. constitution, for example, preserves such individual freedoms. By extension, one might argue that each of us has the individual right to set personal mission and life goals. Unfortunately, it can be too easy to dismiss God in the equation believing that God is aloof and uninvolved in daily human affairs. Yet, each soul has chosen at least one life mission, to accomplish while living on school earth, that has been pre-established by God. Although missions may vary, they are all founded on the principle of unconditional love. We are to learn how to love in all its facets: respect, humility, caring, forgiveness, sacrifice, and so forth. Unfortunately, we cannot give the excuse "I didn't remember what I was supposed to do" when we die. Opportunities to serve in love are boundless. Within these opportunities people discover their mission. We do not even have to embark on a great life search for purpose, as the overall architecture of mission has been carefully pre-planned and assigned to us. The fixed plan includes, but is not limited to, country of birth, family of origin, family, religion, gender, race, sexuality, socio-economic status, and health. More difficult to tease out, due to life's inherent complexity, are the people and events strategically placed into our lives.

Perhaps our mission(s) can be likened to a river flowing through a canyon. Sometimes the river tumbles and turns over boulders and other times it flows placidly over smooth stretches. In other words, the direction of our mission depends, in part, on the steepness and bends of the canyon created before us. Unlike a real river, however, there are countless forks in our journey. This is where free-will becomes important. Unfortunately, many people blindly follow the poor contours of life, like water flowing down the path of least resistance. But those, in concordance with the Kingdom, can intentionally redirect their flow.

Freedom and determinism have long been debated in philosophical circles. From reading near-death experience accounts, both appear applicable. Free-will, chance, and determined outcomes churn and shape our lives into dynamic journeys. Leonard learned something about cause and effect from a life preview (the opposite of a life review):

> Most people have a life review after they have lived their life. In my case I was looking at a life I hadn't lived yet; I was shown the complete life I would possibly lead. I say possibly because we all apparently have freewill, making not only mine, but everybody's future fluid and flexible. (Leonard R. NDERF #2552)

Another NDEr, named Tracy, likewise wrote about a life preview:

> It was all seen! Everything! Meanings, events, pain, sorrow. Not just that, but why we are here! What I'm to do. My purpose and how important my return was to all of mankind and the effects of now, future and after life. How everything we do or don't do affects everything and everyone by how it all ripples through time-space. Nothing was hid during a life preview. Not that anything was set in stone; life was destined and yet was not. Everything we do matters from the smallest to the largest! (Tracy T., NDERF #1648)

Are we truly the captain of our lives? If life is partly pre-determined, then perhaps people should reevaluate individual freedom. Using a Star Trek analogy, we may think we are sitting in the captain's chair when our course destination has actually been set by ship's computer. In similar manner, God sets the template for our lives before we are born. The following NDEr echoed what others have said upon returning from death:

> I came to understand that we all choose to come to earth to fulfill a plan of some sort or even learn about a particular interest. We choose our bodies, parents, and life plan. (NDERF #1653)

Although we participate by making many individual choices, we are placed in certain bodies to learn certain things that we lack. Perhaps the school analogy might still be useful. I had to complete a core set of curriculum to graduate college with a psychology degree. My final transcript was similar to other psychology students, even if the sequence and day-to-day experiences during my college journey were unique. For instance, I delayed taking the dreaded statistics class for several semesters. Yet, I still completed all the standard coursework, including statistics, in order to graduate. In similar manner, we are all faced with painful experiences on school earth that we dread. Although souls have the freedom to delay or refuse experiences, they cannot spiritually grow without them. If souls want to graduate to the next level closer to God, then they must complete and benefit from the life courses set to be completed.

The school analogy, although helpful, does not capture the vitally important fact that individual mission is connected integrally to a larger group mission. As discussed earlier, we each share responsibility in promoting group ascension toward God. Movement applies not only to humans but, probably, to all intelligent beings in the universe. Ultimately, all species are connected as brothers and sisters to the Father. Each step toward God allows us to love each other and commune more deeply; a stairway in heaven, if you will. We achieve maturity by inching our lives toward the One. In other words, we learn to act in concordance with the Father. This reality is difficult to appreciate while living on earth where materialism predominates. Too many people define their purpose in isolation. Their life parameters usually involve exerting power, hoarding money, or seeking attention. Hubris is illusionary within a unified reality based on love. With this in mind, perhaps a more sacred word is in order to describe mission.

Covenant

Our life goals are not really ours because they were established in covenant with God. Laura, who initially argued to stay in heaven, learned about her covenant during an NDE. She wrote:

> In all of Creation, He said, your infant son chose you to be his mother! None other! Together you made a covenant to fill these roles in your lives on earth. This covenant is and was very sacred, not to be taken

lightly. Suddenly I could not wait to return to Earth. (Laura M., NDERF #2995)

The term "covenant" should convey that the stakes are high in life; our choices matter. It is ignorant to claim, "It's my life; I can do whatever I want." Although we can choose to reject the path of God, it will lead only to failure, spiritual stagnation, and darkness. God rejoices when we choose to abide by our divine contract to learn, teach, and act in love. Laura continued:

> There is a contract with our lives that involve our own needs and the needs of others. The term covenant is a very sacred, holy term. As God made a covenant with Moses, God makes covenant with each one of us before our lives even begin. This is why suicide is a very negative action – it breaks the covenant. (Laura M., NDERF #2995)

Any disregard of our sacred mission breaks a promise we give to God. It is like a college student who attends college only to sleep through morning class. If parents are paying for college, then the student has broken his or her agreement. In this manner, any immediate investment in the student's education, in time and money, were wasted. One person who attempted suicide received this stern message:

> He said in a stern voice but that was still like a father speaking to a son, "Your life is not to do with as you please. Did you create yourself, give yourself life? No. Neither can you choose death." (NDERF #14)

The next NDE submission was written by an avowed atheist, named David, who tried to escape life challenges by committing suicide. Meeting Jesus on the other side, he basked in the bliss of heaven and demanded to stay. In other words, David tried to opt out of his mission contract. Jesus had no patience with David's pleading and brusquely sent him back to earth. The following conversation ensued:

> "No! I wanna stay!" Jesus replied, "You promised you would do this. And you have much left to do." With that, I was slammed back into my body and I awoke, gasping for breath. (David, NDERF #3240)

Note that Jesus told David, "You promised to do this. You have much left to do." In this manner, Jesus conveyed urgency toward mission.

Having neglected his promises, David needed to make up for lost time. After all, mission does not just impact the one, but everyone in the One. How many people did David influence, either overtly or indirectly, in his life? According to many NDE accounts, countless souls are touched through the interconnected tapestry. Because of this unified purpose to our lives, we cannot claim our mission as our own. Jesus conveyed ownership when He drew in the life experiences of Bridget. During her NDE, Jesus said: "I'll take that, it's for me" and He took the beam from me and touched me. (Bridget F. NDERF# 1654)

In the Gospel of Thomas, Jesus conveyed a similar message:

Angels and prophets will come to you and give you what is yours. And you, too, should give what you have and ask yourself, 'When will the time come for them to take what is theirs.' (Verse 88)[2]

Our life experiences are incorporated within the tapestry when we die; an eternal testament to our small corner of creation. Although our input is cherished, the Creator has ultimate decision in the mission design of the created. It is our job to execute the plan. The egoist, claiming life for him or herself, has become seduced by a mirage of earthly distractions and has forgotten mission. We are like a soldier in the midst of battle, agreeing to secure an enemy-held position. The soldier accepts the challenging assignment as his/her personal mission. The soldier realizes, however, that he or she is willing to fight or be killed for a larger purpose. At one level, the soldier's mission is tied to the survival of the platoon. At a larger level, his actions are tied to the overall war mission conducted by nations. In like manner, we accept mission as ours, to learn and give love from our being. Yet, we also understand that our mission most directly impacts the souls closest to us. At a larger level, our mission impacts the entire tapestry of creation over eternity. In this way, our personal and larger missions work in tandem. At some point the soldier returns home to a ticker-tape parade. In like manner, we are honored for accomplishing divine mission. I refer the reader back to the last chapter on the topic of heavenly celebration. That is not to suggest that our mission accomplishment equates with mastery. We have eternity to evolve spiritually toward perfection. Still, every step, even if small, is honored.

Jesus, in particular, reinforces the importance of accepting and completing our assigned mission during NDEs. Carmel, from her NDE, wrote:

He started to talk, explaining that he was Jesus, and that my great grandfather and I were there by accident and that I needed to go back. I asked him, "What for?" He told me that I had a big job to do for them all. (Carmel B., NDERF #1920)

Carmel decided to return to earth after she understood the meaning of her life. Carole was equally impressed by Jesus' message:

I was SO special that God had told me I had more to do. What else is better than that to make an awkward thirteen year-old feel important? Nothing else mattered what people thought. God loved me enough to send me back here because what I was going to do was so important. I now teach nursing; I teach others how to care for others and how to make a difference in another person's life. (Carole, NDERF #1834)

Carmel and Carole learned that their lives had cosmic importance. Although they were authors of their life, they were not freelance authors. They learned that their specialness was rooted in unity. Carole's understanding of divine purpose transformed her life course. She became a teacher of nursing in order to make a large difference in the lives of others. She began to burn with mission.

Burning with Mission

Our covenant with God, established before birth, was not designed to be easy. Growing in love always brings forth struggle and challenge. The materialist may find this perspective of love confusing. After all, isn't love synonymous with an easy-good feeling for the self? Biological feel-good states, although possibly a byproduct of love, are insufficient to describe the complexity of divine love. Real love is hard work, as evidenced by the selfless life and sacrificial death of Jesus. It requires caring for the careless, respecting when disrespected, forgiving the unforgivable, and sacrificing all that you have. When I examine the life of Jesus, I think, 'I could not do that'. Although it may be impossible to achieve mission completely on our own, there is help for the asking. First, we can read about Jesus' ministry and emulate Him the best we can. Second, we can be transformed by the Spirit. As explored throughout this chapter, transformation occurs by the refinement through the fire of Christ. In the Book of Mark, Jesus said, "For everyone will be purified with fire."

(Mark 9:49) Jesus continues to tend the fire today through covenant as a collaborative process. It is our responsibility to collect the dead wood and ignite a spark. It is God's responsibility to fuel the flames with Spirit and consume the dead wood in a blistering heat. Although slow and painful, new growth emerges in the process; it shoots up alive and vibrant.

The journey toward God can occur quicker when we are open to the transformative power of the Spirit, the refining power of adversity, and the freeing power of awareness. For me, this power became better realized when I opened myself to new possibilities to my earthly purpose, or my mission. This chapter was written in order to help people become better aware of their mission. Recall the servant/master analogy provided by Julian of Norwich. The servant runs off to earnestly serve the master, only to fall and writhe around in a dell. Perceiving disconnection, the servant felt uncomforted and spiritually lost. Don't be like this servant who couldn't see past his or her immediate surroundings. Know that Jesus tends a fire that refines your eternal being behind the scenes. His power comes from the unified Kingdom of God. The skeptic may say, "I don't see Jesus, God, or the Spirit! Show me a spirit and I will believe in the Kingdom." Of course I cannot prove the Kingdom by scientific measurement. As Jesus explained in the Gospel of Thomas:

> The disciples asked him. "When will the Kingdom come?"
>
> Jesus answered, "It will not come by watching for it. No one will be saying, 'Look, here it is!' Or, 'There it is!' The Kingdom of the father is spread out over the whole earth, and people do not see it." (Verse 113)[2]

I cannot prove that the whole earth, and by extension the universe, is the Kingdom of the Father. A person who lacks faith will never believe that Spirit underlies the quantum power bringing forth existence. I can, however, argue that the Kingdom of God is demonstrated through the words and deeds of Jesus in the Bible. I can also say, anecdotally, that my life has been transformed with the burning of mission coming from within and without. In addition, there is another venue available to better understand mission. It is the way of the near-death experience. Jesus frequently addresses individual mission by interacting with visitors in the spiritual realm. In the next chapter, we will explore specifically what Jesus says about accomplishing our mission through the process of change: we will focus on how Jesus continues to tend the fire he set two thousand years ago.

CHAPTER SIX

JESUS, SPIRIT, AND THE CHANGE PROCESS

Imagine a suited man, leaning over a tall pine-colored pulpit, preaching to a congregation over booming speakers. "Accept Jesus into your heart!" he commands. "Heed this invitation to be saved by the blood of Christ. Today is the day to transform your life anew!" If we all need saving by Jesus, then what must we do? Like many readers growing up in the Christian church, I have listened to an assortment of sermons over the decades. Unfortunately, I have found most references to transformation to be vague—either altar calls or moralistic sermons. The messages that resonated most for me were references to the greatest commandment issued by Jesus: we are to love God and our neighbors with all our heart. Are we primarily called by God simply to love everyone? Indeed, this maxim has been repeated not only by Jesus during his ministry, but by the ascended Christ. To illustrate, Jesus communicated the power of love during Yvette's NDE:

> The power of love is the biggest power. Loving one another is essential for our spiritual growth. Everything was created by Love and with Love. (Yvette, NDERF #2600)

It seems interesting that Yvette associated love with spiritual growth during her NDE. After all, spiritual growth is all about change. Indeed, we are all constantly in motion like a blazing fire. In the last chapter, we learned about the transforming fire of Jesus. Although fire appropriately symbolizes a person's radical changes toward love, it does not tell us much about the process. Evangelical Christians often emphasize that the human heart is transformed by the power of Jesus. Although I applaud the recognition of Jesus as a mystical renovator through the Spirit, I think this view is overly simplistic. When it comes to being transformed by love, the Spirit interacts with human psychology like a pair of ballet dancers. We make the first move through our intention, for God doesn't force love on anyone. But if we choose to dance, the Spirit quickly takes the lead and eventually moves us through beautiful poses. Yet, transformation places many demands on the novice dancer tripping over his or her own feet. Unfortunately for the impatient, the acquisition of the Kingdom is partly a nuts-and-bolts affair: learning delay of gratification, controlling rash impulses, utilizing complex interpersonal skills, and reigning in the relentless ego. All of these skills, as one might imagine, require a great deal of learning and experience, even from the school of "hard knocks." In other words, love does not always come automatically or even easily. Rather, love sometimes must be taught. In this chapter, we will review the process of change on several levels. First, we will explore the process of change as a psychological strategy. On the more mystical side, we will next explore the process of change through the transformative power of Spirit. Lastly, we will tackle fear, the poisonous potion that sickens the process of change.

The Process of Learning Love

I often thought that life would be easier if the practice of love came with an instruction manual. I now recognize that I own such a manual through the biblical teachings of Jesus. Jesus taught and modeled the most important qualities of love, such as unconditional regard, service, forgiveness, and sacrifice. As discussed in chapter five, Jesus was sent to this world by the Father in order to be emulated. Yet, Jesus did not retire from teaching after his death on the cross. Jesus continues to teach in other ways, including through near-death experiences. As ambassadors from the spiritual realm, NDErs are returned to their bodies to share knowledge for our benefit. In a sense, they are modern-day apostles. David is one such apostle. During his near-death experience, Jesus provided David with the following life instructions in fulfilling his mission:

> You must live your life for three reasons. The first is you are meant to do something which you have not yet done. The second is you are meant to influence someone you have not yet met. The third is you have not learned enough yet to accomplish the other two. (David, NDERF #1947)

Living through the 1980's, I remember the Nancy Reagan billboard campaigns that directed the reader to "just say no to drugs." Such advice, although harmless, leaves out all the messy details necessary for change. The same can be said about clergy telling their congregations, "Just go out and love everyone." Note that Jesus did not command David simply to fulfill his mission. Rather, Jesus organized a step-wise process for David to learn how to love. It is insufficient for David, or anyone, to proclaim that one can turn love on like a light switch. The hippie movement was based on peace and love in the 1960's. It did not survive, despite the promising speeches and slogans. Likewise, many wedding vows fizzle over the years. I am often amazed how many people perceive love to be an emotion: a warm, fuzzy feeling of contentment or, even more off the mark, sexual infatuation. It is no wonder that people fall in and out of love so easily. As pleasurable feelings inevitably dissipate, so do relationships. The problem is that people need to know how to love before they can act in love. Specifically, they need to *know* how to be humble, caring, forgiving, and respectful. Moreover, they also need to know that unconditional love requires a great deal of service toward others that involves personal sacrifice.

David doesn't need a slogan. David needs to acquire various skill sets to develop a fuller, deeper understanding of love. For illustration purposes, let's examine the attribute of respect. It is easy to respect reputable people in society. It becomes far more challenging to respect the socially undesirable, like the homeless person or the drug addict. Perhaps we are in no position to judge others, especially if we don't know their stories. It takes a well of courage and an attitude of openness to explore other people's tragedies and pain. The acquisition of knowledge requires a complex skill set that includes discernment, mental flexibility, and the synthesis of complex information. Through this process, a more balanced, holistic perspective can be appreciated.

But where do we learn these important skills? Fortunately, the world is filled with mentors and teachers for those who seek and listen. They are the bright embers flying out from the fire. They may include, but are not limited to, parents, extended family, mentors, clergy, scriptural texts, authors, and various love-based institutions. Some teachers explain, while others model. Blessed are the students who receive both.

Ignorance doesn't transform anyone. Knowing different facets of love, such as respect, starts the engine of change. Unless the knowledge of love is applied, however, it rests as a kind of potential energy, worthless until used. As we will explore later in the chapter, fear often becomes a barrier to activating our love. God wants people to crack open the encasement of fear so that their love can shoot up toward the Light. In other words, we are boldly to express our love in the world, armed with the power of knowledge. Let's return to our illustrative NDE journeyman, David. Jesus told David to "do something which you have not yet done." Jesus' proposition may sound risky for those unsuccessful in love, especially for those who never have been loved. Yet, people are nevertheless commissioned to gather their courage and take a risk. Specifically, it is our mission and covenant to serve God. Similar to David, Ed, during his NDE, was instructed to serve God in this sequence:

> First, acquire knowledge for you will use it to better serve me. Second, learn to love for you will need to love to serve me. And third, do good works so that you may better do them in my name. (Ed H., NDERF #599)

David and Ed were both instructed first to acquire knowledge and secondly to utilize these learned skills to serve God. Regarding our example of respect, the love-bearer serves God by activating several multifaceted skills, such as empathy, verbal sensitivity, encouragement, teaching, sharing of resources, and advocacy. Each skill can be broken down into smaller skill sets. For instance, advocacy requires knowledge of resources and the utilization of social contacts. Despite the diversity, all these skill sets share the same foundation: love, a concept embedded in God's unity, is central to our purpose and very existence. Bringing love to fruition becomes easier when we keep our foundation focused in mind. Appreciating love through unity can be difficult, however, when we feel disconnected. This is particularly the case when we don't love or respect ourselves.

One NDEr, named Judi, derided herself as being unintelligent. She developed this self-concept after being subjected to ongoing barbs of criticism by her family; she internalized all the distorted bullhorns blaring in her life. Fortunately, Jesus draws wisdom from a different Source. Judi, along with her unique life work embedded in love, was respected immensely by Jesus during her NDE. If she was judged by the Well of Truth rather than the dry pits of the world, her success in life mission was not contingent on brilliance, but rather on a loving heart. Along these lines, Jesus told her:

> "Judi, none of those things really mattered. You have all you need." He just assured me that I was not stupid, was not "slow" as I was called by my family. He said what I was doing was more important. He explained that because my sister and ex-husband were educated better than I, did not mean I was not even more educated on things of the Lord. I was in such peace, the Lord laughed, not at me, but somehow with me. I just knew He was conveying to me that I had a purpose for HIM. (Judi C., NDERF #596.5)

Jesus taught Judi self-respect, even if she did not measure up to divisive standards of the world. The only thing that mattered was acting in accordance with the Father. This realization allowed Judi to strengthen her mission to love with confidence.

There have been points when I felt alienated and misunderstood during junior high school. Consequently, I felt unimportant compared with the popular students. I reacted by isolating myself. I stand in a different place now. I respect myself by realizing that God's values are rarely respected in a competitive world clamoring with ego. God sees what is important in me, even when other people can't see beyond their narrow material views. I also realize that this maxim holds true for many others, like Judi. With this realization, I have moved beyond focusing on a circle of self-absorbed thoughts. Now, I reach out to others with respect from an anchored position of self-respect.

Like respect, forgiving requires a complex skill set. This process is explored in more depth in chapter seven of my book, *Psychology and the Near-death Experience: Searching for God*.[1] There are several models of forgiveness, but I prefer the version developed by psychologist Everett Worthington. In his book, *Dimensions of Forgiveness*, Dr. Worthington wrote a five step process of forgiving he called REACH.[2] The process of activating forgiveness is as follows:

1. Recall the hurt
2. Empathize with the perpetrator's point of view
3. Forgive the perpetrator as a gift
4. Commit by forgiving publicly
5. Hold on to the forgiveness

The REACH method succeeds when the forgiver has completely dedicated him or herself to the process. To be frank, most people resist forgiveness. Instead, they relish stewing in their anger and fantasizing about revenge. This is a tiring process. The victim not only harbors anger toward the perpetrator, but carries the toxic burden within; its negativity seeps through in drops of irritability or spills over in rage, particularly toward loved ones. In other words, the sharp edge of a grudge cleaves off all inner peacefulness like an axe. The first rectifying step, then, is for the forgiver to gaze within and note the damage caused to their soul. The forgiver also needs to look outward and know the "big picture" of spirituality. By knowing the unconditional loving nature of God, the victim realizes that the perpetrator truly exists as an eternal spiritual soul, a being of God, who is forever cherished by God. The forgiver can also look outward by analyzing the motives of the perpetrator. Often there are understandable reasons why the perpetrator acted hurtfully. Perhaps the perpetrator lashed out from a buried place of insecurity or fear, possibly a consequence of earlier mistreatment. Perhaps the perpetrator was reacting to a hurt, real or imagined, first unleashed by the victim. Or, perhaps the perpetrator never learned how to love. These are just three examples from a lengthy list of possibilities. The main point being that forgiveness requires the forgiver to empathize with the perpetrator; knowing and appreciating the perpetrator's history, feelings, developmental maturity, and life experiences.

In the next NDERF submission, a young man named John felt tormented for years. He joined a monastery hoping to escape his problems, but to no avail. He became so consumed with resentment and self-loathing that he contemplated suicide. On the night before John was going to take his own life, God came to John during sleep. He wrote:

> He then told me to look closely, and it was then I could see a light around my body during every one of the events. I could feel God's love for me as a little boy and he told me that he had always been right next to me, and he had never left my side. I was overwhelmed by his love for me at this point; it was completely overwhelming. It was then

that everyone who had ever hurt me, from my childhood all the way to some of the personalities in the monastery I was having trouble dealing with, I saw, and they too had a light around their bodies.

I could see that we were all wounded children, and the reason we were here was to love and forgive one another, and to help one another through this spiritual journey. I could feel the love and compassion that God felt for not only me, but for everyone I had ever encountered. I was filled with compassion and forgiveness for everyone. (John K., NDERF #3628)

John became transformed by a vision from God: he was led to implement a type of REACH. With God's assistance, John recalled decades of hurt, understood his perpetrators to be wounded children, empathized with his perpetrators' condition, gifted them with an act of forgiveness, publicly announced his forgiveness through an NDERF submission, and held on to forgiveness through the power of the Spirit. Transformed by this process, John replaced years of debilitating pain with compassion, forgiveness, and inner peace. Not only did suicidal thoughts vanish, but John began to thrive in developing a life mission based in love.

Going back to David's NDE, he was charged with a third task. Specifically, Jesus directed David to, "*influence* someone you have not yet met." Influencing someone, in this context, refers to impacting the life of another to the point of inspiring transformation. In the life of Jesus, influencing others meant bringing forth the Kingdom in word and deed. I suspect that Jesus appointed David to follow His lead, for we are all commissioned to influence others in accordance with divine purpose. Influencing should not be confused with coercion. Influencing respects free-will. Coercion involves one will dominating another, whether through quiet intimidation or overt threat.

As discussed in the last chapter, Jesus set the fire and we are its spreading embers. Once the dead wood has been burned, will new seed germinate? That depends on the receptiveness of the receiver; seeds sprout only in fertile soil. Many Judeans angrily rejected the message of Jesus. Certainly we can expect the same reaction. Furthermore, the spreading embers require potency. During college, I witnessed many "mall preachers" berate their audiences and promise them fire and brimstone in the afterlife. Their embers were hot with rage, but not potent in love. Their strategy was consistently met with dismissal, anger, and ridicule. No one, to my knowledge, was "saved" by their proselytizing. To be truly effective in teaching about Jesus, one must be proficient at love. Yet, proficiency takes time.

In their landmark textbook, *Motivational Interviewing*, psychologists William R. Miller and Stephen Rollnick analyze the process of change in relation to therapy clients.[3] Specifically, they note that adaptive change usually does not occur naturally. For change to take root, a person needs to be motivationally prepared to enact newly learned behavior over time. This is not easy. New behaviors may feel awkward and uncomfortable at first. Moreover, weeks of practice are required to learn new skills and minimize mistakes. Only after the behavior has become ingrained within the client's daily repertoire does it begin to feel natural. With time and diligence, hopefully the new behavior will be maintained automatically. The same process is involved in each attribute of learning love. Before love can be enacted, as discussed, the foundations of knowledge and motivation must be laid. In the activation phase, unconditional love still takes a long time to master. Only after love becomes part of our everyday repertoire does it become natural and spontaneous. Perhaps the effortless expression of love, emanating from our being, serves as the litmus test for spiritual maturity.

To better examine how love can be maintained, let us return to the attribute of forgiveness. Brian, during his NDE, was provided specific instructions on how to maintain forgiveness:

> This being began telling me that I had some things to do. I was given three specific instructions. First was that I had to learn to forgive others, as it was one of the hardest things for me to do when crossed. I had to forgive myself also. God knew I had a real problem with forgiveness of others and for me to learn it; I have to also teach it. I was told that if I just said that I forgave others that it would not be from the heart. In order to show my truth in forgiving, I have to constantly be working on it. Second, I had to do something about my anger. Third, I had to go talk, teach, preach, write, and do a video of my experience. (Brian C., NDERF #3827)

To maintain forgiveness, Brian was instructed to forgive from the heart. Moreover, it was paramount that he keep practicing. Sincerity and practice are part of REACH. However, a couple of additional steps can be sorted out. First, Brian was tasked to forgive himself in order to forgive others. Forgiving oneself can be seen as the backside of the forgiveness coin: it is difficult to forgive others when the mind becomes plagued by self-directed attack. Second, Brian had to teach forgiveness, not just by talking, but by writing and videotaping his experience. Teaching gives repetition and meaning to the behavior. In this manner, forgiveness becomes solidified as part of Brian's being; now he can become a fiery ember that transforms others. In addition to the psychological constructs discussed, an unseen power was at work: maintaining forgiveness opened Brian up to the power of Spirit. It is a state of being where his ego could finally take a back seat to his soul.

The Quiet Transforming Power of Spirit

David, our spiritual sojourner, was tasked with a mission to learn, express, and teach love. His multifaceted task seems daunting. Fortunately, David does not have to walk alone because the Spirit of God always accompanies his journey. The same may be said of us. What is Spirit? Called Ruwach in Hebrew, Spirit translates as the Breath of God.[4] The Breath of God is boundless. A writer of Psalms asks, "Where shall I go from your Spirit? Where shall I flee from your presence?" (Psalms 139:7) The answer is nowhere, for the Spirit of God exists everywhere as Is. The author of the Gospel of Phillip describes the omnipresent nature of Spirit in this fashion: "Father and son are simple names. The Breath is a double name, for it is everywhere: above, below, in the visible, in the invisible." (Verse 33)[5]

Likewise, Jesus conveyed the wonder of an omnipresent Spirit in the Gospel of Thomas:

> If the flesh came into being because of Spirit it is a wonder. But if Spirit came into being because of flesh, it is a wonder of wonders. Yet the greatest wonder is this: how is this Being, which Is, inhabits this nothingness. (Verse 29)[6]

As humans exhale invisible breath, God exhales invisible Breath. However, the former is small while the latter is infinite. In fact, many NDErs have described Spirit as a universal force embedded within the fabric of the universe. In other words, the Spirit is God's essence, which has been made manifest throughout every facet of creation. As Jesus exclaimed, it is utterly amazing that the Spirit makes its home in all things, including all that we perceive as nothingness. Although the Spirit can be seen as a universal ethereal force, orthodox Christians also view the Spirit as a person. NDErs also report a similar experience during their brief stay in the spiritual realm. However, the individuality of Spirit can easily be misunderstood. Perhaps the best way to avoid confusion is to understand Spirit within the context of Unity: the Spirit is the inseparable expression, both in thought and love-force, of God consciousness.

It would be incorrect to claim that the Holy Spirit acts independently of God; that would be seeing separation where none exists. If God and Spirit are united, then why use separate concepts? In other words, why not just say it is all God? There are many compartmentalized concepts we use for God, including the person of Jesus, that allows us, as finite creatures, crudely to visualize the infinite. By creating Spirit as a construct, humanity can grasp the broad notion of God as a pervasive force, breathing spiritual nurturance and revelation into all living things. This may be another reason why the Spirit has a double name. Although our insights into God are dreadfully crude, certain concepts like the Trinity provide humanity with tidbits of conceptual reference. As explained in the Gospel of Phillip, we can never understand the infinite until we become united with the infinite after death:

> The one who hears the word God does not perceive the Real, but an illusion or an image of the Real. The same applies for the words Father, Son, Holy Spirit, Life, Light, Resurrection, Church, and all the rest; these words do not speak of reality. We will understand this on the day when we experience the Real. (Verse 11)[5]

Although our understanding of the infinite is meager, even grasping a scrap of divine truth is better than nothing, provided we don't pretend that we know more than we do. Ron, during his NDE, learned about the God's Breath within the broader context: he experienced Spirit as a universal force having a loving, benevolent purpose. He wrote:

> Imagine, if you will, that this formless force was vastly infinite and evenly dispersed throughout infinity. Though it is perfect, singular, and whole, for the sake of clear rhetoric, I must describe it has having three properties. It is universal, unconditional, and benevolent. (Ron K., NDEF #724)

Many profess the power of the Spirit. Some claim they are living in the Spirit. Yet, how many people know the Spirit through experience? Among those who know of Spirit by doctrine, how many truly believe? Until I began receiving brief visions of image and light, I viewed Spirit abstractly through the lens of doctrine; it was an interesting Christian possibility that seemed absent from my experience. Frankly, it is hard to *know* what to believe, since the Spirit has no obvious material presence. How does one separate Spirit from brain-driven thoughts and hormonally-produced emotions? It is for this reason that the Spirit takes a back pew to God and Jesus, at least in many congregations. Perhaps connecting Spirit with life experience may shine a revealing light into such an enigmatic shroud. How does one do this? Rather than relegating Spirit into some attic box of religious mysteries, I suggest bringing the God's Breath and knowledge front and center. It is the aim of this section to explore how this may be accomplished. First, we will explore the purpose of Spirit. Second, we will apply its purpose to the process of change.

As Ron shared, the Spirit is universal, unconditional, and benevolent. These are qualities of God. If the Spirit is actually God's essence breathed into our souls, it follows that we can begin to know God through our relationship with the Spirit. Our relationship is not just an abstraction. The Spirit is our rusty key to life and the entrance into the Kingdom. With a little polishing, the key of Spirit can actually help reveal the nature of God and, because of our unity with the One, our own nature. The writer of the Gospel of Phillip wrote, "In his Breath, we experience a new embrace; we are no longer in duality but in unity." (Verse 74)[5] By understanding both Spirit and self, a greater unity is achieved. With greater unity comes greater communion. In this manner, the Spirit can become alive as an ever-loving friend, advocate, and source of knowledge in our lives. In the book of First Corinthians, the apostle Paul wrote: "But we know these things because God has revealed them to us by his Spirit, and his Spirit searches out everything and shows us even God's deep secrets." (I Corinthians 2:10)

The Son of Man's secret to success was the power of the Spirit: Jesus tapped into the steady Breath of Spirit through His unity with the Father. The Spirit consistently responded by revealing divine truth and appointing mission for Jesus. In the Gospel of Luke, Jesus even shared that His entire ministry was predicated on revelation by the Spirit. Jesus said:

The Spirit of the Lord is upon me, for he has appointed me to preach Good News to the poor. He has sent me to proclaim that captives will be released, that the blind will see, that the downtrodden will be freed from their oppressors, and the time of the Lord's favor has come. (Luke 4:18-19)

The Spirit of God was not an abstract concept to Jesus. It was the source of his mission parameters, power, and knowledge of God's deep secrets. Accordingly, Jesus never worried about straying from his mission; He was guided during every step of His human journey by connection with the Father. Just because we cannot see Spirit, doesn't preclude similar guidance in our lives. Unfortunately, we usually do not perceive that which sustains us due to our spiritual immaturity and disconnection. For some, it is enough to take the biblical word of Jesus. Others may want more to sustain their belief. It might help to know that there are near-death experience testimonies about the Spirit. For a few sojourners, the invisible was made visible. What did they see? Interestingly, most NDErs perceived Spirit manifested as pure waters; a deep, rich substance flowing freely without borders. Yet, they were amazed to find this watery substance exhibiting consciousness and divine power. Ann, during her NDE, wrote:

I was standing motionless above a large body of water. The water was a brilliant deep cobalt blue color. The water was alluring to look at, like it was alive. (Ann T., NDERF #1919)

Linda had a similar experience:

I remember picking some of the water up with my hand. It did not feel like water. It came into my hand and I could feel great strength and health enter my body. This water was alive and offered life. (Linda K. NDERF #1817)

As suggested by these submissions, the role of Spirit can be likened to expansive waters. I am reminded of the Christian tradition of baptizing through the Spirit by using water. The writer of the Gospel of Phillip describes the symbolism of baptism, at least during the early centuries of Christianity:

None can see themselves in water or in a mirror unless there is light; none can see themselves in light unless there is a mirror or water to reflect them. This is why we must be immersed in water and light. (Verse 75)[5]

Although the congregational celebration of Spirit has symbolic purpose, the Christian view of Spirit can sometimes be too narrow. For instance, the role of Spirit is much more expansive than compelling people to jump around or speak in tongues as they do in some charismatic Christian traditions. Rather, the Spirit is both the Source and giver of spiritual life. Without it, we are spiritually dead. As Jesus said to Nicodemus:

The truth is, no one can enter the Kingdom of God without being born of water and the Spirit. Humans can reproduce only human life, but the Holy Spirit gives new life from heaven. So don't be surprised at my statement that you must be born again. Just as you can hear the wind but can't tell where it comes from or where it is going, so you can't explain how people are born of the Spirit. (John 3:6-8)

How can the Spirit sustain spiritual life and not be perceived or explained? The role of the Spirit, although omnipotent and omnipresent, is eloquently subtle working behind the scenes. From the human perspective, it is the whispering voice behind the brain; a discreet life compass, if you will. Spirit may reveal itself as a nagging tug of guilt, a seed of empathy, an insight of social justice, or in a myriad of other forms. Spirit also produces a sensation of peace within, even during life storms, that erodes our anger with love, replaces our envy with appreciation of equality, and shores up our fear with conviction. In other words, Spirit can be known by our living. Although we may not be able to explain Spirit or observe it as deep waters, we can see Spirit working through our thoughts, emotions, and behaviors. Likewise, we can see Spirit transforming others. What we see has been called the Fruits of the Spirit. These fruits have been superbly defined by the apostle Paul: "But when the Holy Spirit controls our lives, he will produce this kind of fruit in us: love, joy, peace, patience, kindness, goodness, faithfulness, gentleness, and self-control." (Galatians 5:22-23)

Like Jesus, the Spirit appoints us to do the will of God, not through a loud booming voice, but through our interconnection with the Father. The more we become united with the Source of all, the more the

Spirit can work as a transforming fire. The formula for unity begins with a loving desire for reconnection. This typically cannot be obtained through following ideology, but rather by being open to a relationship with God. In this relationship, we first need to be open to listening to Spirit rather than blindly following our selfish biological impulses. Some Christians take an external approach to connection by listening to preaching or studying the Bible. Although such learning approaches may increase knowledge, relying exclusively on external sources becomes woefully inadequate in relating to Spirit in a transformative manner. To truly connect with God, we need enter into a relationship with God by heeding our mission as appointed by the Spirit. The interlacing of transformation and action builds our relationship on solid bedrock. Again, we need to emulate Jesus. The Bible speaks less of Jesus going to synagogue and more of His ministry. Likewise, we also need to learn that acting in the Spirit surpasses worship, although both are important. Spirit represents an individual connection with the divine and cannot be accessed by communal ceremonies or sacraments. Acting in the Spirit takes many forms. Not only do we need to listen and heed the appointments of Spirit, but we need to speak back to God. After all, any strong two-way relationship involves open dialogue. By dialogue, I am referring to the interaction between prayer and response.

We have access to the power of living water through prayer. Sometimes we pray while wondering if God is listening. God hears all. According to the Gospel of Phillip, Jesus said, "Enter into your chamber, close the door, and pray to your Father who is there in secret." (Verse 69)[5] By the power of the Spirit, the divine realm is at our disposal provided our requests are pure. Purity in prayer means that our intent must be concordant with God's Unity. As eloquently put by Julian of Norwich, "We know the fruit at the end of our prayer, which is to be united and like our Lord in all things."[7] Requests for derivatives of ego, such as fame and wealth, is not asking to be like the Lord in all things. Yet, all requests for the Fruits of the Spirit will be honored. In essence, the Fruits of the Spirit are a natural consequence of life lessons learned. As discussed, learning can be a challenging process. One does not seamlessly learn love, joy, peace, patience, kindness, goodness, faithfulness, and self-control. (Galatians 5:22-23) By asking for the fruits of the spirit, one is asking for God to help us fulfill our divine mission purpose. The Spirit gladly obliges, even if the learning of life lessons requires placing the requester on a more difficult and winding path. So be careful what you wish for. If you ask for self-control, you may receive new temptations. If you ask for patience, you may receive frustrating challenges. The same process applies to the other fruits as well.

Although mastering the Fruits of the Spirit can be quite challenging, the outcome will be most rewarding. As mentioned, the Fruits of the Spirit are integral to the divine Unity. Consequently, growth in the Fruits of the Spirit connects us with God by bridging divisions between people. Whereas the byproduct of division is selfishness and anger, the byproduct of unity is compassion and peace. I knew a woman who had lived selfishly. At a turning point in her life, she took a bold step forward into love. Seemingly out of nowhere, she collected over a dozen computers from businesses for disadvantaged children. She was astonished by the impact, not only for the children helped, but for the change she experienced within. She described a pleasant light feeling that washed over her. Unknown to her, it was the Spirit blanketing her with a quiet calm. This was not a calm obtained by meditation, but within the loving action of service. NDErs often report the same purification experience when they encounter the Spirit in heaven. Steve, during his NDE, wrote about a feeling of peace he experienced while bathing in the waters of the Spirit:

> I have come to call on the cleansing waters of no return. This is where all the collectively stored impurities were to be filtered from my conscious energy so that only the purest form of my energy could continue the journey home. Suddenly, everything in view began to cascade around me, almost as if it was melting, and I was immediately swept away into the warm beautiful waters as they enveloped me... In the twinkling of an eye, however, the fear was gone. All I felt was complete peace, serenity, and most of all, the tranquility of pure unconditional love. (Steve B., NDERF #441)

Steve's NDE description of serenity echoes to an ancient Christian concept called *repose*. Repose refers to freedom from worry, resulting in a dignified calmness in the face of adversity. Unlike the state of meditation, a person can achieve repose while engaging in everyday life. According to the Gospel of Thomas, Jesus said, "If they ask you what is the sign of the Father in you, say: It is movement and it is repose." (Verse 50)[6] Repose is the natural state of being filled with the Spirit of God. It has been described as warm, serene, and peaceful. Although not equal to the state of bliss discovered in heaven, repose orientates physical beings in that direction. Although this sensation feels wonderful, repose serves a practical purpose: it serves as a reinforcement contingency to accomplish mission. Let me explain.

One cannot simply experience repose at will. I have tried. Rather, repose is integrally tied into our mission to love. Let's take a closer look at this interaction. The first step is for us to open ourselves up to Spirit. In doing so, the Spirit will guide us toward opportunities to love. By choosing to act in love, we experience a certain degree of peaceful lifting, like the woman collecting computers for charity. Such actions are reinforcing and are likely to recur with more frequency. In this manner, we become motivated to love more. In other words, our opening to Spirit will result in the Spirit's opening up to us. Through this reciprocal relationship, we journey steadily toward the divine in a cyclical, upward path towards purification. The following NDEr, named Derry, interacted with the purifying power of the Spirit while walking with Jesus. She wrote:

> The water was so sparkling clean. I remember wanting to bend over and take a drink from the stream that was running through this garden we were walking through. When I tried to scoop up the water in my hands, the water ran through my hands, literally, and it was not wet. Jesus stopped walking and looked at me while I was bent over trying to drink this water. I could feel His eyes on me. My thirst for this water, even though I wasn't able to put it to my lips and drink it, was gone. (Derry, NDERF #53)

Repose, as a state of dignified peace, allows us to accept the varied flow of life events. It allows us, as Jesus said in the Gospel of Thomas, to be a "passerby" in life. (Verse 42)[6] Meaning, we do not need to have any dependent attachments to worldly yearnings, material possessions, or temporary tribulations. Although the Spirit is available to purify every soul, it is up to each person to choose to be purified. Like Derry, we need to interact with the waters of the Spirit before our spiritual thirsts become quenched. Although many delay the opening of opportunity, we are all meant to drink the waters as part of our ultimate destiny toward change. In this manner, the power of Spirit will eventually unify the universe and bring every soul back to the Source. In the Gospel of Phillip, it was written:

> The Breath leads all things to their repose. It aligns the energies: the obedient, the wild, and the solitary ones. It gathers them together so that they are no longer dispersed. (Verse 40)[5]

The interplay between the individual soul and the unifying force of Spirit is quite interesting. Somewhat paradoxically, we are meant to achieve unity through our own individuality. The Breath also has a double name because it exemplifies a singular love force made manifest by infinite expression. In other words, the unity of Spirit becomes expressed through countless personalities, including yours and mine. Again, one can imagine an arching monolithic rainbow interconnected by different colors. Individuality within unity has important ramifications for our lives. To emulate Jesus, I do not have to love exactly like Jesus. I can express all the attributes of a singular love in accordance with personal strengths, interests, and polished character. During my life review in heaven, I will be able to observe how my irreplaceable life thread fits neatly into the universal tapestry. Although unique, my thread will be a golden strand integral to the Whole. Unfortunately, some people lack confidence in the value of their own thread. Lacking esteem, they live at the whims of worldly forces, meaning they live disingenuously. The universal love force of Spirit will be stymied when we act in a disingenuous manner, even if we think we are acting in love. In the Gospel of Phillip, it was written, "Whoever gives without love experiences nothing of interest." (Verse 45)[5] Barbara learned this difficult lesson when Jesus asked probing questions during her life review. The related dialogue ensued:

FIRST QUESTION BY JESUS: "How have you helped others?" I answered Him excitedly, telling Him what I had done. He replied, "That's good."

SECOND QUESTION BY JESUS: "What did you learn in this life?" I told him what I had learned. He replied, "That's good, but there is more you need to learn."

THIRD QUESTION BY JESUS: "In what way did you give of yourself?" I began to answer but became confused. (NDERF #2855)

Some people are externally motivated to accomplish good deeds; they seek attention, praise, and material reward. We only delude ourselves by calling such deeds acts of love. Love has roots in freedom, not obligation. Interestingly, the writer of the Gospel of Phillip asserts, "In Hebrew, Yeshua means freedom." (Verse 47)[5] I learned previously that the Hebrew name for Jesus means "to deliver." Perhaps the writer proposes that Jesus delivers us from bondage. In this manner, deliverance from spiritual bondage can be equated with true freedom. As previously discussed, Jesus obtained his freeing powers from the Spirit. Through Jesus, the Spirit becomes the key that unlocks the doors to God's Kingdom.

Before we conclude this section, I would like to present a tangible illustration of transformation through the Spirit. The scene is dire. A woman, named Robyn, has been seriously assaulted by a husband who intends to burn her to death using gasoline. Beaten to submission, she prays for deliverance. Jesus delivered her in tandem with the power of Spirit. Her story proceeds as follows:

> "Please Dear God, Let this cup pass from me"... It was at this point that I "knew" I was in two places at the same time. I left my body and passed through a tunnel of light which took me to a door of brilliant light. The door opened. I knelt down (and saw that I was dressed in a dark robe of some sort). As I knelt I looked up to see Jesus in front of me nailed to the cross. He looked down directly into my eyes. I've never seen eyes like those before or since. As he looked into my eyes I asked him, without speaking words, "What do I do?" He answered without speaking words, "Forgive him." As he "said" the words it was done. The forgiveness happened in that very instant.

By emulating the forgiveness of Jesus, Robyn opened herself up to the power of the Spirit. She was subsequently returned to her body and the Spirit took command of her voice. Robyn continues:

> I opened my mouth and started to speak using words that I did not consciously choose or have any control over whatsoever. The first words that came out of my mouth were, "The water will make everything okay." When I said the word "water" I noticed that he put the razorblade down and seemed to almost go into a trance.

Robyn then repeated the words, "The water will make everything okay." In essence, she manifested the power of loving waters, the Spirit, and thereby negated her husband's hatred. With her husband confused, Robyn eventually escaped and ran to safety. She now reflects back on her experience with these important insights about the power of forgiveness and change:

How has this concept of forgiveness affected me since? I taught my three sons to forgive so that when their father got out of prison they were able to communicate with him from a place of peace within their own spirits. Forgiveness releases us from the burden of judgment. As human beings, we are not equipped to judge, and to do so can cause great harm to ourselves and to others. As with the brutal assault that happened to me, my husband had judged me to be the "enemy" and had rationalized killing me. The pendulum had swung so far in that direction that only a divine intervention could bring it back into balance. Forgiving him robbed him of all his power over me. He planned to pour gasoline over me, but instead I poured water over him...and all was healed. Jesus proved to me that his words are as alive today as they were 2000 years ago, "Forgive him, for he knows not what he does." And yes, Love is the greatest power in the universe. (Robyn F., NDERF #3666)

Many become fearful, depressed, and angry after violent traumas. Robyn seemed to have the opposite response: repose. From the violence, she established that love is the greatest power in the universe. Robyn's discovery exquisitely conveys the transforming power of Spirit. First, Robyn learned that we are not equipped to judge. Secondly, Robyn learned that forgiveness robs evil from having power. These lessons demonstrate the important role of Spirit in any journey toward change. Although we may not experience change so dramatically as Robyn, the Breath of God changes everyone through the power of unconditional love. All we are required to do is be open to receive our mission appointments and pray to receive the Fruits of the Spirit.

Barriers to Repose

Opening oneself to the Spirit is a no-lose proposition; repose is a beautiful state of being. I find it ironic that people search for the secret of happiness through power, sex, intoxication, material possessions, and other indulgences. Ever thirsty, they stick their nose up to the very waters that can quench their thirst. Their rejection appears counterintuitive, at first glance. Yet, one can appreciate the appeal of self-defeating behaviors by factoring in biological needs: the Spirit requires hard work, whereas the world supplies pleasures with little effort. Rather than delaying gratification for growth, most people rush toward worldly bling.

Primary reinforcements, or powerful conditioned behavior impelled by biological drives, are not the only barriers to repose. As a psychologist, I recognize that life choices can be complicated by abuse, biology, poverty, illness, mental illness, incarceration, trauma, and other tragic variables. As a therapist, I also recognize that healing can be long and complex. Although the process of healing can sometimes feel overbearingly painful, all that is not well will become well in the end. It is important always to recognize that worldly forces cease at death whereas the transformative love force of Spirit endures eternally. Although the road to happiness may be long and indirect, our natural connective state is to reconnect with God's omnipresent Spirit.

It is beyond the scope of this chapter to explore all the obstructions to Spirit. This topic would provide great source material for a thicker book. Nevertheless, I will brush quickly over one crucial factor underlying much of the human disconnection from God: the emotion of fear. Fear may not be the first factor considered. Some may favor evil-rooted explanations, such as selfish malice and cruelty. Although evil seems, at least to the human mind, dialectally opposed to good, many heinous behaviors have hidden roots in fear. I am not alone in this assessment. In the Gospel of Phillip, it was proclaimed that, "Jesus uprooted fear, which is the root of evil, the poisoner of our lives." (Verse 123)[5] Fear not only poisons righteousness, but it also damages our daily decisions, sours our emotional well-being, and spoils our best plans to accomplish divine mission. It is the aim of this section to address how the substrate of fear impacts our most basic human actions, compromises mission, and disrupts the process of change.

Human motivation often hides beneath our awareness. In other words, daily decisions are tied to complex cause and effect chains we barely perceive. Fear-based motivations direct many activities, even the mundane. Casper, during his NDE, learned about the pervasive power of fear from a spiritual being. He shared:

> The angel communicating with me taught me how we are 99.99% emotion and how every decision we make is based on fear. A good example would be, if we do not work, we do not eat... Most of us work out of our own fear of being hungry, homeless, or not being able to keep up with the Jones's. Consequentially, by living day to day in fear, it provides us with different motives for working and living other than the ones God has planned for us. Although attractive at first, this type of behavior can often lead to our downfall. Once the angel took the

fear factor out of the equation, I had the honor of witnessing all of the things that God had chosen for me to enjoy in this lifetime, but that I denied myself out of stubbornness or fear. (Casper, NDERF #2048)

If what the angel said is true, then only .001% of our decisions are based on motivations other than fear. Thus, practically all of our negative emotional states, ranging from anger to envy, are rooted in fear. It is important to note that all human emotions have evolved for an adaptive purpose. Stopping at a red light is highly adaptive; I stop out of fear of being run over by a truck. Thus, the aim is not to eliminate fear, but to manage its expression in order to accomplish what God has planned for us.

Self-monitoring is key to the management of fear. A prudent question becomes, how do we know when fear predominates in our lives? Pervasive fear becomes problematic when it obstructs our mission to love. After all, sending out love is an inherently risky endeavor, whether it involves building better relationships or a better earth. Our level of anxiety can be used as another good barometer. Anxiety can be defined as a fear of the unknown. In other words, the anxious person focuses their attention on future hypotheticals rather than living in the here and now. They constantly wonder "What if this happens?" or "What if that happens?" Ironically, hypothetical catastrophes rarely happen. Even when they do occur, worriers typically underestimate their inner strength to cope and find solutions. Unfortunately, the worriers barely recognize their strengths, even after successes. Becoming accustomed to living in constant fear, the poison flows and eventually grips their spirit. After a time, the fearful lose their ability to assess situations objectively.

Love is realized in the present; it is expressed moment by moment rather than as a future hypothetical. The anxious are not attuned to what God wants them to do now, in mission, because they are mentally living in the future. Instead of being, they agonize about their becoming. Jesus taught otherwise: "Don't worry about tomorrow, for tomorrow will bring its own worries. Today's trouble is enough for today." (Mathew 6:34)

It is very difficult to enact Jesus' directive to focus on the here and now. After all, the world is filled with unpredictable events and potential dangers. Some respond by falling into a pattern of avoidance. Unfortunately, ventures not risked just maintain the status quo, resulting in a life of stagnation. Those who maintain a cyclical pattern of poor choices do not witness all the blessings God has meant for them. Rather, their lives are defined by routine, boredom, and self-defeating choices. Consequently, the fearful learn not to have faith in themselves. One can see a downward cycle develop. Anxiety leads to avoidance, avoidance leads to failure, failure leads to poor self-esteem, poor self-esteem leads to increased fear, and greater fear leads to heightened anxiety. Over time, a person's life becomes greatly diminished by a downward cycle rooted in fear.

The path of avoidance does not lead toward the Kingdom. The fearful cannot love by avoiding situations and other people. How does one veer back on the right path? The prescription for fear should not rely solely on popping anxiolytic or antidepressant medications. From a psychological perspective, many psychotherapists would work toward alleviating fear by challenging irrational thinking and assigning risk taking. From a spiritual perspective, many clergy would work toward alleviating fear through faith in Jesus. Both approaches, I believe, have merit. I would add, based on near-death experiences, that fear can be alleviated when we realize that there is nothing to fear. No scary event, including death, has a lasting sting. Nothing is as it seems. You and I are not helpless human beings, subject to harsh environments and death. Rather, we are really magnificent, eternal spiritual beings impervious to decline. During her near-death experience, Anita Moorjani wrote:

> I saw that I'd never loved myself, valued myself, or seen the beauty of my soul. Although the unconditional magnificence was always there for me, it felt as though physical life had somehow filtered it out or even eroded it away. This understanding made me realize that I no longer had anything to fear.[8]

Earth, the world of division, erodes all our trust in a greater good and leaves us lingering in fear. Anita Moorjani's quote resonates with these words from Jesus, "We have been rescued from our enemies so we can serve God without fear." (Luke 1:74) By enemies, perhaps Jesus is referring to any perceived threat in life, real or imagined. If we have faith that God will take care of us, we can boldly go forth in mission and meet our potential. Jesus asks two relevant questions: "Look at the birds. They don't plant or store away in barns, for your heavenly father feeds them. And aren't you far more valuable to him than they are? Can all your worries add a single moment to your life?" (Matthew 6:26-7)

Anxiety is not the only emotion rooted in fear. There is a darker side to the flight or fight response. When a threat is perceived, real or imagined, the fearful may attack. Tragically, we sometimes attack loved ones more vehemently than a stranger. We may also attack outsiders encroaching on our illusory bubble of safety. Racially-motivated hate crimes are one of several glaring examples. If humanity truly wants to make the world a safer home, then we need to appreciate that hate, and all its violent derivatives, is rooted in fear. Moreover, fear and division go hand in hand, resulting in the "us against them" mentality. Renee learned this powerful lesson during her NDE. She wrote:

> The separations we have created here has been nothing more than an ignorant mindset to create fear. There has to be an opposite something always. Life-Death, Good-Bad, Happy-Sad. There is nothing separate in the infinite universe, and that would include the terrorist standing right next to you. We are all pieces of one created puzzle. It is true that love is the answer. (Renee M., NDERF #2588)

Therapy and psychotropic medications are human attempts to heal the mind. As a psychologist, I attest to their efficacy, however limited. Yet, the mind is integrally connected to the omnipresent spirit. Complete healing power ultimately comes from unconditional love. As Renee learned during her NDE, "Love is the answer." Similarly, Jesus taught: "Such love has no fear, because perfect love expels all fear. If we are afraid, it is for fear of punishment, and this shows that we have not fully experienced His perfect love." (John 4:18)

Amazingly, Jesus taught that perfect love expels *all* fear, not just some fear. How can that be? Who among us lives without fear? We fear, as Jesus said, because human love is imperfect. Remember, perfect love is a multifaceted force requiring vast skills and eons of practice to master. The unconditional facet of love may be the hardest element to control. As we have explored, our growth toward God is based on achieving unity. Consequently, overcoming fear means overcoming division; valuing everyone with the highest respect. For instance, we are to forgive those who hurt us. Obviously, the world teaches the opposite. The path of the world is the way of fear; to punish perpetrators or attack potential threats. This is why Jesus' commandment, "Love your enemies," seems so alien to the human psyche. The path of the Kingdom, conversely, is to recognize that enemies are fellow beings of God. Humanity can only move toward unconditional love by realizing that division is illusionary. We need to learn that there is nothing to fear if no one can really hurt us. Only then will humanity achieve a state of repose.

As human beings, we have two paths to choose. We can either stagnate in a state of fearful division, or we can grow in unity toward God in a state of repose. I choose my abode in God. I understand that my goal has yet to be realized; I face a long journey ahead. Yet, my voyage will become smoother and quicker if I understand the process of change and know that God is always with me to help. As Joe shared from his NDE:

> The Light said, "I will follow you and will never leave your mind"…and the Light was Jesus Christ. (Joe, NDERF #1127)

Although change is difficult, there is hope for everyone. Each person has the ability to change contained within their soul. Moreover, our hope increased many times through the modeled life of Jesus and the power of the ascended Christ through the Spirit. In this chapter, we have explored both psychological and spiritual processes of change. We have also explored fear as a barrier to change. In the next chapter, we will continue our investigation into change, but focus more on the outcomes of spiritual transformation: we will explore what amazing change looks like when people emulate Jesus and become transformed by the Spirit.

CHAPTER SEVEN

JESUS AND HUMAN TRANSFORMATION

D o people emulate Jesus when they threaten others with hellfire and damnation? People who return from death say "no."
The consequences of "sinful" behavior cannot be judged because no person can foretell the future. Might a prostitute love her
children? Might a father attending church abuse his children much
with his strength? Might all of us learn the best lessons by making the
worst mistakes? Because people are incapable of understanding the
big picture, our notions of "sin" cannot be judged by anyone but God.
Fortunately, God chooses not to judge. As detailed in chapter four,
unconditional love negates all judgment. For instance, people are not
judged based on their mistakes, beliefs, sexual orientation, ethnicity,
occupation, or national culture. As a human, Jesus repeatedly demonstrated this divine principle by welcoming the leper, foreigner, heathen,
tax collector, and prostitute into His circle. To be alive in the Spirit,
one needs to emulate this central Gospel principle and welcome every
"sinner" and proscribed out-group.

God evaluates the human heart. The love-based fabric of the universe would collapse if every action were determined to be equal. For
example, I have yet to read an NDE report where spiritual beings en-
gaged in envy, hatred, or violence in the spiritual realm. Still, God's

organization should not be confused with value judgments or penance. Even the difficult path is for the Good. After all, we are meant to make mistakes because this broken world is our training ground to learn love. Although God's anger and punishment are not the wages of sin, there are painful, natural consequences in choosing disconnection. We see that every day in our world through the isolation and emotional turmoil of many people. In other words, some paths are much harder and more painful than others. Some people even wander into dead end trails and must be redirected to restart parts of their journey toward God.

Having grown up in northern New Mexico, I loosely compare the journey toward God with hiking up a tall mountain in the Southwest United States. Imagine starting out in the semi-desert in July, where yuccas and small juniper trees poke out of the sizzling, rocky soil. Far in the distance looms a shaded mountain teeming with pine, aspen, and pristine waters. The jutting blue mountain peak, with its expansive views, appears to be the destination of all the rested hikers excited to start their adventures. Various paths lead to the top, allowing hikers from different geographic areas access to the mountain using different routes. Regardless of their location, all hikers are welcome to journey on these public lands. Indeed, there are many types of hikers that choose to make the ascent. Let's take a look at just a few types of journeyers.

Some novice hikers fear tripping over boulders, so they keep their eyes down on the rocky terrain without bothering to look at their destination. Eventually they follow a safe, downward sloping path that leads to a dead-end, dry gully. This is the path of fear. Some avoid risks in life to avoid difficulties on their ascent toward the divine. They latch on to the comforts of the world, ranging from various self-soothing activities to entertainment diversions. Embracing safety in numbers, their world shrinks into locked gated communities and fancy church sanctuaries. Life becomes comfortable by following a predicable routine. Unfortunately, contented people lose sight of their demanding mission to heal the world. Although they sing about love alongside church choirs, full love is barely realized without risking personal comfort for the Kingdom. In other words, they search for water in dry streambeds. In the end, they thirst.

Some hikers are reckless. Excited to explore the entire mountain, they seek any thrilling diversion without discernment. Making it to the lush environs, some veer off into thickets beckoning with bright-red, poisonous berries and quickly become entangled into the thorny branches. Bloodied with cuts and nauseated by sickness, the reckless journeyer becomes painfully delayed. This is the tantalizing path of worldly illusion. To fulfill the self, many construct a monument to ego by collecting worldly trophies: power, money, attention, status. In more extreme cases, highly reckless hikers race over precarious ground and fall over cliffs. They are thrill seekers in life searching for constant pleasures. Unfortunately, earthly power is illusory, trophies rust, and pleasures are momentary. The reckless traveler becomes bruised, cut, and spiritually sickened by their self-destructive behaviors.

Some hikers keep their eye on the main path and ascend toward the summit at a measured pace. Although steep ravines have to be climbed, the resilient hiker gladly endures pain and fatigue as a necessary part of the journey. The journeyer, vigilant to the surrounding terrain, eventually becomes rewarded with cool streams and brilliant views. A cool breeze brushes against the hiker's face while sitting under a shimmering aspen tree. Resting in repose, the journeyer looks up at the destination; the tall peak looks so much closer now. The hiker becomes encouraged by his or her progress, despite the steepness of the trail, and looks fondly back on the journey, even the struggling up hot ravines. Sipping water, the hiker finally stands up refreshed from his rest and treks forward. This is the path of transformation. Transformation is all about our steady journey toward the divine. Every soul must strain and sweat before arriving at their final destination, living in concordance with God. Somehow the journey becomes more rewarding, in retrospect, because it is difficult. After all, there is little satisfaction gained by trekking over a flat, short path. In the end, the transformed can say, "By the grace of God, I worked for everything I am. I treasure every moment of the long journey."

We discussed elements of our mountain trek metaphor in the last two chapters. In chapter five, we explored how Jesus transforms our being, through the Spirit, with a tended, forging fire. In chapter six, we delineated steps which needed to be transformed by Spirit. In the coming chapter, we will continue exploring the process of transformation by applying our journey to human life choices. Expressly, we will describe what transformation looks and feels like in the world by emulating Jesus. First, we will explore how the process requires a renunciation of the worldly paths so that we are not diverted into gullies and briar bushes, or over cliffs. Second, we will examine what renunciation looks like in terms of behavior. Specifically, we will examine lifestyle changes chosen by transformed people, especially from those changed by near-death experiences. Let us begin by examining the renunciation of the world.

Renouncing the World

The spiritual quest for non-attachment has roots in both Eastern and Western religions. Unlike Eastern religious thought, the path of Jesus does not endorse avoiding all attachments by embracing solitude, painful austerity, and meditation. After all, Jesus maintained a very social and active ministry. The approach modeled by Jesus seems consistent with NDE reports of mission and divine covenant. As reviewed throughout this book, NDErs are commissioned to transform the world through loving service, not complete renunciation. Humans are meant to savor all aspects of life anchored in love including socializing, exploring, and just having fun. There are the learning experiences such as serving, sacrificing, and suffering. Yet, paradoxically, we are also meant to renounce our adoration of and dependence on the world, particularly in relation to any unloving pursuit. Specifically, we are not to hoard wealth, harm others, seek power, or otherwise live selfishly. According to the Gospel of Thomas, Jesus instructed the Apostles to "Be Passerby." (Verse 42)[1] From this simple passage, Jesus taught that people should not form worldly attachments destined to fail. Think about the world around you. Not only does the physical life creak and grind, but everything will ultimately diminish and disappear. Yet, we need not wallow in fear or despair, for the human condition pales compared with the eternal condition. We have only to embrace the Spirit to live in a state of repose in order to find happiness on earth.

Many people do not live in a state of repose; inner peace seems rarely achieved. Perhaps most are missing the main point of being human. Like the hiker wandering down dead-end pathways, many are attracted to transitory pleasures. Specifically, they saturate their senses with sexual ecstasy, vicarious violence, heady feelings of power, competitive thrills, big shiny things, and other pursuits that lack depth. Although me-centered people may be overstuffed with transient fulfillments, they are spiritually starved, or worse, spiritually dead. I am reminded of my spiritual vision, as described in chapter one, where I witnessed a spiritual wasteland lying beyond sanctuary walls. I understood the wasteland to represent the state of the world. I also understood that sanctuary walls can be erected only through God's loving grace. The Apostle Paul warned the church in Rome, two thousand years ago, about the dangers of individuals conforming to the world. He wrote:

Do not conform any longer to the pattern of this world, but be transformed by the renewing of your mind. Then you will be able to test and approve what God's will is – his good, pleasing, and perfect will. (Romans 12:2)

Note the implied gulf separating the pattern of the world and God's perfect will. One is perfect while the other is starkly deficient. Jesus spoke more bluntly than Paul. In the Gospel of Thomas, Jesus said:

Whoever knows the world discovers a corpse. And whoever discovers a corpse cannot be contained by the world. (Verse 56)[1]

Although it is easy to find fault in the world, is it really spiritually dead? Let's take a critical, sobering look at the world today. The ethic, "might makes right," can readily be observed in corporate practices, the legal system, and intrusive government. Although the most blatant abuses of power typically occur in autocratic societies, corruption and exploitation runs rampant in democratic, capitalistic nations as well. One only needs to watch ten minutes of national news to note daily examples of business and political immorality. Added are other symptoms of societal sickness, such as rampant crime, homelessness, drug addiction, violence, and prisons bursting at the seams. Looking around the world, people justify the most ghastly acts of violence in the name of belief, ranging from ethnic cleansing to religious extremism. What would cause human beings to be so disconnected from God and cause each other so much suffering? Scott, during his NDE, discovered that separation from God underlies much of the pain in the world. His deceased mother told him, "Son, our pain is directly proportionate to the level of separation of our Spirit." Furthermore, Scott learned that people repeatedly create their own false truths because they reject divine truth:

I saw how we've wasted it with petty crap, hatred, war, abuse of control and power, lies, and hurting others. We have spent time being so separated from love and our truth, that we have taken it from others because we can't stand that they may have it and we don't. I saw that we have created false truths and realities because we loathe what we think is the truth. We have nearly, if not completely, ruined our lives, hearts, minds, and souls to keep feeding the illusions. (Scott W., NDERF #3885)

Rather than embracing the Real, humanity has created quick-fix illusions to soothe our pain, fear, and anger. People will believe in anything that feels good or feeds ego. Illusions are reinforced in many ways. The ecstasy of sex and artificial highs creates the illusion of happiness. Status and possessions create the illusion of ego, or self-importance. Society readily meets the demand for false truth by simulating warped reality through undeliverable enticements. For instance, the media promotes all types of sham excitements by showing violent hero movies, gross materialistic acquisition, gossip television, competitive sports, sensationalized news, and pornography. After a mundane day at work, it seems that many people just want to be bathed in sex, voyeurism, competition, and violence. According to the Bureau of Labor Statistics, a typical American spends about three hours a day, on average, watching television.[2] Likewise, they spend, on average, two and a half hours surfing the Internet for their personal use.[3] That covers most people's free time. If we devote the vast majority of our free time to using electronic media, how much time are we spending with friends and family? How much time are we devoting to our mission to serve others? As Jesus said in the Gospel of Thomas, "The harvest is abundant but the workers are few. Pray to the master to send more workers to the harvest." (Verse 73)[1] Unfortunately, workers seem to be in ever shorter supply as society becomes numbed by virtual overstimulation.

People who become connected to God and mission, like many NDErs, soon discover a shallow impermanency that pervades most human activity. Heartbreakingly, they uncover a spiritual corpse. According to many NDE reports, Jesus frequently asks the recently deceased visitor to heaven, "What have you done with your life?" How tragic it would be to look Jesus in the eye and truthfully answer, "I watched a lot of TV." I hardly consider myself a psychoanalytically-oriented psychologist. Yet, I must admit, Sigmund Freud touched on an important theoretical construct when describing the *id*. The id represents the unconscious part of our psyche driven by sex and aggression. The media, recognizing Freud or not, certainly exploits our animal urges. Through their titillating sensory assault, people become enslaved to the world through conditioning. I suspect that some people recognize, at some level, that their need to be entertained becomes unhealthy at some point. Yet, they still indulge, sometimes out of compulsion or addiction. It is no wonder that people become cynical of the world and fall into despair. As the writer of the Gospel of Phillip wrote:

The bad root bears its fruits in us and in this world; it will dominate us and make us its slaves so that we do what we do not want to do and are no longer able to do what we want to do. (Verse 123)[4]

I find the concept of slavery appalling at all levels. My dismay brings up a few questions about society at large. When did we accept virtual reality as the source of our living? As a community, how did we accept this as normal or healthy? I do not fully know the answer to these questions. However, I know that freedom involves connecting to God by embracing a life path of service—a lifestyle modeled by Jesus. In the Gospel of Phillip, the writer instructs Christians thus: "You who are with the Son of God do not love worldly things; love the Teacher, so that what you produce will resemble the Teacher, and not some other thing." (Verse 112)[4] If a person chooses to follow this advice, whether Christian or not, he or she will experience freedom from being contained by the world.

Not Contained by the World

I acknowledge my comprehensive criticism of the world. Believe it or not, I do not consider myself a moral crusader. First of all, I don't judge any particular activity in terms of sinfulness. Sinfulness is a black and white term that incorporates ideas of shaming, righteous anger, and punishment. God represents unconditional love, not revenge or division. Secondly, I recognize the rigid environmental and biological constraints placed on the human animal. Humans cannot deny their physical inheritance or transcend their DNA, even if everyone decided to live in a monastery. Not to seem hypocritical, allow me to use my own behavior as an example. Have I recently enjoyed the competitive nature of a basketball game? Yes. Have I recently felt the excitement of watching a suspenseful movie? Yes. Do I fill most of my free time with these things? No. My last answer is vitally important to being "passerby" in life. Jesus did not say to avoid being part of the world as a hermit, but rather He instructed us not to become attached to the world in a state of dependency. The central management question becomes: do I control my biological impulses, or do my impulses control me? What is the focus of my life, physical pleasures or mission from God? Perhaps spiritual growth does not require the denial of human nature, but rather our striving toward a higher existence while still being human. It is a matter of trajectory guided by the loving heart and connection to God.

If we choose to embrace our biology, rather than Spirit, we will continue to live according to the animal part of our nature and become slaves to instinctual drives and primary reinforcement contingencies. Unfortunately, most people seem to embrace biology over our higher Spirit, regardless of their religious or philosophical persuasions. The world hasn't changed much from the Roman period of gladiators, orgies, and political intrigue. As stated eighteen centuries ago in the Gospel of Phillip, "There is no lack of animal-human, they are many and they revere each other." (Verse 84)[4] I share in the Gospel's observation that some people seem to be driven more by the id rather than their higher nature. With high reverence for each other, the animal-human appears to have a lower reverence for the ways of God. Enslaved to their biology, they also remain disconnected to their true nature of soul.

Despite the enticements of materialistic culture, a small number of people refuse to become contained by the world. They do not endlessly pursue immediate pleasures, but rather walk paths centered on community, worship, justice, and service. The writer of the Gospel of Phillip describes their transcendence from the world in the language of freedom:

> Whoever is free of the world can no longer be made into a slave there. They have risen above attraction and repulsion. They are master of their nature, free of envy. (Verse 61)[4]

For the spiritually transformed, freedom means having the opportunity to grow toward God rather than becoming mindless moths attracted to the material flame. Becoming freed from worldly prejudices, they are no longer repulsed by the poor and oppressed, but embrace their cause. In sum, they strive to master their baser impulses and nurture their higher nature. Once liberated from the chains of worldly trappings, they begin to live in repose within the parameters of being human.

As stated earlier, there are biological and environmental bounds in being human. Although transformation always remains the goal, full and immediate Christ-like transformation seems unrealistic. For this reason, God doesn't expect any of us to be perfect; nor are we judged on what is unobtainable. Thus, we have no reason to loath ourselves or fear damnation. Living the transformed life is somewhat like walking a tightrope. We are to walk in the physical world, to be a part of it, yet try not to lose our balance and fall. The writer of the Gospel of Phillip describes this balance in relation to the physical, especially our desires of the flesh:

> Do not fear the flesh nor be enamored of it. If you fear it, it will rule you. If you love it, it will paralyze and devour you. (Verse 62)[4]

Let's take a look at the last passage in depth. By fearing the flesh, we avoid our duty to understand normal biological human needs in order to control its expression. In our ignorance, our repressed impulses eventually surface to control us. But if we love the flesh, then we give it power and our spirit becomes paralyzed by worldly desires and addictions. Unchecked, the flesh takes complete control and the integrity of our spiritual life becomes devoured. How do we accept the human condition yet not be ruled by the flesh? Again, we need to be "passerby," unattached to the physical trappings of the world: living in our flesh without becoming a slave to it. Part of the answer involves achieving balance between flesh and spirit. Betty Edie wrote:

> To become as perfect as a mortal being can become, we need to bring the mind, body, and spirit into total harmony. To become perfect in the spirit, we must add to that harmony Christ-like love and righteousness.[5]

Those bonded into slavery need not despair. Not only does God automatically forgive, every damaging thing can be made well with time and effort. Ironically, becoming enamored with the flesh can ultimately become a catalyst for growth. After all, great wisdom can be learned from the experience of embracing a corpse, especially if the deed becomes revolting over time. Transformation can occur when the lost finally realize, through tragedy, that the flesh becomes devoured in the end. Enlightened, the lost will have opportunity to transcend the flesh by seeking the Kingdom; they learn to be "passerby."

Not only is non-attachment important regarding the flesh, but we need to be "passerby" with other aspects of the world, such as ego, power, fame, and wealth. In the Gospel of Thomas, Jesus said, "Whoever has found the world and become wealthy, may they renounce the world." (Verse 110)[1] In order to renounce the world, we need to know what we are renouncing. A poor man has little insight into renouncing wealth. But a rich man knows exactly what he has lost. Knowing is the first step toward transformation. Applying that knowledge fulfills meaning in life. J.R. learned this lesson after talking with Jesus during his NDE. He wrote:

> I believe that God is our mentor, teacher, and guide. He loves us and wants to watch us grow. He knows we can't walk without skinning our knees; he knows that we cannot love without the knowledge of hate. (J.R., NDERF #195)

J.R's point seems to be that people can't know what is meaningful and permanent if they don't know what is pointless and transitory. Sometimes the spiritual novice must bite into the apple of knowledge before the rotten fruit can be tossed for a more sustaining fruit. Those who repeatedly choose to eat rotten fruit will become increasingly sick and eventually die. To remain spiritually healthy, they need a long term plan to increase self-motivation, self-examination, and self-discipline. They do so by harvesting the Fruits of the Spirit, which include love, joy, peace, patience, kindness, goodness, faithfulness, gentleness, and self-control. (Galatians 5:22-23) The Fruits of the Spirit are a blessing to humanity, as they are available to all. They keep us alive. We just need to pick them from a divine Space. The writer of the Gospel of Phillip wrote:

> This world is an eater of corpses. Everything eaten here has the taste of hatred. The truth is fed by that which is alive, and those who feed on truth are alive. Yeshua (Jesus) comes from that Space, and he gives this food to those who desire it. They will not die. (Verse 93)[4]

By bringing the Light into our lives, God illuminates the rottenness in the world. Jesus was heaven's ambassador to show us how to separate the good from the rotten fruit. Those who are transformed by Jesus through the Spirit discover a corpse and thereby become revolted. Seeking spiritual life over death, they embrace the Kingdom and discard worldly treasures like cheap plastic toys from a vending machine. Jesus taught about finding real treasure in Matthew 13:46. Teaching through parable, Jesus described a man purchasing a pearl of great price with all the wealth he owned. The pearl represented the Kingdom whereas his wealth represented the treasures of the world. Jesus taught a similar, but less known, parable in the Gospel of Thomas:

A human being is like a good fisherman who casts his net into the sea. When he pulls it out, he finds a multitude of little fish. Among them there is one fine, large fish. Without hesitation, he keeps it and throws all the small fish back into the sea. Those who have ears, let them hear! (Verse 8)[1]

By renouncing the world as "passerby," a transformed individual can now focus on the Real, the singular truth of God's creative love-force filling the universe. By emulating the divine as modeled by Jesus and others, the transformed person clutches the large, fine fish and discards the inferior fish back into the sea. What does a changed life look life? Rather than competing with others, the transformed person celebrates others. Rather than hoarding wealth, he or she gives in service. Rather than being entertained by sex and violence, the enlightened individual spends much of his or her energy and time healing the world. By discovering the gift of Jesus' life, he or she can no longer be contained by the world's hedonistic values and culture of drivel. Personally, I would rather be dead than live in a loveless, pleasure-seeking world. Fortunately, I share my human existence with pockets of like-minded people who want to heal the world. Some have seen the Light of God by embracing love through their own seeking. These individuals, regardless of religion, are walking the path of mission by seeking the Kingdom on earth. Many people who have had near-death experiences represent a subset of this group, for they have seen the Light directly. For those have touched heaven, transformation has been profound.

The NDE and Transformed Lives

In the midst of darkening times, friends might try to comfort you by saying, "Well, at least you have your health." When life goes completely awry, they may comment, "Well, it beats the alternative." The "alternative," of course, may be spoken as a euphemism for death. Perhaps people's deep fear of pain, incapacitation, and death underlie these offhand comments; most people would rather suffer any tribulation rather than that dreaded trifecta. Yet, God sees existence differently. Love trumps all earthly experiences in God's Kingdom. No physical process in life has great importance, including death itself. Maintaining such a detached "passerby" perspective can seem impossible living on earth. For us, physical life seems omnipresent whereas spiritual reality seems intangible. Spiritual life is truly omnipresent while the physical life is transitory. The question becomes, how can humans maintain a focus on spiritual eternity when we are constantly being diverted by our physical transience? As discovered in the last chapter, gaining spiritual knowledge is the first step. Unfortunately, an open pursuit of spiritual knowledge seems relatively rare on earth because people do not remember their unified existence in heaven with God. Typically, people cling to a weak, desperate faith. Even the rare strong human faith pales compared to true experiential knowing. One should not be surprised that the greatest level of transformation often occurs in people who have experienced God's Kingdom firsthand. By experience, I do not mean just tapping into the Spirit through prayer, but through face-to-face communication with spiritual beings like Jesus.

I do not claim that the direct experience of God is the only path to spiritual knowledge and transformation. If that were the case, there would be no reason for me to write spiritual books. Everyone is being transformed on a daily basis, even if just by a little. Some people are profoundly transformed during their earthly journey without having an NDE. It would be a disservice to downplay their growth. I suggest only that NDErs have a distinct advantage in remembering the Real, knowing God and knowing their purpose. Historically, people have relied on religion and their own center for guidance. In the dawning of a new spiritual age, people can enhance their spiritual discovery by reading thousands of near-death experience accounts. With an attitude of openness, they can emulate these people's life experiences that resonate with their own mission. For these reasons, this section will focus on a few NDE accounts that describe life changes subsequent to NDEs.

Through reading over four thousand accounts of near-death experiences, I discovered that the overwhelming majority of NDErs underwent a major life transformation after they returned to their physical bodies. For the purposes of this book, I will focus on sharing inspired NDE testimonies from those who interacted with the ascended Christ. For instance, Elizabeth, during her NDE, reported a life overhaul after simply being held in the arms of Jesus. By experiencing the purity of Christ's love, Elizabeth became empowered to emulate Jesus upon return to her body. Reflecting on her NDE, Elizabeth elaborates:

> My life is better than it ever has been. I am grateful for everything and everyone. I try to do my very best every day with everyone and I do something nice for someone every day. I drop/skip the small stuff. I

have no time for anger or resentments. I have made amends to anyone I may have hurt along the way. Life is really good right now—even with cancer! (Elizabeth E., NDERF# 3298)

Something amazing happened when Elizabeth was held by Jesus. Specifically, Elizabeth remembered her own divine nature: an eternal, encompassing, interconnected spiritual being made in love and for love. Realizing her unification with Jesus and the divine, it was only natural for Elizabeth to become more Christ-like when she returned to earth. The transformative process toward unity was explained by the writer of the Gospel of Phillip back in antiquity:

> It is impossible for anyone to see the everlasting reality and not become like it. The Truth is not realized like truth in the world. Those who see the sun do not become the sun. Those who see the sky, earth, or anything that exists, do not become what they see. But when you see something in this other space (spiritual realm), you become it. If you know the Breath, you are the Breath. If you know the Christ, you become the Christ. If you see the Father, you are the Father. (Verse 44)[4]

Elizabeth became more united with the Real by lying in the arms of Jesus. By knowing Christ, Elizabeth's life became grounded in love rather than worldly attachments. In this manner, she adhered to Jesus' commandment, "Be passerby." By checking ego, Elizabeth detached herself from the petty fights, competitive comparisons, resentments, and pride that often characterize many human relationships. Elizabeth also made amends with anyone she hurt. Finally, she made enough space for love to permeate her daily interactions, even treating the stranger with respect. All these experiences allowed her to emulate Christ and achieve inner peace through the Spirit. Even the ugliness of cancer did not dent her repose, for she knew that physical sickness and pain are not part of the Real. In this manner, Elizabeth remained grateful and graceful while facing great adversity.

From my perspective, repose in the face of tragedy speaks volumes of the power of the Spirit. No earthly event, not even death, can conquer our divine residence within the Real. As part of normal grieving, most people become angry and depressed when diagnosed with a serious medical ailment. Elizabeth largely bypassed the usual grieving process. Imagine if everyone focused their lives on eternal reality rather than temporary illusion. Most mental ailments, such as severe anxiety or major depression, would largely disappear. Knowing that we are eternally connected to God, we would have nothing to fear. Decreasing division by appreciating Unity, we would have little to envy. I would gladly welcome such a worldwide transformation, even if it meant finding a new profession other than psychologist.

Many NDErs develop greater repose when they return to their bodies. Their transformation may seem elusive, at first glance, because the Spirit does not automatically transform a human being into a perfect saint. In other words, NDErs continue to have a full range human emotions and thoughts, both constructive and hurtful. The power of the Spirit directly impacts being while indirectly influencing feelings and thoughts. For instance, a person can experience feelings of sadness and still remain in a steady state of repose. This is also true for positive states, such as happiness. After her NDE, Rachel explained, "I am happy when I am happy. I am happy when I am sad. I am happy when I am sick. I am happy when I am sick and tired of life." (Rachel, NDERF #3875) Stormy emotions are often transitory; we all lose control from time to time. By becoming centered in the Spirit, however, we remain grounded in the long run despite our failings and transitory feelings. Despite our being fallible human beings, failures eventually decrease over time when we become grounded in Spirit.

As discussed in the last chapter, God-concordant behaviors develop in a stepwise process based in knowledge, motivation, and experience. Similarly to Elizabeth, David learned to find a dignified peace facing lung cancer. He described three gifts of knowledge that bolstered his state of repose:

> The first gift was acceptance. I knew who I was and could accept that I had faults and strengths. I no longer needed to beat myself up over failures. Instead, I could learn and accept and make myself a better human being. I now understood how my life could touch others without knowing it. I also know that I am in the perfect place at all times. The second gift was tolerance. This was very new to me. I liked to cut my swath through life. Suddenly, I now had a way of respecting and recognizing others' beliefs or practices. I can now see that others in their life path are experiencing what they need for their growth. Tolerance allows me to allow them to walk their paths. The third gift was my truth. Those two days I was living with my heart wide open. I was experiencing everything through an open heart. When I say an open heart, I mean the light that you experience when in the presence

of that unconditional love. With these three gifts my new life started. I began to change. I didn't view everything the same anymore. I started to work on myself ...Yet because of my ministry and experience, acceptance of the cancer was immediate. It brought me back to my center and balance of self and Spirit. (David B., NDERF #278)

Consider David's three blessed gifts: acceptance, tolerance, and truth. In regard to acceptance, David bore his imperfections with repose rather than becoming devoured by anxiety and shame. He moved forward in confidence rather than insecurity. Not only did David accept his own core worth, he became more tolerant of others and their imperfections by recognizing the value of diversity within God's unity. In this manner, he began to acknowledge different beliefs and traditions. Furthermore, he began to empathize with other people's pain without thinking, "They had it coming." Combining self-acceptance with tolerance brought David to a new place of Openness. Explicitly, David opened his heart to the rainbow and learned to love with fewer conditions. Although David was part of the world, he was no longer enslaved to his old worldly views. Rather, David found a balance between self and Spirit. His judgments and prejudices, in turn, faded.

Not only did David receive three gifts related to transformation, but he learned that death does not exist. With this fear removed, David felt liberated to apply these gifts for the remainder of his life, even while facing lung cancer. Rather than wallowing in self-pity or lashing out at others, David converted a "hopeless" situation into something beautiful: he began ministering to others dying of terminal cancer. In other words, he transformed his own pain into a mission of ministry for terminally ill patients.

Where most people view cancer as tragedy, both David and Elizabeth viewed their illness as opportunity to serve God and, by extension, their fellow brother and sister interconnected in God. Because they were acutely aware of their sickness, they shared a sense of urgency to accomplish their mission before death. Everything else paled in comparison; they clung to their one fine fish. Similar to David and Elizabeth, none of us have the luxury to ignore our finite time on earth. After all, even a long life seems momentary in retrospect. In a world of hurt, there is so much to do with so little time. To be fully connected with the divine in service, we need to share in a compelling sense of urgency in prioritizing our choices. Christopher, from his NDE, elaborated:

My near-death experience has radically changed my life. I will devote every minute that I have left serving my neighbor as if he or she were myself. (Christopher R., NDERF #932)

Devoting one's life to service seems extremely rare today. Although Jesus commanded us to love our neighbor as ourselves, the concept seems more intellectualized than taken to heart. It doesn't have to be that way. Nor does a person have to be dying to embrace radical transformation. Everyone has opportunity to connect to the divine by loving other people. Sometimes I do a double-take when people wonder what they are meant to accomplish in life. A bolt of insight is unnecessary to find direction, for the simple answer can easily be accessed, within our soul, within every moment of now. It is just a matter of choice that we care. In a world filled with hurting people, there are countless community organizations that would welcome any person with a loving attitude: churches, charities, support groups, hospitals, hospices, food banks, jails, shelters, and various non-profit organizations. Special talents are usually not a prerequisite. If a person has the ability to put a can of food in a box, then they have necessary skills to be of service. In the next NDE submission, a woman named Joy profoundly illustrates a life transformed by love. She wrote:

I have truly developed a new outlook on life. I am in full-time ministry. I am a volunteer chaplain at one of our local hospitals where I do rounds visiting the sick and dying, and comforting the family members of loved ones who have lost someone. I also work as volunteer server and counselor at the mission soup kitchen, which caters to the poor, homeless and working poor of our community. I do this only once a week, on Wednesdays, but I truly enjoy it. Additionally, I am a member of the jail ministry team, a group of volunteer Christians who visit the local juvenile detention center once a week, on Thursdays, to mentor and offer bible study to the young inmates. I will be hosting a foreign student from Korea beginning August 10th. (Joy C., NDERF #99)

Few people seem to volunteer regularly. Far fewer volunteer like Joy. Clearly, not everyone shares Joy's life commitment to emulate the service path of Jesus. Perhaps we do not need to feel ashamed if we do not quite measure up. God does not measure worth based on human standards. For this reason, even our most simple acts of kindness and humility have enormous value and are greatly celebrated in heaven.

During her near-death experience 700 years ago, Julian of Norwich learned this lesson from Jesus:

> He wants us to know that he takes heed not only of things which are noble and great, but also of those which are little and small, of humble men and simple, of this man and that man. And this is what he means when he says: Every kind of thing will be well. For he wants us to know that the smallest thing will not be forgotten.[6]

God knows our situation intimately. Accordingly, God only asks that we stretch ourselves according to our circumstances and stage of spiritual development. Moreover, not everyone shares in the exact same mission to serve. For instance, some people have children to raise and support; their free time may be limited beyond serving their family. Although community service may not be everyone's primary mission, every person has been tasked to reach out and serve in love in some fashion. It is a copout not to serve at all. More importantly, it represents a failure to follow one's life mission directive from God. For those who deem themselves lacking in this area, I recommend selecting at least one helpful cause to heal the world, be it a person, profession, or organization. In the last chapter, I shared about a woman who suddenly collected computers for disadvantaged children. Her transformation was immediate; she felt happy and peaceful. Among thousands of NDERF submissions, she is hardly unique. Perhaps the state of happiness and repose are universal responses to being filled by the Spirit.

Some people give excuses why they can't serve, ranging from a lack of time to some innate inability. Reading this section, they may counter the call by saying, "I would love to help, but I am no Mother Teresa or Mother Joy." Unfortunately, they would be self-handicapping themselves; diminishing their God-given human ability while deifying the traits of others. Mother Teresa and Mother Joy are just ordinary people, not perfect saints. Sharing in the human genome, they readily express common human failings. They act in love only because they have opened themselves up to the Spirit and closed off their rampant ego and selfish desires. More generally, they have unshackled themselves from the World; they can no longer be contained by a corpse. Instead, they breathe life into the world by servicing the oppressed, the weak, and the hurting.

Joy never claimed to be better than anyone. Her passion for service derived from valuing everyone, even those the world rejected in judgment. In other words, Joy perceived unity where most comprehend division. She elaborated:

> At any rate, I feel that I have come to a complete understanding of my purpose in life, and that is to serve and love others. I do not judge ANYONE - 'for men have judged and judged wrongly.' And, besides, we are all measured by the measure which we meet. In other words, if I judge, I will be judged equally. So, I have let that go in all aspects of my life. (Joy C., NDERF #99)

Even a small alteration in daily behavior, like dieting, is difficult for most people to sustain. Joy's ability to withhold judgment was monumental. Igniting dead wood into a funeral pyre requires a fundamental shift in motivation, attitude, and life perspective. From my point of view, such transformative life testimonies provide supportive evidence for the authenticity of the near-death experience.

Transformation by Testimony

A single testimony has power in a court of law. Most juries would relish three or four corroborating testimonies when weighing evidence. Imagine the power of thousands of corroborating testimonies, like the kind of consistency shared by those who have had near-death experiences. Reliability of self-report is further bolstered by observable confirmation, primarily through people's everyday behavior. The few examples shared in this chapter are commonplace; such testimonies reverberate a thousand times throughout the NDERF website. These individuals don't just talk the talk, but they walk the walk. Anecdotally, I have directly witnessed radical transformation by talking with over a dozen people who have experienced NDEs. It is my strong impression that they also are walking the walk. I would bet that millions more do the same world-wide.

Skeptics often claim that NDEs are hallucinations associated with the dying process. Indeed, a brief surge of electrical activity has been measured in some dying brains of rats.[7] Can hallucinations radically transform one's life orientation toward love? In over twenty years of practice, I have never evaluated a psychotic patient who reported positive life changes based on a hallucination. Hallucinations typically present as disorganized, involuntary, cryptic, shallow, negative, scary, and surreal. Conversely, near-death experiences are typically described as organized, freely interactive, complex, meaningful, positive, blissful, and seemingly more real than earthly life. Hallucinations are also highly associated with mental illness, poor adaptive behavior, and broken lives. On the flip side, NDEs are associated with stable mental health, highly adaptive behavior, and fulfilled lives. Beckie became a believer after her mother met Jesus. She wrote the following testimony:

> Jesus told my mother she had to come back, as she had things to do. This is the remarkable part. She had always been very depressed. The next four months were the most difficult of her life physically and yet everyone she met was told of the Lord's love for them. She sang hymns all the time and witnessed constantly. If she peed she thanked God for it. It was an unbelievable change. (Beckie H., NDERF #632)

Beckie's mother was told to return because she had "things to do." How would you react if Jesus commissioned you to do something? Personally, I would be compelled to try my best. As one might imagine, NDErs not only view their near-death experiences as highly meaningful, but highly motivating. They often return to earth eager to apply their mission in every aspect of life. By studying thousands of NDEs from the NDERF website, I have noted many themes related to spiritual transformation. Please note that this list is neither exhaustive nor mutually exclusive. The list reads thus:

1. A sense of shared purpose and interconnection between living beings.
2. An understanding that love drives creation as a universal force.
3. Increased sensitivity, kindness, and gentleness toward people. Relatedly, an increased interest in social causes and community outreach.
4. Differentiating between the meaningful and the superficial.
5. Increased urgency to complete mission.
6. Less interest in exerting power and control over events and other people.
7. Less emphasis on material acquisition.
8. A rejection of violence prevalent in society, ranging from a dislike of violent entertainment to abhorring war.
9. Increased sense of repose, or dignified peace, during tribulation. On the flip side, decreased feelings of dysphoria, existential despair, and suicidal ideation.

10. Increased ability to forgive significant wrongs perpetrated by others.

11. Less fear and anxiety knowing that death does not exist.

12. Strong belief in a higher power and consciousness, either described as God and/or some universal love-force. Relatedly, an increased perception of the sacred, not just with God, but within all creation.

13. Increased spiritual connection to God. With connection, communication becomes an ongoing dialogue rather than a laundry list of requests. Correspondingly, the content of prayer becomes more focused on personal growth and the wellbeing of others.

14. Increased sensitivity to a greater spiritual presence. These sensitivities include, but are not limited to, spiritual dreams, spiritual visions, sensitivity to people's emotions, sensitivity to people's intentions, and interaction with spiritual guides.

15. A feeling of being misunderstood by most people, especially by those who do not understand spiritual transformation and all that it entails. Relatedly, a yearning to return to the spiritual realm while still holding the earth mission as sacred.

16. Hearing the call for global transformation.

It is beyond the scope of this chapter to review the presented list in detail, especially since many of these themes are addressed throughout the book. However, I would like to expand on the last point, hearing the call for global transformation. I wrote more on world events in the final chapter of my book, *Psychology and the Near-Death Experience: Searching for God.*[8] For our purposes here, let me offer an opinion that NDE testimonies are strongly tugging on the human tapestry. It is very likely that NDErs, knowingly or not, are spearheading a spiritual revolution. During her NDE, Yvonne internalized this simple but profound insight, "Knowing and standing for the truth matters." (NDERF #3854) Through testimony and quiet activism, people like Yvonne have been slowly stirring up real change throughout the world, not through external ideology, but from inner conviction.

The general populous has yet to realize the world impact of the NDE, and the inherent power of direct interactions with God, Jesus, deceased family, and other spiritual beings. Nor have they recognized the power of understanding their own life purpose. Descriptions of the afterlife, as well as testimonies of transformation, will travel around the world like embers blown from multiple forest fires. Many will be deaf to the call. Some will reject NDE testimony based on their beliefs in materialism. Still others will dismiss accounts based on religious ideology. Whatever the rationale, objections will likely be rooted in fear. People who seek ego and power have the most to fear, for spiritual transformation is based on the loving principles of the Kingdom, not on the self-centered principles of the world. Most egoists will continue to embrace the corpse, not recognizing a rotting body of death, because the carcass is dressed up with fool's gold and dazzling lights.

Although many will persistently reject transformation, others will hear the call. Will these numbers be enough to transform the world from an unsustainable path toward a viable direction? I wish I knew. Yet, I sense a growing dissatisfaction by the general public regarding worldly trends: political, economic, cultural, environmental, religious. The time is ripe to try. Harkening back to my vision described in chapter one, those seeking life want an alternative to seeking refuge in a dilapidated sanctuary while being injected with ideology. Not to be contained by a corpse, they want to live fully in the Spirit. I believe their ranks will include spiritually-inquisitive agnostics, spiritually-minded scientists, and people from various faith traditions. During her NDE, Karen spoke of spiritual transformation after meeting Jesus. Furthermore, Karen shared her desire to transform the world, as a small ember, through her routine daily interactions. She wrote:

> I'm a kinder, more gentle person, and since the experience, not materialistic any more. I donate & volunteer more than ever, and love to share my story with whoever will listen to me. Maybe it can somehow get people to think that the body is just a shell, the real self is within; in the soul itself. I can at least plant a seed, if anything, to make people think about eternity; not just today, this weekend, or the near future. I have a totally different outlook on life now. (Karen W., NDERF #2665)

Karen understands that her testimony, whether heard by a few or many, greatly contributes to the tapestry. Imagine throwing a stone into a lake. Although the stone quickly submerges, ripples swell to the lake's shore. Compound Karen's testimony by millions like it; the result will involve groups of people who can no longer be contained by the world. For, having seen the divine Light directly, they have become Children of the Light. Like Karen, they cannot help but live as burning embers and seed bearers. In similar vein, the writer of the Gospel of Phillip concluded his gospel by describing the Children of the Light:

> For them, this world has become another world, and this Temple Space is fullness. They are who they are. They are One. Neither shadow nor night can hide them. (Verse #127)[4]

Children of the Light do not hide God's brilliance under a pot, or some other cover. They shine their light broadly because they are not of this world. Rather, they are people filled with the ever-presence of God, the Temple Space. As will be explored in the next chapter, there are many paths to becoming Children of the Light. With global spiritual transformation simmering, there is hope that more people will embrace the Kingdom, whatever their path, rather than be contained by a corpse. If enough people become transformed, then perhaps humanity can save this broken world.

CHAPTER EIGHT

JESUS AND RELIGION

How do we discover our greater reality? Some seek religion for answers whereas some rely on science. I choose not to rely exclusively on one over the other, as both answer different types of questions: science solves *how* reality works whereas religion pursues answering the intangible *why* questions. Similar to religion, the near-death experience pursues "why" questions. But unlike religion, the NDE relies on direct observational evidence and, to some degree, lends itself to empirical study. I refer the interested reader to Dr. Jeffery Long's excellent book, *Evidence of the Afterlife: The Science of the Near-death Experience.*[1]

Because the near-death experience impinges on traditional religious turf, it may be viewed as a competitor by certain religious devotees. The NDE has recently become the "elephant" in the sanctuary within the last generation. In conservative religious corners, the degree of NDE acceptance will ultimately rest on its congruence with narrowly-defined doctrines. A cold reaction seems likely over time due to a certain level of discordance. Although the NDE shares much in common with religion, differences will disturb some people, particularly conservative believers. But for the open seeker, a comparison may garner a mutual understanding of different sources of spiritual knowledge.

Volumes could be written on comparing the NDE and religion. It is beyond the scope of this book to address each religion individually.

Although I often approach religion generally, my focus here centers on Christianity. There's a couple of reasons for this narrowed method. First, an exploration of Christianity appears most appropriate in a book about Jesus. Secondly, I know more about the expression of Christianity, having attended churches since I was a baby. Still, this chapter was not written only for Christians. Non-Christian readers may find it useful to apply various concepts to their own faith, or in helping to understand the reasons behind their lack of faith. It seems to me that most, if not all, religions germinate from the same need to seek the divine. Thus, it is likely that many of my points will generalize nicely. I'll leave the readers to make their own comparisons.

The purpose of this chapter is to compare the teachings of the ascended Christ with popular Christian belief and expression. I'll begin by exploring a few disconnections between the church, as a human organization, and the life and teachings of Jesus as well as the ascended Christ. A similar discussion follows regarding the church and the Holy Spirit. Such critical comparisons involve exploring the tarnished side of the religious coin. However, the brighter side of the religious coin will also be explored within the chapter. Next, we will explore how NDErs try to reconcile discrepant views between the Christ in religion and the Christ they experienced in heaven. As the chapter proceeds, we will examine the power and limitation of religion during the human process of spiritual transformation. Finally, we will consider the possibility of increased interfaith cooperation, including the religious incorporation of the NDE. First, let us take a look at the human side of religion.

The Disconnection between Jesus and Christianity

A sizable segment of any religious following asserts that their religious beliefs are the one and true word of God. Belief becomes a black and white affair while the gray is ignored. The belief in infallible doctrine assumes that God somehow produces the doctrine. One may question the logic behind this conceptual maneuvering throughout religious institutions. Who writes scripture, interprets holy books, writes liturgy, defines sin, structures ritual, defines heresy, canonizes church laws, raises money, supports political agendas, nullifies threats, and evangelizes? People do. Human beings organize and execute the business of religion. It cannot be, objectively, all of God's doing. If the Christian God was at the helm, orchestrating the application of a singular divine truth, there wouldn't be 33,000 denominations within Christendom alone.[2] If God does not steer the business of religion, then what can we say about religion? As with any human endeavor, religious practice and belief falls short of perfection.

According to the Pew Research Center, Christian affiliation has dropped 7.8% in the United States during the last seven years, with the Millennial generation showing the smallest level of Christian affiliation.[3] I suspect that a self-righteous chorus may have something to do with the falloff. If a sanctimonious attitude sours me, as a Christian, I can only imagine the response of non-Christians. In some Christian corners, our material world, the spiritual corpse, has been embodied with opulent cathedrals, moneyed reverends, exploiting capitalists, right-wing political advocates, and moral crusaders. Ironically, some opulent church mega-buildings may be spiritually hollow inside. I cannot help but be reminded of the barren sanctuary in my dream with its blown out stained glass and crumbled roofs. Love, poverty, service, and tolerance are the foundational messages of Jesus. These messages have somehow become twisted to their opposites: ego, wealth, greed, and judgments. Ironically, all this is done in the name of Jesus. Is there anywhere in the Bible where Jesus pursued wealth, hate, politics, or exclusion? On the contrary, Jesus became angry at the religious elite who represented these very attributes. He called them snakes. Interesting to me, many of the people who affiliate with such groups seem oblivious to the disconnection, despite memorizing verses in the Bible. Perhaps a biblical reframe is in order: Jesus never became angry at anyone during his ministry except the behavior of the powerful religious elite and anyone else who profited from the name of God. Specifically, Jesus never admonished people with different traditions, like the Samaritans, ignored people with lowly occupations, like the taxpayer, condemned sinners, like the prostitute, shunned the social pariahs, like the leper, or argued against people of differing philosophies, like the gentiles. Jesus was only ferociously opposed to the religious elite who twisted the Truth for their own selfish purposes. For instance, when an adulterer was about to be stoned by a mob stirred up by the Pharisees, Jesus conveyed their hypocrisies by writing in the sand. The story begins with the Pharisees bringing the adulterer before Jesus. They said:

> "Teacher, this woman was caught in the very act of adultery. The law of Moses says to stone her. What do you say?" They were trying to trap him into saying something they could use against him, but

Jesus stooped down and wrote in the dust with his finger. They kept demanding an answer, so he stood up again and said, "All right, stone her. But let those who have never sinned throw the first stones!" Then he stooped down again and wrote in the dust.

When the accusers heard this, they slipped away one by one, beginning with the oldest, until only Jesus was left in the middle of the crowd with the woman. Then Jesus stood up again and said to her, "Where are your accusers? Didn't every one of them condemn you?"

"No, Lord," she said.

And Jesus said, "Neither do I. Go and sin no more." (John 8:6:11)

Note that Jesus did not approve of the accused woman's behavior. He knew that adultery partly disconnected the woman from knowing God and thereby caused her undue misery. But unlike the religious mob, spitefully condemning her to death from a position of judgment, Jesus only tried to redirect the woman's behavior from a position of compassion. There cannot be a starker contrast in spiritual intent. Jesus, the benevolent transformer, never rejected anyone. Rather, he modeled a path for humanity to be more concordant with the Father, to develop a state of loving repose, because he empathizes with our weighted pain of being disconnected from God.

Might modern-day Pharisees act selfishly and coercively? It is not for me to judge any given person, church, or denomination. However, I perceive that a nest of vipers thrive within the Christian church today. Unfortunately, these individuals seem to grab most of the attention. Consequently, they contribute greatly to society's growing distrust of Christianity. Often charismatic and wealthy, their loud ambitions darken the reputation of genuinely motivated clergy, the quiet humble majority, just through the mere association of religious faith.

The disconnection between the ministry of Jesus and institutional religion has not been lost on people who have had near-death experiences, especially for those who communed with the ascended Christ. Having experienced the purity of Christ's love, they return feeling unsure how to bridge the gulf between the Jesus of heaven and the Jesus of dogma. Bridget describes her first-hand experience of Jesus by highlighting some of these contrasts:

It was not the Christ we see in paintings or pictures, it was not the Christ we hear about from evangelicals, it was not America's Christ or any other representation of Christ I have come across. This was a being so pure and so benevolent, and so non-judgmental, I could barely comprehend the level of compassion this being possessed in the small, yet brilliant, light that it was. (Bridget F., NDERF #1654)

One might assume that frequent NDE reports of Jesus would be celebrated by Christians. After all, people who return from near death have interacted with Jesus somewhat like the Apostles. I can't think of more compelling evidence supporting the case for Christ! From my experience, efforts to share this good news have garnered wary stares from most conservative Christians. Apparently, I am not alone in this assessment. Such a negative Christian response to the ascended Christ often takes NDErs by surprise. Jill wrote about her experience:

I found it interesting that the people who gave me the hardest time about my retelling were self-professed Christians. I never understood that...One woman said I was in hell. Well, if that's hell, sign me up. (Jill, NDERF #2922)

Another NDEr, named Catherine, wrote:

No church has ever been open to hearing what I have experienced. They seem more like artificial forms of social control rather than real connection to God on earth. (Catherine M., NDERF #571)

Although I have not had an NDE, I have sensed the same closed mindset whenever I share my own mystical experiences. Conservative Christians generally interpret my beautiful revelations as demonic. I was initially perplexed by this repeated attack, since my experiences have always guided me toward a greater love. "Come on," I say. "Demons do not encourage righteousness." Whatever my counterargument, they remained unconvinced. Then I realized the unbending psychological mindset, the existential need, of my audience. Their response represents a predictable reaction to fear. They are only preserving an established, clear order of unquestioned beliefs. Ambiguity raises uncertainty and uncertainty raises anxiety. The spiral of fear seems particularly salient when associated with meaninglessness in life and death. It is better to stuff Jesus in a small, tight enclosure of ideology;

a protective armor of certainties. In this manner, personal faith, the traditional key to salvation, can be protected from tough questions or unfamiliar visions like mine. Pondering this possibility, another consideration came to mind. Some adhere to dogma in order to feel special; they can perceive themselves as cosmic heroes righteously standing at the right side of God. For these elect, special blessings come only to those who attend the right type of church. Wonderful divine experiences cannot come from quasi-heathens like me. Ergo, they conclude that unfamiliar, amazing experiences that happen to the wrong people must be the work of the devil.

Although dogma can be protective, it produces debilitating psychological and spiritual side effects. Most strikingly, dogma stunts a person's growth toward the divine. Spiritual growth equates to one's individualized journey tied to free will. Confined by strict ideology, religious devotees live by the standards of the institution. By offering their will to another, they end up living inauthentic lives. In the next NDERF submission, Stanley, who happened to be a devout Catholic, learned about following strict religious doctrine at the expense of living honestly. At the beginning of his near-death experience, Stanley followed a crowd into a heavenly cathedral. He shared the following events:

I, too, ascended the staircase and, as I took the last step before finding myself on the floor above the church's main area, I became aware that we were all proceeding into a confessional. As I had been born into a Roman Catholic family, I knew I needed to confess my transgressions, or sins, while in the confessional. So I began searching my mind for things to say. My turn arrived, and, having entered the confessional, I knelt down and began with, "Bless me, Father, for I have sinned..." Before I was able to go any further, the screen window opened and a man's arm and hand extended toward me. I knew that I was to place my hand into his. I seemed to know that this arm, although it was covered with cloth, was of light olive-toned skin with dark, perhaps black hair.

As I placed my hand into His, I immediately found myself in a world of unconditional Love. Today, I feel that the hand was the hand of Jesus the Christ, Son of God. While my hand was in His, I discovered, felt, or believed that I was inside the mind of God. Although there was complete darkness, I felt that there was never a need for forgiveness here, that only unconditional love existed. At that moment, it seemed to me that I was in the presence of all existing eternity. I believe to

148

this day that what was communicated to me was simply this: "Don't lie to yourself, nor to anyone." (Stanley S., NDERF #2718)

Stanley learned that living by strict Catholic rules, conceived in antiquity, required him to sacrifice freedom of thought and individuality. In other words, the choices Stanley made conformed to a mass societal template. By living inauthentically, he was lying to himself and others. Enlightened and transformed by meeting Jesus, Stanley realized the disconnection between dogma and what spiritually matters. His NDE story continues with a confession of remorse:

While in the cathedral I felt sorrowful and remorseful, as if I were responsible for spreading the lie about the Holy Roman Catholic Church; that the Catholic Church, and ONLY the Catholic Church, is the way to God. I came to realize that this was not true when I had my hand in the hand of Jesus. There was total unconditional love, the likes of which I have never felt in this earthly life... The true church, if there is one, is within us all; in our hearts, and in our souls. Therein is everlasting life. (Stanley S., NDERF #2718)

Interestingly, Stanley's near-death interaction with Jesus echoes the words of Jesus within the Gospel of Thomas:

Jesus' disciples questioned him. "Should we fast? How should we pray? How should we give alms? What rules of diet should we follow?"

Jesus answered, "Stop lying. Do not do which is against your love." (Verse 6)[4]

Jesus revealed that salvation derives from deep within our souls, where a reservoir of love should abound, and not from religious convention. The real church lies within our caring hearts. It does not reside in ritual or law. Nor does it reside in the Roman Catholic Church, Judaism, or any other religion. Jesus' message can easily be embraced by people who are on fire through the Spirit. It is a pity that so many Christians seem to carry cold cinders in their hearts; they hear the pounding of the pulpit easily but appear quite deaf to the quiet inner voice of Spirit.

Inconsistencies between Spirit and Religious Legalism

Mahatma Gandhi watched imperial Britain subjugate the Indian sub-continent into servitude. Within the halls of political power in a past age, imperial Britain professed a divine right to enforce Christian doctrine, along with a servitude work ethic, onto native populations around the world. Still, Gandhi was a great admirer of Jesus. He accepted Jesus' message of love while rejecting his supposed overlords' unloving behavior toward the Indian people. He was frequently asked why he did not convert to Christianity. Gandhi indirectly answered the question in a 1931 essay titled, *The Jesus Love*. Here are two excerpts from his important work:

> It seems to me that Christianity has yet to be lived, unless one says that where there is boundless love and no idea of retaliation whatsoever, it is Christianity that lives. But then it surmounts all boundaries and book teaching. Then it is something indefinable not capable of being preached to men, not capable of being transmitted from mouth to mouth, but from heart to heart. But Christianity is not commonly understood that way.

Gandhi ends his essay with these thoughts about Christ celebration:

> I have never been able to reconcile myself to the gaieties of the Christmas season. They have appeared to me to be so inconsistent with the life and teaching of Jesus. How I wish America could lead the way by devoting the season to a real moral stocktaking and emphasizing consecration to the service of mankind for which Jesus lived and died on the Cross.[5]

Similar to many NDErs, Gandhi noticed the disconnection between the Spirit of Jesus and some Christian institutions. On a more contemporary note, Jonathan Merritt, a Christian activist formerly associated with Jerry Falwell and the moral majority, wrote about the culture wars in an excellent book titled, *A Faith of Our Own*. He concluded that movements to legislate conservative Christian values are doomed to failure. Taking encouragement from the forces of transformation, Mr. Merritt noted that a new generation of Christians was taking a more Jesus-consistent approach to healing a broken world. He wrote:

Rather than lamenting everything that is wrong with the world or retreating into a corner filled with Christian schools, Christian movies, Christian music, and alternative Halloween parties, today's Christians are rushing into places where you wouldn't have found them a generation ago. They know you can't impact the world while holding it at arm's length.[6]

Mr. Merritt rightly highlights the difference between following a moral code and following the Spirit of Jesus; one excludes whereas the other unites. As suggested, today's youth may represent a generational divide between these poles. Although a new generation may give hope for religious transformation, this same opposing polarity has separated Christians since the time of Constantine, seventeen hundred years ago. Emperor Constantine stopped the persecution of Christians by the Romans, transforming an underground spiritual movement to a powerful religious institution throughout the world. Although the Roman Catholic Church exerted immense secular power, the spiritual embers tended by Jesus still remained hot. While Popes waged religious war, friars ministered to the poor and attended to the sick. The Christian religion still seems beset with these types of contradictory opposites today: welcoming and intolerant; generating new ideas and exerting dogmatic control; serving the poor and creating hardships on others; liberating the lost and bonding the faithful; facilitating acts of love and generating fear; endowing hope while leaving some in disappointment. Let's look at a couple of contradictions of Christianity within the United States. The same institution that contributed 15-20 billion dollars in charitable services in the U.S. [7] once supported slavery in the South.[8] The same institution that promotes religious expression today also promotes the censorship of science.

I also witnessed such polarity recently during my faith journey. While my family attended a Church with an active ministry for the poor, my son was restricted from church attendance due to involuntary behaviors associated with Tourette Syndrome: he would have very loud vocal tics and blurt out inappropriate words. Some people in the congregation complained. Although the clergy were quite apologetic, they remained firm in their decision to exclude a vulnerable child from their faith community without trying any meaningful efforts for accommodation after complaints were lodged. I found their lack of effort disconcerting, particularly since various secular institutions had successfully accommodated my son's disability. When I brought my concerns to their attention, one clergywoman made a startling congregational comparison. She stated that most clergy would not even have discussed the issue because churches are not bound by the American Disabilities Act (ADA law). Sensing that my son was being treated like a leper, I thought frequently about the chasm between the ministry of Jesus and the Christian church throughout the ordeal. Jesus served lepers. Apparently, this vibrant Christian church did not. Although I might have left bitter, I took into consideration the business of religion and general human fallibility. In other words, I maintained some respect for the institution that rejected my son, even if it had been tarnished. After all, many of the members were heavily involved in charities and overseas missions. The Spirit of Jesus was alive there. How does one reconcile such polarity within one institution? I recognized that this church, like any other, was an organization where the Spirit and market pressures mixed. No doubt the latter suppressed the former in the case of my son.

It is not my intention to rant against religion. In my experience, non-religious critics tend to focus too much on the negatives. It seems unfair to label all Christians as fanatical or criticize religion for all societal ills. It is important to note that Christianity is not a monolithic institution, but a host of denominations adhering to a wide spectrum of positions, ranging from ultra-conservatism to liberalism. Some congregations respond to the call for global transformation by serving the greater social good, including the poor and downtrodden. Conversely, some religious elements promote earthly agendas: financial, political, national. While some sects denounce all violence and acts of revenge, others turn a "blind eye" to the death penalty and, in some cases, war. Whereas some congregations provide sanctuary for illegal aliens, other groups advocate closing borders and banning illegal aliens. One could write a book on hundreds of such differences. It is beyond my purpose to advocate or denounce various beliefs. This is not a book on Christian politics. My only point is that Christians develop very human responses to human-generated problems. As long as religion remains a financial business dabbling in human power bases, there will be some religious elite who veer from the inner transformative power of the Holy Spirit. The Spirit will instead manifest within those members who serve in love, as emulated by Jesus.

Religious ills are not a God problem, they are a human problem. Unfortunately, religious dogma can generate conflict in the world whenever religion and politics mix. In the worst cases, devotees relentlessly coerce non-believers into ideological submission. There are no limits to such efforts when religion wields political power and devotees are willing to die for doctrine. Although most Christian sects have less secular power today than in centuries past, a similar mindset persists in some corners. Like followers of the Pharisees during Jesus' time, some well-meaning people confuse the will of an egotistical human with the will of a loving God. From my perspective, people who consistently claim to know what God wants are acting in hubris. Only God knows what God wants.

Most NDErs apply the lessons of heaven to their assigned earthly mission when they return to society. This mission may or may not involve religion. It may not be surprising that many returnees have difficulty connecting with established religious institutions, especially those steeped in narrow dogma. In the next section, we will discuss a number of NDE responses to religion: we will explore those who follow a non-religious path as well as those who incorporate religion into their lives, not as dogmatists, but as quiet reformers.

NDE Responses to Religion

Although the basic elements of the near-death experience are universal[9], returnees apply knowledge differently depending on personality, spiritual maturity, culture, and personal history. For example, NDErs vary in their attitude toward religion. Considering that NDErs were unconditionally accepted while visiting the spiritual realm, it should not be surprising that they harbor mixed feelings toward religious institutions. After all, they just returned from a divine place of perfect love. A few NDErs focus on the more negative elements and consequently reject religion outright. For example, Shea abandoned the church because she believed that religions limit God and exclude people. Voicing her opinion, she wrote:

> I was not happy with a church that limited God or excluded other people. I went on a church hunt and never found such a place. (Shea, NDERF #2974)

One person who felt excluded was Francois. Following his NDE, Francois felt a profound disconnection between his meeting with Jesus and his religious experience. He wrote:

I saw Jesus who was smiling at me and loving me... I don't believe in church, because church, and this is personal, is crammed full of dogma, of principles that prevent and sometimes outdated ideas, and ideas on the fringes of our era. And I'm also homosexual and it is difficult for me to nowadays hear the bias of church about this. There is a total disconnection between my experience with my very intimate encounter with Jesus and God, and the vain encounter with church, wherein I don't fit as others may not fit today. (Francois O, NDERF #3495)

Francois experienced pure unconditional love from Jesus. Jesus never judged his life, never evaluated his homosexuality. Some Christians would counter, "You cannot possibly claim that Jesus approved of Francois' homosexuality. Being gay is wrong because the Bible says so. Clearly Jesus would condemn him for engaging in an unnatural act." To make this claim, however, one must project his or her conditional perspective of love on to Jesus. In reality, perfect love is unconditional. The unconditional love of Jesus, however, does not negate the moral order of the universe. According to NDE accounts, spiritual beings are not engaging in angry, exploitive works in heaven. Likewise, God does not encourage people to develop their own moral compass on earth. Such an attempt would represent a blatant exercise of ego and pride. Still, the divine moral code does not follow any institutional system of disciplined conduct or moral legalism. Rather, the Jesus code was written in broad, loving strokes. Love is good and the absence of love is not. Although describing morality in terms of love may sound unsophisticated, it is anything but simple. Remember, love is not a feeling but a series of complex skill sets that involve respect, unconditional acceptance, humility, forgiveness, and sacrifice. Once these skill sets become mastered, the true Christian life falls into place.

The ideal Christian life takes more than a lifetime to master. Living the perfect Christian life, rooted every moment in love, appears far beyond human capability. If perfect love were easy, then human existence would be orchestrated differently. School earth was created to give us opportunity to learn; to gain what we do not yet possess. Consequently, humans are not expected to ace the love test. God knows that we act within our elementary school level of spiritual development. It is a pity that human religious systems develop stringent pass-fail "righteousness tests" and assign individual worth accordingly. Fortunately, God does not care about arbitrary human moral systems or rules of ideology. In the Gospel of Thomas, when the disciples asked Jesus whether circumcision was useful, He replied:

> If it were useful, fathers would engender sons born circumcised from their mothers. Rather, it is the circumcision in Spirit that is truly useful. (Verse 53)[4]

In today's Western society, the same question could be said about dancing, social drinking, eating pork, homosexuality, premarital sex, new philosophies, scientific study, and so on. Within Islam, there are prohibitions against listening to instrumental music, drinking alcohol, and exposed head hair for women. The differences between Christian and Muslim rules serve as examples of how standards vary across religion, culture, and time. In other words, the origins of relative religious prohibition may stem from dominant cultural/religious opinion more than divine proclamation.

The skeptic may challenge, "Are not ethical standards central to the success of society?" After working 20 years in prisons, I would answer "yes" to that question. Without laws, anarchy would destroy the fragile threads holding society together. However, rules governing social order are qualitatively different from rules governing harmless personal practices. Although religious prohibitions against cultural taboos may seem benign, strict ideology and moralism crushes freedom of expression and limits individuality. Perhaps more importantly, it stymies individual mission. Blinded from the larger reality, group coercion slows the individual's quest to reconnect to the One who is infinite. Jacob Needleman, in his thought-provoking book, *Lost Christianity*, wrote from his own personal experience:

> As a young man I had been repelled and frightened by a religious moralism that seemed to kill life in the name of the creator of life. That is why I turned not to pleasure or sensuous indulgence but to science, which seemed to me then to accept life in all its movement and forms.[10]

It is no accident that culture and science blossomed when Catholic control loosened during the European Renaissance. It is no accident that certain religious terrorist groups want to beat the world back to a pre-scientific era. Taking notes from history and current events, we can see that rigid moral systems become increasingly destructive when differences are squashed with threats of violence and hellfire damnation.

Rather than creating a divine utopia on earth, dogmatic activists create a culture of fear and repressed stagnation through a continuum of intolerance: distrust, exclusion, hostility, vigilante violence, mob brutality, and religious war. In other words, the human connection to God becomes suppressed by rigid legalism. Moreover, moral servitude keeps the human species from evolving. Jesus did not support the moral rigidity of the religious elite during His ministry. He had a different path. In the Gospel of Thomas, Jesus said, "I come from the One that is Openness." (Verse 61)[4] In similar measure, NDErs have also discovered that they are magnificent spiritual beings who come from the One of Openness. No wonder they become frustrated when they try to reconnect with constrictive communities of faith.

Based on NDE submissions, it appears that many NDErs yearn to be part of a faith community. Yet, many become wary of religious organizations that teach division rather than unity. Personally, I have found that a number of Christian congregations welcome diverse beliefs and lifestyles. Indeed, open faith communities have attracted many NDErs. The influx of NDErs into open congregations may be mutually beneficial. After all, NDErs bring a fresh Christ perspective to the communion table. One NDEr expressed learning a fresh Christ message after his NDE:

> I love Christ's message, but I believe our chosen religion has nothing to do with reaching AT-ONE-MENT... This experience does not connect to anything I learned about "heaven" or God in my religion, but I feel it is more real than anything I've read. I can now read the Bible and Christ's words and hear them differently based on my experience and relate better to them, and the current world. (JMH, NDERF #1827)

A similar testimony was conveyed by Miles, who converted to Christianity from the New Age movement following his NDE. Rather than joining a church to embrace strict theology, Miles joined the broad ecumenical Christian community to share in God's far-reaching love. Miles wrote the following about his interfaith transformation:

> I had been searching and seemed to find something in New Age spirituality at the time but most definitely without our father and our Christ. This has now changed for some time. I now find myself so confidently assured of my faith in our Father and our Christ, that I search for signs of them in other people, creatures, the environment,

ecologically, historically and prehistorically in the forms of spirituality. I don't affiliate myself with only one denomination as I believe there are many aspects of our Father and our Christ in each and every one of them. (Miles, NDERF #3321)

Those mistrustful of organized religion might wonder why Miles, looking for Christ in all life, would participate in human religious institutions. Recall the dialectic, or polarity, previously discussed. Just as religion can bring out the worst in people, it can also bring out the best. In regard to Christianity, most churches teach facets of love through sermon and scripture. In this manner, the foundation of God's love remains intact despite fallible human beings messing up its application. I am reminded of my dream, in which I stood firmly in a dilapidated sanctuary. Spiritual life continued in the sanctuary, despite the missing roof. Furthermore, most churches provide communities for believers to socialize, minister to each other, and contribute to the larger good. Along these lines, many faith communities engage in diverse charity work. In an age of dwindling social services, the church remains the largest non-governmental bastion of help for the homeless, sick and downtrodden.[11] Perhaps most importantly, I have found that most congregations are sincere in their efforts to help connect people to God. For many members, the church operates at the center of most major life transitions: birth, baptism, marriage, and death. In this manner, the Christian church often becomes a beautiful partner throughout the process of life. Let's review several NDERF submissions of people who returned to the Christian church after their NDE. In the first submission, Annmarie recognized the value of the church despite its imperfections:

Religious organizations will always have conflicts and leaders that are stubborn and rigid. They are human and imperfect. But, many people gain a Christ-centered life through organized religion. (Annmarie F., NDERF #251)

In the next submission, Jean re-evaluated her initial decision to leave the Church:

I had stopped going to church about a year before my NDE. My NDE showed me there are many ways back to the Great Light. After a few years of philosophy and deep inquiry, I realized that my church was

157

one of the ways back to the Great Light and I didn't have to look any farther. So I went back to church and started again practicing my religious path. (Jean K, NDERF #2555)

In the third submission, Giselle remained in the Catholic Church despite rejecting its dogma of salvation:

I am still Catholic because it is a little less fanatical but I have a different view regarding the beliefs of others. I believe God approaches you according to your individual beliefs, that we are all his children and He speaks to us according to the language that we understand. I do not believe in everlasting damnation for those with different beliefs. I think that hell exists only for those who voluntarily choose to distance themselves from God. (Giselle RV, NDERF #2521)

Note the mixture of rejection and acceptance in all three NDERF submissions. All three NDErs tolerate religious imperfections so that they can participate in a community of faith. In other words, they discovered that their lives were more spiritually fulfilled with religion than without it. Moreover, they now have an opportunity to share a broader understanding of God with fellow Christians based on their near-death experiences. That does not mean that these women, or other NDErs, become religious followers in a traditional sense. Although they search for a "good fit" between religion and their connection with God, they maintain a spiritual identity larger than any one religion.

God is Bigger than Religion

It is easy to feel small in a disconnected world. Indeed, many people feel insignificant navigating through life's chaos and indifferences. People thereby yearn for certainty and relevance, to somehow supersede the human condition. It is no wonder that many gravitate toward the religious promise of a bigger reality. With its practiced tradition and storied history, highly institutionalized religion can efficiently be packaged and delivered with the supportive endorsement of millions. The inner struggle for truth, the tough soul searching, may largely be bypassed after a religious conversion. The basic religious creed may be summed up in a flyer, or using some other packaged conveyance, ready to be consumed by those who believe without question. For the unquestioning devotee, highly institutionalized religion can supply supportive community, personal relevance, and absolute truth. Not only does such religion promise to be big in life, it offers an even bigger future with the promise of eternal salvation. The existentialists would counter that it is all an illusion; religion simply shores up vulnerable psychological needs. Through personal experience and corroboration by the NDE, I know that the existential position is overly reactionary. Still, I submit that there is a big problem with some religious institutions: God is infinitely bigger than any religion.

The infinite nature of God has been addressed throughout this book. We have seen how every atom, physical law, and lifeform collectively expresses God. It is hubris to think that any religious book, or collection of books, captures much of the infinite. Likewise, it seems irrational to believe that any rite or ritual can magically control God, somehow bending the divine Will to human whim. Instead, God's omnipotence and omnipresence suggests a different relationship path with people. Rather than justifying personal aspirations with cherry-picked scripture, it is better to recognize our inability to fathom the will of God. Instead of trying to control God through ritual or bargaining, it is better to surrender to God's perfect will by adhering to our assigned mission to learn love. In this manner, we can love everyone by embracing the diversity inherent to infinity. In sum, humanity needs to relate to God in a relationship marked by dependency, love, and humility. To spiritually evolve, humanity needs to follow a more open religious path.

In the next NDERF submission, Cami conveys her experience of an infinite God:

> God is too big to fit inside one religion. I refuse to cling to any definition of what "God" is! It's certainly not an embodied being or a masculine entity. The systemic imbalance of a single-gender God is absurd on the face of it. Even the word "God" felt like sacrilege to me for years, like condensing the ultimate force into a shoebox with sides: there were so many cultural projections onto the concept of "God" of personification, and my experience was not of God as a separate paternal force. Instead I interpret this potent word as the underlying, glorious, intelligent, sublimely loving force that simply IS, leaping again and again into existence through all of us. By this definition, and by my experience, there is nothing that is not God. (Cami R., NDERF #2901)

Cami's experience of God is hardly unique. Indeed, her story repeats itself throughout the near-death experience literature. Many NDErs testify that God cannot be expressed by using human language. As limited physical beings, humans lack the necessary spiritual reference points. Consequently, most describe God in vague terms similar to Cami's description: "A glorious, loving force that Is."

Appealing to the human need to define the unknowable, religions often create God in their own image. In other words, they don a recognizable mask over the unknowable face of God. In Hinduism, one face of God, Ganesh, looks like an elephant. In Christianity, God is represented as a strong, Caucasian, white-bearded man (think of God touching the finger of Adam in the Sistine Chapel). Although most Christians no longer see God as an old man, many still see God through the lens of human traits. By human traits, I refer to any emotions that bubble up from our own insecurities. For instance, religions may portray God having the propensity toward jealous rage, final crushing judgment, and harsh eternal punishment. Or, they take a paternal view of God: strict, distant, tough. Throughout history, people have projected imperfect human qualities onto God. Perhaps they could not imagine sentient existence beyond the human experience. Or perhaps they feared the mystery. In any case, humanity tends to think small. Big religion, answering the human need to resolve mystery, can likewise think small.

Certainty decreases our anxiety over death. Religion downsizes God so that people can believe in something tangible. The unspoken selling line seems to be, "We can tell you about God." David rejected this claim of divine knowledge after his NDE:

> One thing I have learned through my experience is not to make God as small as my mind. I learned that the scientists and religious leaders of today also make God as small as their minds. They try to catalog God, to make Him fit into their concepts of Him. (David D., NDERF #2835)

Humbleness is a prerequisite to learning divine truth and experiencing God. After all, there is little to learn when religions reject new ideas. I never contemplated having transformative awakenings while attending more conservative churches. Looking back, I probably undermined my connective potential with God by limiting my curiosity and exploration. Do most people limit themselves, as I did? Ironically, in order to become bigger in God, we need to accept our smallness. Not only do we lack answers, but we lack the mental capacity to understand most answers. Sometimes it is enough to know the divine fundamentals: God loves us unconditionally; we have a mission to love; there is a unity between beings; we have nothing to fear. Rather than teaching about God or Jesus with conceit, the religious elite might increase spiritual awareness by presenting the good news with humility. After all, we lack knowledge and power apart from God. According to the Gospel of Thomas, when the disciples asked Jesus when He would appear to them, Jesus answered:

> On the day when you are naked and newborn infants who trample on their clothing, then you will see the Son of the Living One and you will have no more fear. (Verse 37)[4]

Becoming like newborn infants requires approaching God with humility; accepting our ignorance and helplessness. Dancing does not cause rain. Rubbing rosary beads does not bring forth forgiveness. Bargaining does not reverse sickness and death. Please note, I am not suggesting that God refuses to answer prayers. Rather, I am asserting that we usually do not know what is best for ourselves and others. Out of this human ignorance, we cannot control God. Rather, our life missions depend on allowing God's perfection to work through open hearts, humbleness, and willing obedience.

Different Paths up the Mountain

The fallibility of religion, coupled with divergent ideologies throughout the world, serves to create doubt for the logical, inquisitive mind. It is no wonder that many scientists question the existence of God, especially when established scientific principles are vigorously attacked. Thus, I understand the negative reaction some people have toward religious doctrine. However, a negative response does not necessitate a retreat into agnosticism. People who have actually seen God and Jesus through the NDE typically do not express religious zeal. Quite the opposite, most do not even believe exclusively in one religion, even if they actively participate in one particular community of faith. Interestingly, some sojourners into death ask spiritual beings about the exclusivity of religion. They consistently receive the same answer. Jean shared the response she received:

The first question I asked was, "What is the right religion?" I was told, "They all are. Each religion is a pathway trying to reach the same place." I was shown a mountain, with each religious group trying to reach the top, separated from each other by distance, but each one was trying to get to the same place. I was then told that people choose to be born into whichever religion or group that will help them achieve the lessons they are sent here to learn. (Jean, NDERF #2932)

Even Howard Storm, an atheist who became a Christian pastor after his NDE, received a similar answer to the same question. He asked Jesus and other spiritual beings, "What is the best religion?" They answered, "The religion that brings you closest to God."[12]

The answers Jean and Howard Storm received underscore two important principles. First, no religion has a monopoly on truth. Second, many religions can facilitate positive spiritual transformation in accordance with our individually assigned curricula while on school earth. Christianity resonates for me because of Jesus' emphasis on love and grace. Buddhism may resonate more for someone who is passionate about non-violence and introspection through meditation. Native American beliefs may resonate for someone who respects harmony and interconnection with creation. And so on. Many religious beliefs have merit because they contain elements of divine truth. David wrote this measured assessment about religion:

There are dozens of religions in the world, many claiming to be "The One." I think they are all right AND wrong at the same time. In other words, in man's attempt to describe the nature of God and the after-life; he has gotten the gist of it, but has given his own different interpretations and revisions. (Daniel E., NDERF #103)

Religion has spiritual value despite being right and wrong at the same time. As discussed, religion provides people with community, avenues of study, and loving outreach. However, religious affiliation is not the only vehicle for spiritual connection. There are many paths up the mountain, and not all of them are religious. God has gifted humanity with free will to explore different life possibilities. In this regard, Tanya wrote:

I asked about the Bible, Jesus, gays, and lesbians as well. I asked all sorts of questions and I received every answer. I asked what religion was the correct one. They told me that I did not have to choose. (Tanya BB., NDERF #3392)

If there is no one right religion, then why I am writing about Jesus? Based on the teachings of Jesus and the ascended Christ, I firmly believe that Jesus completed a special God-mission on earth; He was purposely inserted into history to change the spiritual evolution of humanity. Moreover, Jesus continues to nudge the evolution of humanity today in accordance with divine will. I propose that the contents of this book speak well to these positions. However, the special mission of Christ does not imply exclusivity. Other individuals have intervened in human spiritual history, to varying degrees, as well. Christian groups only limit their understanding of God by categorizing dissimilar beliefs as heretical. When Susan was asked whether she met any spiritual beings in heaven, she answered:

I saw Christ, Saint Mary, Buddhist monks, angels, and Native American saints (I was aware of some dancing movement). They said they are always with me and looking out after me on my journey, whether in the physical or not... We are all connected was the message. (Susan H., NDERF #2543)

Why would Jesus "hang out" with Buddhist monks and Native American saints? From a fundamentalist Christian perspective, monks and saints from other religions should be burning in hell for leading heathen cultures astray. To counter such exclusive ideology, Susan was introduced to an intercultural pantheon. In other words, it was important for her to learn, and share upon return, that all beings, no matter how diverse, are interconnected through God's unifying love. Buddha is a son of God like Mary is a daughter of God. Likewise, I am a son of God as my Muslim friend is a son of God. Ideological divisions only create artificial separation where there should be infinite diversity within a connecting unity. This lesson becomes echoed again during Linda's NDE with, of all beings, Jesus:

He was explaining the different things of life on Earth, why it was that life on earth was not perfect, and why it was that way. He also explained what people on earth had misconstrued about life and living. He said that there were many different religions on earth, as one faith would not take care of everyone's spiritual needs. (Linda S. #1864)

Based on Linda's NDE, Jesus did not evangelize in His own name, but rather supported the viability of non-Christian religions. It seems ironic that Christians who believe that Jesus is the only means to salvation, assert a different point of view. If what Linda and others say is true, then perhaps Christians claim to know more about the function of Jesus than Jesus. I recognize this message serves as a radical departure from orthodox Christianity; it goes against what people have learned from the church. I am not suggesting that every Christian should radically change their views about Jesus. I have not radically changed my views. As will be presented in the next chapter, Jesus remains my Savior in many respects. Rather, I suggest that people consider reframing Jesus, and Christianity in general, in a more inclusive manner, as a part of God's manifestation of the All. In doing so, humans might have an opportunity to take a developmental step toward living in a divine unity shared by all living beings.

A Religious Step toward Divine Unity

Imagine a cooperative world existing without war. Indeed, God encourages us to imagine and embrace peace. If humanity embraced diversity within unity, perhaps most conflicts could be avoided. Based on the world track record of violence, one might argue that humanity never learns from self-induced tragedy. Although history supports the pessimists, I say that everything is possible with God. Before such change can occur, however, societies must fundamentally change. Intolerances must be fought at every source, including divisions created by religious dogma and moralism.

Only through teaching love can humanity be catapulted to a higher spiritual level. Perhaps love might not only quell the turmoil without, but the turmoil within. Many people do not love, or even respect, themselves. As explored in earlier chapters, proponents of God's wrath tend to cause shame and fear in others. In other words, they cause others to think small about themselves. If everyone recognized their true royal heritage, eternal and magnificent, then no one would have to worry about passing the salvation test. The questions "Did I do enough?" or "Did I believe enough?" would be moot. People can better fulfill their mission from a state of confidence rather than from a state of doubt and fear. Catherine, from her NDE, shared how important it was for her to move beyond fear:

164

I used to fear that if I did not worship Jesus I would burn in hell because, like most people describe, "Jesus is the only religion." I did not want to believe in a religion that was conditional. I felt deep down that God unconditionally loves (in a non-spoiled manner). God guides and helps us grow toward mastery and peace. God does not condemn, restrict, or torture. Now that the fear is gone, I feel at greater ease. If I do choose to be religious, I will do it for the feeling of the Light that I had felt and not because "if I don't, I'll end up in hell." I now believe that religious teachings are stepping stones to the Light. There are different pathways to it as there are different religions. It is how you interpret the teachings that take you to the Light, not what the religious teachings say. (Catherine P., NDERF #2534)

Real spirituality, the soul's connection with God, does not blossom from states of self-doubt and fear. Does a child's love for a parent deepen when that parent threatens physical violence? Likewise, does a person's love for God grow deeper when the church threatens eternal torture in hell? When fear is removed from the equation, humanity will enter a new spiritual age; a transformative fire will spread across the nations: more people will gravitate toward God in a sincere way, like a child deepening his or her love with the gentlest parent. As gentle love germinates, the suffering of others will become more important than the measuring of sin. I believe that God has long planned for such a worldwide transformation through the power of the near-death experience.

In a modern age plagued by serious planetary challenges, it is no accident that God has revealed so much to humanity in such a short period of time. Just in the last sixty years, ambassadors from heaven have partially relayed the meaning of life, nature of heaven, evolution of being, unity of spiritual beings, person of Jesus, and nature of God. As medical technology continues to advance, a growing number of ambassadors will reenter their bodies transformed. When NDE numbers reach critical mass, their influence will be unstoppable. Even now, many NDE books have become bestsellers and even Hollywood has begun to make movies. How has religion responded to this sudden avalanche of spiritual information? For the most point, they have ignored the NDE. Perhaps they are hoping it will all go away like a fad. I have no doubt the opposite course will unfold. Like the Pharisees of old, religious leaders will miss out on a massive spiritual movement if they ignore near-death experiences. As old orthodoxies are questioned, I predict that fundamentalist religious leaders will soon attack the NDE in earnest. Although they will have strong support from likeminded adherents, churches will probably continue to lose members in the long run. One cannot cork God's efforts to bring in a new spiritual age. Perhaps it would be better if the Christian church tried to come to terms with the NDE, even embrace aspects of its message.

To accept the near-death experiences does not require abandoning religion. I have always viewed the NDE as an expanding and unifying force, not a corrosive energy. True, there are notable differences between NDE reports and the strict orthodoxies of any particular religion. Yet, there are many more similarities than differences. As David pointed out earlier, humanity appears to have acquired the gist of God. There is no need to abandon religion. As a Christian, I find a remarkable consistency between the NDE and the Bible. Personally, I have no desire to create a new religion based on NDE accounts. Nor have I met any NDErs who have endorsed starting an NDE religion. Perhaps churches have little to fear if they are willing to broaden and synthesize their concepts of Jesus and God. Possibly the same could be said of other faiths. A different David proposed an interesting idea from his NDE. He wrote:

> And I know all religions fall together and should grow together. There is no religion that is better than the other. (David A, NDERF #2501)

Will religions eventually grow together? Perhaps the whole of humanity is not ready for such a monumental change. That does not preclude transformed people from starting a "grass roots" spiritual revolution. With time, societies may become more ecumenical and embrace the unity that defines God's creation. Indeed, the unity vision underlies a primary purpose of my own writing. Perhaps the combined efforts of likeminded people will stop the destructive wake of human division. I can only hope these efforts are not too little nor too late.

In this chapter, we compared religion, particularly Christianity, with the testimonies of those who met the ascended Christ. In addressing related topics, divisions created by dogma and moralism have been examined. I recently had a dream about the church trying to clean up human sin. In this dream, I was hovering over a ceramic tile floor caked with dirt, food crumbs, clipped grass, pieces of feather, and other diverse, unwanted particles. The dirty floor, as I saw it, represented the sins of the world. Above the mess, eight mechanical arms, reaching out of a large, thin, rusty machine, were busily scrubbing away at the grime and dirt. At the end of each arm were hand grips that moved brooms, dust pans, mops, and mop buckets. Although the cleaning was fast and furious, none of the activity seemed coordinated; the machine had no central control system. Brooms were mixing up dirty mop water and dust pans were tangling into mops. The machine, as I saw it, represented the state of religion. In an effort to control human morality, different religions, like mechanized automatons, were just transporting globs of dirt from one area in life to another. Unfortunately, these efforts were not coordinated by the rules of love. If religion cannot help humanity move to the next level, then how are we to be saved? In the next chapter, we will examine how Jesus saves humanity from itself.

CHAPTER NINE

JESUS AND SALVATION

The word "salvation" often elicits charged emotions and thoughts. After all, our futures depend on the legitimacy and function of salvation. Do we die with the body, float around earth, ascend to heaven, or suffer in hell? Unfortunately, consensus about the process in achieving salvation, or even its existence, seems lacking in the world. Yet, religious circles maintain their own ironclad beliefs about salvation. Christianity holds that believing in Jesus is the key to salvation.

For many orthodox Christians, salvation exclusively depends on each person's "accepting Jesus into their heart." The process involves a commitment of faith, preferably through public proclamation, that Jesus is the Son of God. In this manner, the saved are renewed by the power of the Holy Spirit. This process is necessary because God, perfect in nature, cannot tolerate sin or sinners. Only by God's mercy was Jesus, the Father's only Son, sent to die so that human wretchedness could be cleansed. Meaning, Jesus' execution served as a blood sacrifice for anyone who accepted Jesus as their Lord and Savior. Everyone else will burn eternally in hell for their sins.

Attending several Baptist churches throughout my youth, I felt a celebratory comfort whenever unsaved people answered the Sunday service altar call. Likewise, I became saved enthusiastically in the church at the age of twelve. For me, it was an easy decision based on logical deduction. I was incredulous that anyone would risk burning in a lake of fire, like all those atheists, agnostics, Buddhists, Muslims, Jews, Hindus, Catholics, and other heathens. Besides, the cost/benefit ratio seemed extremely favorable for me as a Christian. Becoming saved was not only easy, it was free! I had only to say a few heartfelt words to receive my golden ticket into heaven.

My belief in salvation by faith became more muddled as I matured. Looking back, I can now point to two clouding events. Most important was the death of two grandfathers. Both men were decidedly not Christian, despite concerned family members confronting their beliefs in order to save their souls. Despite their faithlessness, they were consistently ethical and loving. Ironically, they seemed to act more Christ-like than some of the very Christians who were pressing Jesus on them. Around this time, I started attending a state university and was introduced to students representing various countries and religions. They seemed mostly to be friendly, ethical people. I certainly enjoyed their presence more than the "mall evangelists" volleying hateful threats of hellfire toward passing students. Because of these life eye-openers, I became plagued by unsettling questions. Through my struggle with doubt, eventually I arrived at a few liberating answers. I concluded that I had no right to judge anyone, whether I was armed with scripture or not. I could not readily see any division of virtue in myself or others. Were my grandparents suffering hell at the hand of God? I decided that was not possible.

During my uncharted journey of youthful spiritual discovery, I began to wonder what kind of God condemned people to hell simply because they did not publicly proclaim, "Jesus, I accept you in my heart as Lord and Savior." Given God's perfect love, how could God condemn the majority of humanity, and possibly multitudes across the universe, to unending torture based on religious belief alone? I would refrain from making such harsh judgments if I wielded omnipotent power. Indeed, I would be forgiving, despite my narrow ability to love, because I care too much about people. In fact, I would not even send my worst enemies to be endlessly tortured. Would not God exhibit a greater love than me? Phillip Gulley, the author of *The Evolution of Faith*, conveyed similar concerns. He wrote:

> How can the same God who urges us to freely forgive be so resistant to forgiveness that he would demand the spilling of blood in order to pardon others? How can God demand a mercy of us that he himself is not willing to extend to others? This is nothing less than divine

hypocrisy, inconsistent with the gracious character of God, who freely and generously forgives.[1]

Based on Gully's logic, there is either a problem with God or a problem with our understanding of God. I accepted the latter position during my spiritual searching in college. But I didn't stop there. I also questioned whether the evangelical view of salvation was even based on a singular act of faith. I was especially suspicious about the recurrent Christian phrase, "Once saved always saved." Such words suggest that any saved person can behave dreadfully, lose sight of their faith, reject love, and still be welcomed into heaven, whereas non-Christians, who try to embrace love and behave morally, are doomed to hell. The ramifications are troubling. Such an exclusive club position advocates that the mere proclamation of faith controls God's judgment and forgiveness. In other words, evangelical Christians assert that a few heartfelt words have power over salvation and, by extension, the will of God. I am reminded of the magical rituals of ancient mythology: gods providing bounty if a person performs certain rites in perfect rote. My reaction—my epiphany—was that rites and rituals do not control the omnipresent and omnipotent character of a loving, infinite God. If current views of salvation do not relate to God, it follows that these views may be a product of human thinking. Not only that, human concepts of salvation may say more about humanity, and the way we view ourselves, and less about God. Along related lines, Phillip Gully wrote:

> The appeal of narrow salvation rests in our willingness to believe the worst of humanity, not the best.[1]

Indeed, segments of the Christian church view humanity in the worst light, wretched and unworthy of God. Correspondingly, some Christians judge their fellow spiritual beings as deserving of everlasting torture, just because they do not believe as they do. More sadly, they impose their human-based ideology on the divine; they displace human failings onto God.

Perhaps humanity has finally evolved enough to view God, and ourselves, in a more mature light. Indeed, people who have near-death experiences teach new lessons about humanity, the nature of God, and the meaning of salvation. People who have NDEs do not view salvation from the narrow, harrowing viewpoint of being saved from hell. Rather, they see salvation from a positive view of expansive spiritual growth. Primarily, Jesus saves us from the ignorance of our disconnection through the power of the Spirit.

The traditional view of salvation can be likened to an antique table top: two dimensional in complexity, darkly stained in age, and chipped by wrath and judgment. The near-death accounts of salvation can be likened to a cut diamond: multifaceted in complexity and clear with the purity of unconditional love. To reexamine salvation as a cut stone, we will draw on foundational concepts studied in past chapters. It is not my intention to be redundant, but to apply learned principles to understanding a new complex topic. Accordingly, the reader will not only have the benefit of considering something new, but also of synthesizing learned material as the book comes to a close. First, we will explore the meaning of salvation apart from sin. Next, we will examine salvation as an extension of God's mercy through ongoing operations in love. To follow, we will explore how Christ saves humanity through mission adjustment, deliverance, and protection. Finally, we will explore the impact of Christ's crucifixion, as an act of great sacrifice, as it relates to the salvation of all humanity. Let us begin by redefining aspects of sin.

A Bliss for Every Sin

According to Christian creed, sin shuts the gates of heaven and opens the gates of hell for the unbeliever. Ergo, sin needs to be smothered, lest the wiles of Satan bring humanity down toward a tragic fall. Any other suggestion begets rebuke from adherers of conservative orthodoxies. Yet, NDErs consistently veer from the popular track; they risk countering the belief that salvation has exclusively been reserved for Christians. They know that heaven is the home for all spiritual beings regardless of their religious creed on earth. The following NDERF submission summarizes their point:

> The concept of salvation is our attempt to grasp what is already ours. Our understanding of salvation, much as we debate it, doesn't begin to reflect God's reality. (NDERF #4)

Grasping the idea that "salvation is already ours" conflicts with widely-accepted Christian beliefs about salvation. Yet, NDErs are reporting that God does not judge. Without judgment, there is no need to fear. Without fear, penance has no purpose. Without penance, sin no longer becomes a devourer of souls, but rather a blockage for human connection with God. As previously explored, the purpose of school earth is to work through these blockages so that we can know the real self as an interconnected expression of God. Although some lessons may be hard-learned, they provide opportunities for healing and victory. Sin, in this manner, becomes a catalyst for growth. Thus, God does not see sin as a two-dimensional evil, but as something more complex. During her NDE, Julian of Norwich learned about sin while interacting with Jesus:

> All his judgments are easy and sweet, bringing to great rest the soul which is converted from contemplating men's blind judgments to the judgments, lovely and sweet, of our Lord God. For a man regards some deeds as well done and some as evil, and our Lord does not regard them so, for everything which exists in nature is of God's creation, so that everything which is done has the property of God's doing.[2]

One may question sin as a "property of God's doing" given that God exhibits perpetual perfection. Yet, God does not view "sin" as a malicious entity, as people do, but rather as a function of spiritual inexperience inherent to a budding creation. To elaborate, reality unfolds through evolutionary steps, often from the simple toward the complex. This is true not only for species development, but also for spiritual development. In his spiritual writings, the brilliant Russian novelist Leo Tolstoy wrote:

> We are certainly not free if we imagine ourselves being stationary, and if we forget that our life is but a continual movement from darkness into light, from a lower stage of truth to a higher, from a truth more alloyed with errors to a truth more purified from them.[3]

To better understand movement toward light, it may be helpful to understand the nature of time. NDErs consistently report that time doesn't flow in a linear fashion in the spiritual realm like the physical realm. In heaven, the past, present, and future can be experienced as a singularity. Imagine if all time could be represented as a loaf of bread. Then imagine that loaf being sliced in every direction all at once. Consequently, God does not see behavior, including sin, in isolation, but rather developmentally and holistically. Evil is not viewed as a static state, but as a fluid means toward a perfectly evolving future. For this reason, God's understanding of sin differs radically from emotionally-based judgments made by humans living in linear time. Julian of Norwich wrote:

> For our Lord does everything which is good, and our Lord tolerates what is evil. I do not say that evil is honorable, but I say that our Lord God's toleration is honorable.[2]

Although sin may not be honorable, God tolerates "sin" as a necessary and integral part of spiritual evolution in an open system. By "open", I mean that God grants people the freedom to choose their destiny. Seen from the viewpoint of choice and responsibility, sin no longer breathes evil as if it were some external expression of satanic will. Rather than personifying sin, people may better understand sin as a consequence of immature spiritual development. In the Gospel of Mary, the writer recorded this possible teaching of Jesus from oral tradition:

> Peter asked Jesus, "What is the sin of the world?" The Savior said, "There is no sin, but it is you who make sin."[4]

Julian of Norwich echoed this possible Christ message from her NDE. She shared the following:

> I did not see sin, for I believe that it has no kind of substance, no share in being, nor can it be recognized except by the pain caused by it.[2]

From the NDE perspective, religion mishandles sin. By tying immorality to hellfire, doctrine infuses sin with an animate, caustic power. Rather than reframing sin as an opportunity for learning and growth, religion created a living monster out of immorality: a beast devouring our identity as sons and daughters of God. When religion teaches that people are wretched, many respond by enveloping their sin with shame and fear. They begin to attack themselves by saying, "I am a bad person. No one can love me, especially God." Self-defacing beliefs thwart people's ability to grow spiritually. Lacking confidence, they become stuck, instead, in old patterns. Moreover, people with low self-esteem become hypersensitive. They overreact to perceived threats and displace their self-anger onto others. In other words, they regress into more immature emotional states and, in the process, create more "sin" in their lives. Religion typically fails to see this human dynamic. How have Christians reacted in the past? Rather than teaching better patterns through positive reinforcement, the self-righteous have created a state of war against immorality. Such battles usually lead to some suppression of freedom, ranging from moral legalism to inquisition. Ironically, the war against sin does not slay the monster, but feeds it, for the reasons stated above. By no means am I suggesting that humanity embrace "sin" or anything that disconnects people from God. Indeed, it is our mission to work diligently toward loving God and our neighbor more fully. I only point out the dangers of slapping powerful labels onto a nebulous term that we hardly understand, particularly as it relates to salvation. In other words, we need to react to sin with more finesse. Julian of Norwich conveyed a different view of sin, one that involves polarity of purpose:

> And God showed that with sin will be no shame, but honor to man, for just as there is indeed a corresponding pain for every sin, just so love gives to the same soul a bliss for every sin. Just as various sins are punished with various pains, the more grievous are the sins, so will they be rewarded with various joys in heaven to reward the victories over them.[2]

The connection between sin and victory is inseparable. The Baptist church, as I remember, preached that victory over sin occurs during a singular moment of salvation. Julian of Norwich, conversely, speaks of victory over sin as a life process. Reframing victory as a journey toward growth may be our key to the management of sin. Rather than exterminating immorality with anger, like slaying the mythical dragon, we could challenge "sin" by means of strength and endurance, like running a marathon. Before a marathon can be triumphed over, the 5k, 10k, and 15k need to be mastered one stride at a time. Likewise, before sin can be triumphed over, students of school earth need to endure various challenges one decision at a time. Every time the runner masters a longer distance run, he or she becomes stronger. In similar fashion, every time the sinner chooses light over darkness, he or she becomes spiritually stronger to live in accordance with the Kingdom of God. In both cases, it is the little victories that matter the most. The point being, in order to experience the joys of conquering sin, we need to experience sin in the first place. Some churches create undue fear in people's lives. Given that sin is a property of our evolution, we do not have to feel wretched in the sight of God nor fret over personal salvation. We can, instead, choose a saving path that brings us liberation.

People carry religious beliefs and expectations into heaven. Ironically, it is the ascended Christ that often flips traditional views of salvation during near-death experiences. In the following NDERF submission, Atilla enters a courtroom following a suicide attempt. Facing God as her eternal judge, Atilla awaits trial and a verdict for her life. A defense attorney sits beside her on the court bench. Atilla recognizes the attorney as an ally ready to speak on her behalf, a friend who may be Jesus. She wrote:

> Next I found myself in some kind of courtroom. Before me sat an unbelievably stern, all-powerful, yet very kind judge; absolutely incorruptible. Duty and person were One, and the person didn't exist without the duty. I sat on a bench and near me was a friend or defender. Great love emanated from him. Was it Jesus?
>
> The judge asked me, "What are you doing here?" I was overcome with fear and wanted to wake up. But that didn't happen. I thought about it and remembered that I had wanted to die. At the same moment that I knew this, so did the judge. I felt his mercy and it was like balm for my soul. I realized he wasn't at all angry. I learned how to distinguish between power and anger. The judge thought for a while and said, "But you have a mission." (Atilla, NDERF #1658)

Note that Atilla mentioned that duty and person are one: our being cannot be separated from our assigned mission embedded in God's unity. Atilla knew that she failed in duty by attempting suicide. No wonder she hoped desperately to escape by waking up. Escape from reality was impossible, however, so Atilla awaited God's judgment. Would Jesus make a strong case on her behalf? Would she be sentenced to hell? Before the trial even started, the entire situation flipped. Suddenly, there was a stark disconnect between the contrived courtroom setting, which appeared as if drawn up according to some evangelical blueprint, and the true nature of God. Jesus never had to defend Atilla because God, the Father, was never angry at her for attempting suicide. The underlying message, as I see it, is that God will never become angry at any of our failings. As referenced earlier in the book, Julian of Norwich wrote:

I saw truly that our Lord was never angry, and never will be. Because he is God, he is good, he is truth, he is love, he is peace, and his power, his wisdom, his charity and his unity do not allow him to be angry. For I saw truly that it is against the property of his power to be angry... Our soul is united to him is unchangeable goodness. And between God and our soul there is neither wrath nor forgiveness in his sight.[2]

Wrath and forgiveness are inversely related. People forgive transgressors by letting go of their anger. If there is no transgression, there is no anger. We cannot harm God by our misbehavior. As the omnipotent author of reality, God can take it. Even more to the point, divine love, peace, power, wisdom, charity, and unity disallow God to feel and express anger. Furthermore, God cannot become angry if all creation is an expression of divine will and essence; fallible human beings are a property of God. Rather, God honors our hardships and pain lovingly. By these three lines of logic, the entire doctrine of sin comes into question: salvation does not stem from forgiveness of sins through faith, but rather through operations in mercy. As we will discuss in the next section, mercy acts as a balm for our souls.

Delivered by Mercy

The church defines divine mercy as acts of clemency from sinful transgressions. Based on her NDE, Julian of Norwich reframes God's mercy as a continuous state of compassion toward the human condition. Through God's compassion, mercy offers salvation from human desperation through gracious operations in love. As a result of meeting Jesus, Julian of Norwich concluded the following:

> For we through sin and wretchedness have in us a wrath and a constant opposition to peace and to love; and he revealed that very often through his lovely look of compassion and pity. For the foundation of mercy is in love, and the operation of mercy is our protection in love...That is to say, as I see it, mercy is a sweet, gracious operation in love, mingled with plentiful pity, for mercy works, protecting us, and mercy works, turning everything into good for us.[2]

Salvation can be conceptualized as a process of soul refinement; turning everything for us into good. God refines our essence through mercy much like a sculptor chisels away stone. Like our servant writhing in the dell, God looks upon every personal struggle with compassion and pity. Unfortunately, we do not notice God grieving for our pain nor working on our behalf. Separated by realms, human beings may feel abandoned when making hard life choices. Freedom is not always easy. We cannot be fully connected to the divine, as we exist in heaven, and still have the independence to make mistakes, as we live on earth. Although we may grow from our individuality, life consequences, sometimes harsh, become the price of freedom. Still, mercy abounds for those who seek it. With mercy, sin becomes washed away along with guilt and only profit remains. Betty Eadie elaborates from her NDE, "This new understanding then leads me to naturally abandon the sin. Although the sin is blotted out, however, the educational part of the experience remains."[5]

Those who seek mercy discover it by connecting with their true divine nature. To varying degrees, human life promises periods of peril, fear, loss, and sickness. Finally, it promises death. If we follow the path of love, our true nature, then we transcend temporary tribulations and find eternal hope in God's mercy. Conversely, if we follow the illusionary path of ego, we fall into despair by discovering a corpse. For several chapters, we explored how people are transformed through gifts of the Spirit. To recap, God provides wisdom over obstacles, opportunities to love during mission, repose while under trial, solace when feeling alone, healing when grieving, endurance through sickness, and eternal hope when facing death. Not to belabor these points, it is important to note that ongoing refinement has its basis in a type of personal salvation. When dead wood is slowly burned by the fire of Jesus, new life explodes with fresh potential. Made anew, souls are saved from the stagnation of death by transcending the corpse of the world. Put succinctly, they are saved by becoming alive in the Spirit. As previously discussed, the process of becoming anew is difficult and lengthy. The humble servant therefore knows that he or she cannot progress far toward salvation without divine operations of mercy.

The term "operation" entails a systematic course of outside intervention. Think of heart surgery. Heart surgery requires the careful execution of external, intrusive interventions necessary to save someone's life. When Julian of Norwich talks about operations in love, she refers to a similar set of complex interventions meant to save us by bringing us back to the Source. Unlike a simple heart operation, however, God's operations in mercy far exceed human comprehension in complexity.

Fortunately, the work of God is infinite, so souls never have to worry about being abandoned. After all, humanity is just beginning to crawl spiritually. If human adults do not condemn toddlers, surely God does not condemn us. Rather, God is more interested in healing and making us whole. These operations in mercy are quite personal since we all have divergent personalities, circumstances, strengths, and weaknesses. In this manner, each path toward salvation should be seen as special and individualized. Phillip Gulley offered this interesting assessment:

> There might be as many definitions of salvation as there are human needs, that the specific requirements for wholeness vary for each of us, depending on which things keep us from being well and whole and healed.[1]

God offers salvation by providing souls various opportunities to evolve spiritually: to master what we lack and sustain what we need. The realization that salvation is based on connection, rather than the fear of damnation, cannot be accomplished by ritual or belief alone. To find peace in truth, people must actively seek God's mercy. To seek it, we must be open to God's help. To be open, as explored in earlier chapters, we must shed our ego and become humble servants, like Christ, and be "passerby" to all physical trappings that keep us distracted.

Many of the Old Testament authors conveyed the operation of God's mercy in terms of a life process. Samuel wrote, "The Lord is my rock, my fortress, and my Savior." (2 Samuel, 22:2) To this ancient seeker, God's presence will never falter; it is solid and permanent like a rock. Furthermore, Samuel indicates that God's protection remains steadfast like a fortress. Similarly, King David expressed a fundamental need for God's mercy. Despite his high status in the world, David realized that he was, in reality, poor and needy. He wrote: "As for me, I am poor and needy, but the Lord is thinking about me right now. You are my helper and my savior." (Psalm 40:17)

David understood that his salvation rested in God's continuous mercy, not in his own works. His power was based on humility. The popular epistle, *Clement I,* had once been adopted into some early Christian Bibles. Around 95 A.D., Clement offered this prayer to the church in Corinth, "Open the eyes of our heart, that we may recognize you as the savior of those who abandoned hope." (Verse 59)[6] Feeling hopeless can motivate us to humbly seek God's mercy. When we open our eyes to God's mercy, we become alive in the Spirit. Thus, our salvation rests in understanding and becoming who we really are throughout time. Only by realizing our unified spiritual magnificence can we transcend our physical existence. Therein lies not only hope, but eternal salvation.

Operations in Mercy by the Ascended Christ

As the Father wills mercy the ascended Christ works in mercy. Acting in accordance with His pure divine nature, the ascended Christ adds many pieces to an infinite cosmic puzzle. Recall my vision of Jesus filling the life strands in the universe with golden light in chapter three. In this manner, Jesus exhibits great power and authority to fulfill God's will. Likewise, we read a few NDE submissions in chapter two in which Jesus maintained authority over the angels. Thus, it seems likely that Jesus has power and authority far beyond human comprehension. Bridget, from her NDE, described Christ's responsibility in assisting humanity this way:

> That is when I recognized that he was a part of the greater light and in a way a custodian of our planet, kind of like he was assigned to it. It was his to "rule" and watch over, to guide, protect, love, and nurture. (Bridget F. NDERF# 1654)

Working as an earth custodian, Jesus nudges every open mind and heart toward the Source, even those oblivious to his quiet presence. Howard Storm, when speaking to Jesus during his NDE, discovered that Jesus was afforded an even greater cosmic purpose:

> I asked Jesus, "Are the things written about him in the Bible true?" He said that stories in the Bible are only a small sample of who he is and what he has done. All the books in the world couldn't contain what he has done. The stories about him in the Bible are sufficient for us to know him and what he represents. He is the revelation of the unknowable God. That is what he wants us to know. He has spoken to many people in many times, millions upon millions throughout time in our world, so that people would know the intimate, personal love of God.[7]

In order to speak to millions upon millions of people, Christ must speak to many people simultaneously. Thus, Christ consciousness must somehow be refracted into many channels, somewhat like a rainbow. How can this be accomplished? I once experienced a vivid spiritual dream that may have depicted the process. I saw a brief image of God consciousness, depicted as bright white light, shining through a soul. The soul was reproduced in holographic form on earth. I should clarify that the hologram was more than a mere projection: it was a full reproduction of the original soul in heaven; it even contained individual consciousness expressed through human existence. Regrettably, I cannot explain the process further. If my dream speaks true, herein rests one of countless divine mysteries that can be only partially explained. But that is how it should be. Mystery is part of the divine plan, particularly when it relates to Jesus and salvation.

NDErs do not describe the process of salvation like a recipe of measured ingredients. Perhaps it is more important to know what Jesus represents than to categorize the mechanisms behind His deeds. From the NDE perspective, some of the ascended Christ's deeds can be placed in the context of salvation. These accounts generally fall into two categories. First, Jesus saves NDErs by redirecting their mission upon return to earth. Second, Jesus saves lost souls by delivering them from self-created hells. Let's examine both types of operations by the ascended Christ, starting with the redirection of mission.

Jesus occasionally redirects the mission of the NDEr. Everyone has been commissioned to learn and express love on earth. When the possibility of resuscitation accompanies death, a crucial choice must be made: should a soul find rest in heaven or continue its mission on earth? The vast majority of NDErs press for rest. Not recognizing the larger plan in the moment, they push for a continued state of intense bliss, ongoing celebration, and permanent love. It is the job of spiritual beings, such as Jesus, to counter their understandable enthusiasm. When Jesus becomes involved, the ascended Christ quiets their pleading by explaining the importance of mission. As explored earlier, the entire purpose of human existence is to provide souls with an opportunity to grow toward the Source through free will. Once the NDEr comprehends this message, Christ sends the soul back to the host body.

Sending NDErs back to earth represents a type of salvation: Jesus often salvages the premature termination of mission. From the standpoint of the weary earth student, the rebooting of mission may not feel like salvation. But from God's eternal perspective, missions are critical to the spiritual evolution of both the individual and group. About her NDE, Georgia wrote:

I would have to return to earth, but I did not want to leave this heavenly place. He (Jesus) explained to me that I had not yet performed His wishes that He had set forth for me in my lifetime. (Georgia, NDERF #684)

In the next two NDE examples, Jesus stated that additional time was needed to complete mission:

He smiled at me and said, "It's not your time. Follow me, have faith in me, and I shall protect you." (Kendra NDERF #1750)

He said, "You are not ready to die. You still have work to do." He hesitated, and then said, "And don't be afraid, I will be with you." (Elizabeth, NDERF #2113)

Most NDErs are reluctant to leave heaven and resume life in a battered or sick body. Pain and suffering, however, are potentially powerful lessons on school earth. Although it is difficult, returnees need not despair or fear. Jesus will guide and protect them throughout the dark valleys in life; they will not be given more than they can handle.

Although we are all capable of achieving some success in mission, some people reject outright their commission to love. These individuals represent the spiritually lost. For the spiritually lost who experience NDEs, many receive a stronger message from Jesus other than a kind directive to "go back to work." In fact Jesus may reveal future consequences stemming from their disconnection. Such seismic warnings are meant to jolt the NDEr into a more connected spiritual frame of reference. Paul, during his transforming NDE, shared an ominous alert issued by Jesus:

I remember standing on the edge of a cliff and in front of me I saw a mist, a floating fog, but for some reason I knew it was bottomless. All I could feel, hear, and see was sadness... Looking down into the abyss, I was filled with sadness and I sensed that if I stepped forward I would fall into the abyss of sadness for eternity. It was Jesus holding my hand that kept me from doing so; I believe He wanted me to just see and sense the sadness but not go into it...The sadness that I felt, saw, and heard reminds me every day how nothing in this life means anything to me except for people. No money or inanimate objects or possessions mean a thing to me, I don't care about anything except people, family, friends; they are all that matters in life here. (Paul J, NDERF #1694)

It is important to note that Paul reframed his frightening experience as a gift: Paul returned with a burning passion to love others. Indeed, Paul's frightening experience may have saved him from a path of sadness. Moreover, it may have saved others reading his story from the same.

The realm of sadness, as described by Paul, parallels some of the Christian notions of hell. Indeed, a type of "hell" may exist according to numerous NDE accounts. How does one reconcile the notion of an unconditionally-loving God with the existence of hell? The conflict may partly be resolved by examining the details. Whether NDErs visit or see hell from a distance, they consistently deny that hell is a place of punishment. Rather, hell serves as an alternative realm separate from God. Although this distinction may seem minor, it is profound. According to NDE accounts, people choose their own hell, either on earth or in the spiritual realm. Imagine a person completely disconnected from love, like the criminally-minded psychopath. I have interacted with a number of psychopathic inmates during my twenty-year career as a prison psychologist. I attest that psychopaths are incapable of compassion toward others. Rather, they relentlessly pursue personal gain through sadistic predation; they intentionally cause suffering with relish. Such people are categorically different from most imperfect human souls. They do not merely make mistakes out of spiritual immaturity, but rather embrace evil without remorse.

The psychopath cannot enter heaven. Just as they are predators on earth, they would exploit the divine order, eagerly undermining God's plan by thwarting good works. It would be like mixing oil and water. Instead, psychopaths are separated into a neutral realm with likeminded souls. They could create their own heaven, if they chose. But in a realm without rules, instead they create their own hell by preying upon one another. By outwardly expressing their hatred within, the psychopath's evil becomes manifest without restraint. Just because they are not allowed into heaven, God is not responsible for torturing these lost souls. Rather, lost souls are responsible for victimizing each other. For those interested in learning more about hell and what it represents, I encourage reading the Lost Souls chapter in my book, *Psychology and the Near-death Experience: Searching for God.*[8]

The existence of hell frightens many people. This is not the aim of my book. Instead, I have made a concerted effort to squash this fear, created by millennia of hell-related doctrine, by emphasizing God's automatic forgiveness. I still hold tightly to that premise. As stated, people choose their own hell by rejecting love. Fortunately, only a small percentage of people embrace a life path filled with darkness. As I observed working in prisons, even many criminals maintain some ability to love, however tenuous and immature. Let me address the human fear of hell in another way. Anyone who tries to tap into the power line of love will enter heaven. We are not judged by religious faith. Nor are we judged by the number of mistakes we make in life. Indeed, salvation is a matter of heart and soul. In other words, if we chose Light we will be in Light. If we chose darkness we will be in darkness. In a universe created by free will, God allows us to be who we want to be. Is there a final point of no return? Many Christians claim that the decision point to be saved ends when we die, be it at age 18 or 90. NDE observers counter that God's perfect mercy does not have an expiration date. Consequently, souls can leave hell anytime they want; no one keeps them in bondage. George Richie, from his classic book *Return from Tomorrow*, described the occupants of hell during a tour given by Jesus:

> No condemnation came from the Presence (Jesus) at my side, only a compassion for these unhappy creatures that was breaking His heart. Clearly it was not His will that any one of them should be in this place. Then – what was keeping them here? Why didn't each one just get up and leave? I could see no reason why the person being screamed at by the man with the contorted face didn't simply walk away...And suddenly I realized that there was a common denominator to all these scenes so far. It was the failure to see Jesus.[9]

Tragically, NDErs observe that lost souls often choose the darkness and ignore the Light. Wallowing in anger, they do not notice Jesus who is standing by to save them. Yet, there are exceptions. Some souls cry out for deliverance. Their calls are immediately answered through God's everlasting mercy. Specifically, God sends Jesus down to save souls from their own black creation. Let us review a couple of accounts, starting with Trevor:

> I saw our driver who was a private being dragged away by the dark figures. I called on Jesus Christ to save me. A hole opened in the red skies and through the hole was a blue sky...I felt as though I was sent to hell or purgatory and because of my faith in Jesus Christ I was spared.

I was in a place no one in the whole creation of life knew where I was at and because I uttered His Name Jesus Christ I was immediately transported back to my body. Because of the paranormal stuff has led me into a spiritual battle and stronger faith in God. (Trevor, NDERF #2479)

One of the better-known accounts of hell was documented by Howard Storm. Tormented and torn apart by lost souls, Howard Storm cried out to Jesus to be saved. Jesus promptly arrived and lifted Mr. Storm into deliverance. He wrote:

Tangible hands and arms gently embraced me and lifted me up. I slowly rose up into the presence of the light and the torn pieces of my body miraculously healed before my eyes. All my wounds vanished and I became whole and well in the light. More important, the despair and pain were replaced by love. I had been lost and now was found; I had been dead and now was alive.[7]

In both accounts, Jesus offered salvation through deliverance from predatory, lost souls. Once he had saved them, Jesus protected each individual from further attack. On a related note, there are also a few NDE accounts centering on Jesus' protecting NDErs from demonic forces. For example, Jedraine shared:

I was very critical of religion and God, these things were convincing me otherwise. And I immediately began saying "Jesus loves me!!! The power of God will kill you all, Jesus save me!!" and the beings started to yell and so I continued... the demons continued to yell and curse at me but at the same time they were slowly retracting from me and their presence was minimizing. (Jedraine C., NDERF #912)

Educated in science, I used to think demonic accounts were superstitious. Even during my evangelical church training, I dismissed reports of demonic possessions and spiritual warfare. After reading other NDE accounts, like Jedraine's submission, I have reconsidered my position. Still, I do not fear demons. I know that Jesus, working as earth's custodian, will always protect me from dark unseen forces. Only those people who embrace darkness place themselves at risk.

NDE accounts of hell are uncommon, especially accounts of rescue. Reading thousands of NDERF submissions, I have stumbled across only a handful of times people have been saved from hell. Despite the relatively small sample size, tormented souls were saved by Jesus in all the accounts I reviewed. I am not surprised that the ascended Christ appears to play a significant role given His responsibility as custodian of earth. Did not the Bible depict Jesus bringing lost sheep back into the fold? As Jesus said in the book of Matthew:

> If a shepherd has one hundred sheep, and one wanders away and is lost, what will he do? Won't he leave the ninety-nine others and go into the hills to search for the last one? (Matthew 18:12)

Deliverance from hell, whether on earth or in the spiritual realm, exemplifies the highest love: unconditional caring, inherent respect, and automatic forgiveness. Unfortunately, there will always be people who need sinners to be punished. God doesn't see salvation that way. Indeed, Jesus remains the Good Shepherd in this life and the next. He protects every person, the lost and found alike, through continuous operations of mercy. How should we respond to such valuable gifting? Jesus requires nothing in return, yet gladly accepts our openness and gratitude.

I know that, with Jesus in my corner, goodness will germinate from my efforts to sow seed. With Jesus as my model, I know that I will incorporate Christ-like values into my beliefs and actions. I also have little doubt that others who become transformed by the fire of Jesus will have the same response. Although we are not the primary custodian of earth, like Christ, we all can assume the role of custodian with friends, family, and other people we meet. In other words, we help other people by emulating Christ's compassion and mercy. Although these attributes are transforming, there is another attribute that followers of Jesus can emulate: sacrifice. Jesus was willing to sacrifice everything out of his love for us as exemplified by His death on the cross. In the next section, we will tackle the most elaborate aspect of salvation. Specifically, we will examine Jesus' sacrifice of death so that we may live.

Salvation and the Passion

Most Christians voice that there is power in the blood of Christ. Indeed, the crucifixion of Jesus remains the cornerstone of the Christian faith; the blood sacrifice of Jesus ensures salvation for anyone who believes.

Jesus' sacrifice, known as "The Passion," has also been emphasized in a number of NDE accounts. Paul, during his experience, wrote about his transforming experience with Jesus:

> I was standing in a room with a coffin in front of me. A man was standing next to me. I didn't look at him, but was aware of his presence. I asked him why I was there. He said to me it is my coffin and I should get into it. I said that I am not ready to die, because of all the things I did in the past that was sinful and wrong (my divorce included). He (I then realize it was Jesus) spoke to me and said that He paid for my sins 2000 years ago, that I must not be afraid. I will not die, but I must focus on Him and He will bring me in contact with people and opportunities where He will use me. (Paul S., NDERF #647)

The ascended Christ revealed that He died for Paul's sin two thousand years ago. Christ's message to Paul echoed his living words from earth, "I am the gate; whoever enters through me will be saved." (John 10:9) Note that Paul reported living a life of sin prior to this NDE. Yet, Jesus provided comfort by telling him not to be afraid. Was Paul already saved by Jesus? Had he always been saved? If perfect love is unconditional, then it stands to reason we all have been saved by default. Similarly, we should also be saved if our identities are expressions of God's eternal essence. After all, why would God condemn parts of the God-Self. For these reasons, Paul had been saved as an eternal heir of the Kingdom from the beginning of time. As recorded in the Gospel of Phillip, Jesus likewise taught, "Blessed are those who are before existing; for those who are were, and will be." (Verse 57)[10] In this ancient text, Jesus invites us to evaluate life from a perspective of eternal soul rather than as a human mortal. Before we were individuals, we were of God. Someday we will reunite back with the Source as individuals coexisting in eternal unity. Every instance in between is a blessed moment.

People usually think of eternity going forward, but time flows endlessly in both directions. Unfortunately, the human brain cannot fathom forever. Perhaps it may be helpful, however, to try to peek beyond the material perspective. For instance, does God's eternal blessing suddenly plummet if we fail to say, "Jesus, I accept you in my heart" during this short life? Such a belief may appear too finite when considering all we have done, all that we will do, within the scope of trillions upon trillions of years. Jesus' words in the Gospel of Phillip continue:

A pearl thrown into the mud does not lose its value, and anointing it with oil will not increase its value. In the eyes of its owner, its value remains unchanged. So it is with the sons of God; wherever they are, they are just as precious to their Father. (Verse 48)[10]

Wherever we are, whatever we are doing, we remain precious as sons and daughters of the Father, like pearls of great price. Our value never changes, even when we are writhing around in our self-made messes on earth. Whether we are drug addicted and homeless or married and living on a yacht, our core value remains constant because we are just acting out different roles in the material realm. In true essence, we are really magnificent spiritual beings. Salvation is our birthright.

Salvation through Sacrifice

As we explored in chapter eight, people with different beliefs typically have positive near-death experiences; there are many paths up the mountain of God. Even those creating their own hell have continuous opportunity to be saved. Given the consistent reports of universal salvation in NDE accounts, the pertinent question becomes, "Whom did Jesus die for?" Rather than dying for a narrow set of believers, perhaps Jesus died for all humanity. If this is the case, then Jesus' sacrifice on the cross does not save us from hell, but represents a different mode of salvation. As previously quoted, Howard Storm asked Jesus whether he had been to any other worlds:

Jesus said that he had been to every world in every time and space. He said that he had brought the revelation of God to all intelligent beings. Some beings had been as stubborn as we were to accept him, and many more worlds had gladly accepted him.[7]

Apparently, the human species was given a choice to accept the message of Jesus or not. Jesus would have served humanity either way. If we had gladly embraced Christ, like many worlds, then the human species would have followed His example and lived more in accord with God's will. Consequently, our spiritual evolution would have been accelerated. Interestingly, Storm's revelation creates a bit of a conundrum for those accepting the fundamental Christian viewpoint of salvation. According to doctrine, all of humanity would have been condemned to hell if Christ had not been sacrificed on the cross. I can't fathom how a perfect loving God would allow that to happen.

Unfortunately, the human species chose a harder, more winding path out of stubbornness. By accepting the message of love partial and piecemeal, human spiritual advancement has slowed. Still, the crucifixion of Christ has one overriding benefit. Through the gruesome death of Jesus, God was able to model the greatest pillar of perfect love: sacrifice. The Passion not only modeled perfect sacrifice, but it demonstrated the immensity of God's love for humanity. God was willing to sacrifice himself as the Son, a being fully connected to God's will, in order to demonstrate perfect, unconditional love. Not only did Christ die once, but he would have done it repeatedly. Let's revisit what the ascended Christ shared with Julian of Norwich during her NDE. Jesus told her, "If I could suffer more, I should suffer more." Reflecting on these words, Julian of Norwich added this insight:

> And I contemplated with great diligence to know how often he should die if he would. And truly the number so far exceeded my understanding and intelligence that my reason had not leave or power to comprehend or accept it.[2]

Not only does Jesus' unfathomable sacrifice demonstrate God's perfect love, it serves as an idealized model in how we are to love one other. In other words, we are called to sacrifice for each other within the spirit of unity. We can deliver many from bondage by sacrificing through our giving, caretaking, teaching, and mentoring. Phillip Gulley understood the sacrificial model of Christ as follows:

> Jesus, rather than being the means of salvation through his sacrificial death, was instead the archetype of salvation, embodying this unity of purpose and divine receptivity, and in that power he lived as one transformed, even as he was transforming the lives of others.[1]

If Jesus serves as the archetype of salvation, then emulating Christ requires putting the needs of others before personal needs. Personal sacrifices will transform some people more than others. The radically transformed will learn to treat other people with more love. In other words, our little embers of love have the potential to ignite dry wood into a raging fire throughout the tapestry.

Salvation from Spiritual Death

Emulating the Jesus archetype seems quite daunting. After all, human beings lack the necessary spiritual maturity to follow completely in Christ's footsteps. However, the degree to which one can become Christ-like correlates with one's ability to connect with the Father and, by extension, with each other. It is our connection that remains the cornerstone of our spiritual growth and our impact on others. As discussed in chapter two, spiritual journeys are rooted in reconnecting with the overarching divine unity; our true identities cannot be separated from the One. Entering the Kingdom entails becoming concordant with the One through life experience and transformation. That experience is based on all attributes of love. In the Gospel of Phillip it was written:

> Christ comes again to heal this wound (of separation), to rediscover the lost unity, to enliven those who kill themselves in separation, and revives them in union. (Verse 78)[10]

The deep wounds of human disconnection can be catalogued by our countless atrocities throughout history. Some atrocities are small and repetitive; no one is completely immune from the corpse of the world. Even in times of peace and prosperity, most people embrace power and consumerism by seeking the glorification of "me." Killed by embracing the popular values of self, many stumble through this world like spiritual zombies. They cannot see the truth of unity. Their ego relentlessly hungers to consume without meaningful production. Focused on their own hunger pangs, they become oblivious to the needs of others. Jesus died on the cross to revive us from this kind of spiritual death: salvation comes to fruition for anyone who loves with unconditional regard, humility, giving, service, forgiveness and sacrifice. If the concept of unity seems abstract to you, then search for grounding by empathizing with others. Unity is part of the natural order, experienced authentically through operations in love. Think about how this may be applied to life. If we value everyone deeply as sons and daughters of God, we naturally won't treat anyone as better or inferior. Spiritual zombies can be saved by emulating Jesus and abandoning their divisive, ego-driven life orientation, to honor the sacrifice of the Son.

Jesus fully loves and honors everyone who rediscovers their lost unity. Likewise, Jesus fully loves and honors everyone who chooses to remain a spiritual zombie. Such unconditional love reflects the nature of God's unity. Not only does Jesus love and honor the lost, he feels acutely their pain of disconnection. But, take note, the tendrils of unity travel in all directions. For this reason, we feel the pain of disconnection through the Passion. Communing with Christ, Julian of Norwich witnessed the bidirectional consequences of unity between human beings and Jesus. She wrote:

> Here I saw a great unity between Christ and us, as I understand it; for when he was in pain we were in pain, and all creatures able to suffer pain suffered with him.[2]

Amazingly, Julian of Norwich requested that she suffer the Passion fully during her NDE. Her request was granted as a natural extension of unity. Because we are One with Christ, every person suffers what Christ suffered. People usually do not fully experience Christ's suffering on earth due to our human disconnection. Still, consider this important maxim when contemplating unity. What we do to others we do to ourselves. We become the victims of our own crimes just as we are recipients of our own operations in love. Many NDErs realize this maxim when they experience life reviews. Not only do they re-experience making life choices, but they also relive the consequences of their choices from the recipient's own experience. If they love someone, they feel every ounce of their joy. If they hurt someone, they feel every ounce of their pain. The point being that NDErs relive the lives of other people because, in essence, they are them; we are all expressions of the One. With this mind-bending concept of unity presented, let's delve deeper.

According to the Gospel of Phillip, Christ was born to heal our separation by reviving our true connection with God. Herein rests the reason why Jesus died for our sins: Jesus saved us from the separation of ignorance, through the knowledge of His suffering. By Jesus' death, God held up a mirror to our rooted fears. But remember the other side of the connection coin. While we can partially connect to the suffering of Jesus, God completely experiences the suffering of our disconnection. How does God respond to our violations? God can only respond with perfect compassion and mercy. With this in mind, humans need to reevaluate their religious doctrines of shame. The purpose behind the Passion is not to be saved from shameful punishment, but to allow us to *triumph* over our separation. Ultimately, our triumph will be our salvation. Julian of Norwich wrote:

His Passion was manifested again in this compassion, in which there were two different understandings of our Lord's intention. One was the bliss that we are brought to, in which he wants us to rejoice. The other is for consolation in our pain, for he wants us to know that it will all be turned to our honor and profit by the power of his Passion, and to know that we suffered in no way alone, but together with him, and to see him as our foundation.[2]

By reflecting on Christ's suffering, human beings have the opportunity to know the pain we caused, not just to Christ, but to ourselves. When such understanding becomes internalized, we will profit because our capacity for empathy will increase. Hopefully, over time, we will learn to stop hurting other people; we will become saved from our own barbarous nature. Will our descendants evolve into a higher state of being? Perhaps this will be a long time in coming. The human species will only really start moving in a positive direction when we collectively start emulating Christ. After uniting with Jesus during her NDE, Betty Eadie concluded, "Whether we learn of Jesus Christ here or while in the spirit, we must eventually accept him and surrender to his love."[5]

Julian of Norwich was not the only NDEr to experience Oneness with Christ's Passion. Vinnie had a similar, but reversed, NDE experience. He did not suffer as Christ, but as a perpetrator of His death:

I was sitting on a rock... The only way I can explain it is that it reminds of "memory foam." At this time I was approached by a "Man" that for some reason I believe was Jesus Christ the Messiah... He transferred me to a time during the crucifixion. I remember being in the crowd yelling for him to be crucified, I could smell the blood and I could smell death. I remember as he hung on the cross I remember stabbing him with my spear. But he was already dead. I didn't cry. I didn't regret my sins. I just remember stabbing him. I don't know if this was a vision he was showing me, but I remember telling him, "We killed you. You died. I saw you die." He looked at me and said, "Yes, but I arose on the third day, remember?" I said, "Yes, you did". (Vinnie G. #1094)

Note that Vinnie did not regret his "sins." Although he experienced the crucifixion from a position of unity, he did not feel ashamed. For Jesus arose on the third day; all that was not well was well. Sins are only learning experiences, not stagnating operations in shame. Like it or not, we all have to suffer through difficult growing pains together in our winding journey toward unity. Our salvation lies down this winding path back toward the Source.

In this chapter, we have explored several different mechanisms for salvation. We have studied how God saves people through daily operations in mercy. We have examined the revitalization of mission as a saving force. We have explored how the ascended Christ saves souls from evil. Finally, we have examined how salvation rests in our growth toward unity. Although many sides to the salvation crystal have been explored, love lies at the heart of the stone. Salvation ultimately boils down to developing a loving relationship with God. It begins by knowing God and opening ourselves to the Light of God. The bud of our openness flowers when we extend love to everyone and everything. Leo Tolstoy echoed the point of connection when he had been transformed by the Light. He wrote:

> And then finally, more than ever before, everything within me and around me lit up. "What more did I have to seek?" exclaimed a voice within me. "This is He. God is that without which you cannot live. To know God and to live is one and the same thing! God is life. Live seeking God, and then you will not live without God." This light that had dawned inside and around me never abandoned me. And I was saved.[3]

Like Leo Tolstoy, I know that God has never abandoned me. The Light only grows brighter as I am revived back into God's unity. I know that I am still just a babe paddling through deep spiritual waters. Sensing that I am basically headed toward shore, I slowly keep working on my ongoing salvation. I try to be ever thankful for God's help via the Son. By keeping my eyes on Jesus, I strive to live by his example on my personal journey of salvation. NDEr Sharon Milliman also strives to emulate Jesus in order to be saved. Having met Jesus in a near-death experience, she experienced God's unity, celebration, and mission transformation. In the final chapter, we will conclude our exploration of Jesus and the near-death experience by delving into Sharon's amazing encounters with Jesus.

CHAPTER TEN

THE JESUS ENCOUNTERS
OF SHARON MILLIMAN

I personally believe that human beings can be transformed through a personal relationship with Jesus. Indeed, I have devoted a large portion of this book to this topic. So far, I have taken an exploratory approach to meet this goal. In this final chapter, I hope to personalize the book's content by introducing a woman who reportedly met with the ascended Christ on numerous occasions.

I am honored to present the transcendent experiences of Sharon Milliman. Sharon actually had two near-death experiences, but only the second involved Jesus. She also conversed with Jesus on at least five separate occasions since her return to earth. Sharon recently published a book about all her experiences called, *A Song in the Wind: A Near-death Experience.*[3] I highly recommend reading her account for anyone interested in Jesus and the NDE. It is beyond the scope of this chapter to describe all of Sharon's experiences. The present chapter will focus instead on her interactions with Jesus as they relate to the topics presented in this book.

Encountering Jesus at Church

Sharon first met Jesus at the age of fifteen while growing up in West Virginia. It was a time of great turmoil. Sharon's adolescent innocence was shattered by predatory people intruding into her life. A deceased brother frequently visited Sharon in spirit during this troubled period. Although these visits were a happy diversion from a difficult life, Sharon began questioning her own sanity. Isolated and afraid, Sharon's self-confidence plummeted to the point of considering suicide. Sharon desperately needed sound intervention from a person she trusted. Unfortunately, there was no one she knew who could understand her unusual experiences.

It was a Good Friday afternoon when Sharon met Jesus in a church basement just before service. The visit started when a man started to walk toward Sharon. At first glance, the man could have been a day laborer, even a carpenter. Even from a distance, Sharon sensed that she was in the presence of holiness. Perhaps, she wondered, this man was a biblical prophet. But as the tall figure came closer in the light, Sharon recognized this person to be none other than Jesus, even if He was commonly dressed in a white button-down shirt, blue jeans, and boots. For Jesus' face appeared just like the image in the Shroud of Turin, as did his dark skin, tall, strong build, and long, wavy black hair. But this was not the only reason Sharon recognized this man to be more than a man. Specifically, Sharon instinctively recognized Jesus at a soul level. Moreover, she experienced an indescribable love that could only have come from God.

Jesus walked up to Sharon and four other women and smiled. He gazed at each of them with deep, welcoming, brown eyes. Sharon returned His smile with a stunned look; her mouth opened and her eyes rounded like quarters. She desperately wanted to ask Jesus questions, at least say something, but her mouth became too dry and swollen to speak. She was left, by divine design, to listen in quiet awe. The four other women standing next to Sharon also recognized Jesus by His extraordinary love. They were equally amazed by His presence. Then Jesus spoke to the women in a loving voice. He asked, "Where am I supposed to sit in this church?"

Jesus posed an interesting question relevant to His divine status and identity. Where would you sit Jesus at a church service centered on worshiping Jesus? Sharon and her friends seated Him in a front pew so that He might fully enjoy the celebration of Himself. Following their suggestion, Jesus later sat at the head of the congregation and listened intently to the service. Sharon watched Jesus throughout the hour, transfixed by radiant sunlight streaming down onto His body through a nearby stained-glass window. When the crucifixion-themed song, *Up to Jerusalem*, played, Jesus placed his head in his hands and wept. As for young Sharon, she sang loudly and enthusiastically until it hurt. But we are getting ahead of ourselves.

Before the service started, Jesus healed one of the four women from her painful arthritis while in the basement. He also had an important message for Sharon. At the exact same time He was asking the other women about seating, Jesus spoke directly to Sharon about the visits from her deceased brother. Jesus told her, "What is happening to you *is* happening. You are not crazy. I love you and I am not going to leave you. You are not going to be alone."

Jesus' intervention quickly moved Sharon's life in a positive direction. His validation provided her with the confidence to move forward. Instead of feeling crazy and alone, she now felt blessed and understood. Sharon felt blessed because she had a renewed, genuine relationship with Jesus based on love. He was not some sappy-sweet white-robed guy shepherding lambs, as depicted in the children's Bible. Nor was He the austere King of Kings sitting on a throne worshiped by a host of angels. On the contrary, Jesus presented as a humble man dressed in a white button-down shirt, blue jeans, and workman's boots. Sharon could relate to this "down to earth" guy, even if He didn't wear His Sunday best to church. She was especially touched by Jesus' weeping during the service. Because of His open display of humanity, Sharon and the other four women never felt the need to kneel and worship this humble man. Rather, they felt the need to usher Jesus into a good seat to participate in all the worshiping of Himself. I have been reflecting on this irony ever since hearing Sharon's story.

If Sharon did not see Jesus as a religious icon, then how did she view Him? She reports viewing Jesus as a loving big brother sent to guide her through the briar bushes of life. Her perception was entirely based on her familial relationship with Jesus, rather than on theology. Jesus was not just an amazing new acquaintance, but an elder brother Sharon had loved as a young child. She also knew, within her heart of hearts, that they were part of the same royal lineage dating back to the beginning of time. Although Jesus was much more mature and powerful than she, Sharon understood that their love was bonded and eternally unbreakable.

Sharon felt like a spiritual toddler compared with the adult, mature standing of Jesus. Yet, even their widest differences never weakened their loving bond. Jesus met Sharon as a loving adult might with a toddler playing on the carpet; He spoke to her with simplicity, patience and kindness. In fact, the presentation of the ascended Christ reminded Sharon of the Jesus who lived two thousand years ago; they were basically one and the same person. As a case in point, Jesus came to Sharon to serve rather than to be served. The ascended Christ did not descend in radiant glory. Rather, the ascended Christ came to validate Sharon, heal a woman from pain, and attend church wearing workingmen's boots.

Jesus disappeared after the church service. Sharon and the other women excitedly asked other attendees whether they also saw Jesus. No one saw Jesus except for them. Some of the congregation probably thought them a bit daft. But Sharon knew that she was not stupid or crazy. She felt blessed beyond measure. Indeed, she would need Jesus' blessings during troubled times to come.

Sharon's Near-death Experience

Sharon reported having two near-death experiences in her life. For the purposes of this chapter, I will focus on the second experience, which involved both God and Jesus. Sharon died on the steps of her house when a lightning bolt blew out a nearby transformer. When the transformer blew, a surge of energy traveled beneath her house and into her body. Sharon's soul seamlessly peeled upward into the air. Sharon immediately found herself floating below the ceiling inside her house. But was it really her house? Oddly, the living room was heavily saturated in a burnt-gold light. Other things seemed out of place, as well. For instance, Sharon noted that the furniture and curtains were not hers. She also heard a radio talk show broadcast from around the 1930s. The radio show should have been impossible in real time, she later reasoned, because the blown transformer had caused a neighborhood-wide blackout.

Sharon's new reality shifted further when she found herself floating in a sky filled with billowing pink and gold clouds. Although she did not see anyone, Sharon felt an amazing loving presence both inside and outside her being. Using a metaphor to describe the indescribable, it was as if every cell in her body was bathed in a love that had no earthly precedent. Sharon knew that she had died and was in the presence of the divine.

Sharon's location changed a third time when she found herself floating in a beautiful garden. The garden was unlike any other she had seen. The flowers were more colorful, the grass more lush, and the trees more grand than any garden on earth. Not only did all the colors pop in vibrant richness, everything hummed with a pervasive loving energy. In fact, all creation seemed to be vibrating in unison; frequencies were layered one upon another. All these frequencies combined to create beautiful music. To Sharon, the music was reminiscent of a symphony, except the classical chords were richer, grander, and more beautiful. It was as if all the symphonies in the world were exquisitely playing together in unison. A small stream also meandered to one side and a brilliant city towered in the distance. Sharon breathed deeply and felt the clean, crisp air come into her from a gentle breeze. Everything was lit as if it were a pleasant spring day. A bright, white, shining orb graced the sky. Although appearing somewhat like the sun on earth, Sharon knew that the orb was the conscious, ever-present Light of God.

Sharon experienced a full life review in which she was not judged. Following the review, Sharon heard a male voice say, "What you put out into the universe comes back to you." She understood that this was a message conveyed for all humanity. Clearly, she was not alone for long in the garden. Indeed, Sharon's two brothers appeared and stood before her smiling. Although they had died in infancy, they were now two attractive young adults. The brothers appeared as if they had never died on earth; they were glowing, tanned versions of their father. Sharon also noted that her brothers were wearing clothes weaved with beautiful ivory thread. Not a single thread was out of place. She sensed a larger meaning within the flawless interconnection of the weaves: she realized that perfection was possible only if the weave remains whole. This lesson of interconnection would be expanded upon from a new visitor. This visitor would soon be introduced by her old friend Jesus.

Jesus appeared to Sharon as He did in church years ago. Sharon felt excitement in being reunited with Him. Jesus gazed lovingly at Sharon and smiled. She noticed a twinkle in His deep brown eyes as well as the hint of laughter. Here was a man, she realized, who loved with humor. Sharon's heart melted at the love she felt from Him. Awestruck, she pondered, "That He died for me."

Jesus guided Sharon to the edge of the garden to a stream of living Spirit. Amazingly, countless diamonds sparkled in the water's depths.

In her mind, Sharon knew that each diamond represented the contributions of a single human life within the flow of time. Perhaps her life was represented by one of those diamonds. A kindly man sat next to a log by the river's bank. In some ways, the man seemed ordinary. He wore shoulder length hair, a neatly trimmed beard, and a happy smile. But it was within His amazing blue eyes that Sharon perceived infinity. She knew that she was in the presence of God. Note that Sharon understood that God was not really a human, but rather a conscious force present in all things. Apparently, God manifested as an unassuming man in order to provide familiarity and comfort for Sharon.

Sharon sat on the log beside the man. God asked Sharon, "What would you do if it was just Me and you?"

Sharon stared at the man, bewildered. "What do you mean?" she asked.

God patiently elaborated, "What if there were no parents, no children, no husband, and no friends; just me and you and no one else."

Sharon answered, "I would drive you crazy after a few minutes with all my questions and chatter—and then you probably would not like me very much."

God smiled and motioned for Sharon to follow Him to the edge of the forest. Suddenly the forest split apart and revealed the entire universe. Planets, stars, and galaxy clusters materialized in a vibrant smearing of colors, a cosmic rainbow without beginning or end. To Sharon, the beautiful rainbow represented all the realities and possibilities in the universe. When the showing was complete, God led Sharon back to the stream bank.

Sitting together back on the log, God instructed Sharon to examine a gigantic oak tree towering above them. Peering deeply into the majestic tree, Sharon saw detailed patterns of leaves, roots, and cells. Moreover, she perceived a life-giving force flow through every vein of the tree. The lesson became as clear to her as a perfect diamond lying in the stream. Sharon realized that every element of the tree was interconnected to the whole organism. In other words, every part, no matter how tiny, was necessary for the tree to be complete. From a broader perspective, she also realized how the tree was necessarily interconnected to the larger environment of the forest and beyond.

God's lesson took root in Sharon's soul. She understood that the smallest atom had its rightful place in an infinitely large universe. Every leaf and bird in the oak tree was praising the Creator in song. They were not only singing to God, but praising their own sweet existence. For everything in heaven was conscious, infused with God, and loved by God. God looked at Sharon and asked her again, "What would you do if it was just Me and you?"

Gifted with the insights from her lesson, Sharon referenced the 99 names of God in the Koran (she had no prior knowledge of the Koran). She replied, "God, your 100th name is 'God is everywhere, God is nowhere, and God is in me.'"

God said, "Yes, that is right. And..."

After some thought, Sharon said, "God, you made this tree. You are in this tree. So when I see this tree, I see you."

"Yes, and..."

When I look at my parents and my children, I see you."

"Yes, and..."

With mixed feelings, Sharon added, "When I see people hurting me, like my ex-husband, I also see you."

God said, "Yes, that is correct. And when you look in the mirror, what do you see?"

Sharon wanted to say, "No one special." But when she looked into God's beautiful blue eyes, Sharon only saw the deepest love for her. She answered, "God, you made me, you are in me, so when I look in the mirror, I see you."

"Yes, that is right," God said happily with a broad smile. Sharon could feel God's joy surround her; she was immersed in love.

God then led Sharon to a lakeside where she met two female angels. Within the lake, Sharon was shown future events, like 9/11, and subsequent terrorist violence. More distant events were also shown, including increased wars, political corruption, violence, floods, and economic collapse. Sharon was sent back to her body after the conclusion of these disturbing revelations.

God's lesson about unity applies to every person: we are sons and daughters of the One, just as Jesus is the Father and the Father is in Jesus. So let me ask a question of you, the reader. Whom do you see in the mirror? Do you see a wretched human being or do you see the face of God? Sharon saw the priceless divinity within. Perhaps we should learn from her NDE and do the same.

The Marriage Proposal

Sharon struggled through a difficult divorce and became a single mother. If that was not difficult enough, she was left to take care of her ailing mother who suffered from late stage Alzheimer's disease. Sharon was anxiously pacing around in her parents' backyard when Jesus appeared to her. Unlike his casual attire at church, Jesus was now formally dressed in a pure white suit. Moreover, His wavy, black hair had been neatly pulled back. With complete sincerity, Jesus asked, "Sharon, will you be my bride?"

Sharon stared at Jesus confused and stunned. Here was the Son of God, appearing handsome in the prime of His youth, proposing marriage! Sharon wondered if she was dreaming.

"I can't marry you!" Sharon answered. "And why would you want to marry me, anyway?"

"I want you as my bride."

"I can't be your bride. I have to stay here and take care of my mom and dad."

"I love you and I can wait for you," Jesus replied.

"How can you wait?"

Jesus answered, "My Kingdom is not of this world."

Sharon remained steadfast and Jesus left without pressing the point further. With later reflection, Sharon began to wonder what the marriage proposal meant. She recognized that Jesus was not proposing marriage in a human sense. After all, Jesus was not living in the world and had no need for a bride. The proposal was a metaphor; it symbolized a deep spiritual commitment between her and Jesus.

Jesus did not propose marriage to be flippant. On the contrary, Jesus conveyed the highest love for Sharon. The concept of an ideal marriage roughly approximates divine love in a way that humans can understand. After all, in what other vows of devotion do we say, "I will be faithful to you until death do we part." Likewise, in what other vows of sacrifice do we say, "I will cherish you in sickness and in health." When Jesus proposed marriage to Sharon, He was giving His bonded oath of love sealed throughout time; their love would never lose luster. Based on the Bible and other gospel texts, Jesus proposes the same oath for anyone living in the Spirit. At the end of the book of Revelation, scripture reads: "The Spirit and the bride say, 'Come! Whoever is thirsty, let him come; and whoever wishes, let him take the free gift of the water of life.'" (Revelation 22:17) Similarly, in the Gospel of Phillip, the writer explains, "The soul and the spirit are born of water and of fire. It is with water, fire, and light that the son of the bridal chamber comes into being." (Verse 66)[1] Unfortunately, not everyone chooses to enter the bridal chamber. Some reject Jesus' love with an attitude of scoffing arrogance. In the Gospel of

Thomas, Jesus says, "Many are standing by the door, but only those who are alone and simple can enter the bridal chamber." (Verse 75)[2] Indeed, Sharon was simple in her faith and alone in her suffering. Thus, she was a fitting bride for Jesus. Sharon was also a fitting bride because she understood the concept of unity from her near-death experience.

Sharon saw God when she looked into the mirror. In order to embrace union with Jesus during this difficult time, Sharon needed to quiet her rampant thoughts, let go of earthly stresses, trust in a loving God, and embrace the Real. The writer of the Gospel of Phillip described divine embracement in this manner: "What is the bridal chamber if not the place of trust and consciousness in the embrace? It is a representation of Union beyond all forms of possession." (Verse 76)[1] Sharon was not ready to make such a huge leap in union; she was too wrapped up in the daily turmoil of her world. But Jesus understood her perfectly. Thus, He gave Sharon a promise as a ray of hope for her future: Jesus promised to marry Sharon when she returned to His Kingdom.

Jesus' proposal for marriage, as gleaned from our quoted gospel passages, carries great theological complexity. It's easy to become lost in the complexity, however, and lose the main point. At the heart of the matter, the marriage proposal represents how intimately Jesus loves us all. Jesus does not want a relationship built on academic curiosity, dogma, or worship. Rather, Jesus wants to build a relationship based on spiritual unity. In time, Sharon understood just what Jesus really wanted. In fact, Sharon wore two wedding rings when she remarried: one for her husband and one for Jesus. Sharon wonderfully captured Jesus' message of spiritual intimacy while walking through a vibrant green meadow filled with flowering Queen Anne's lace. Words began to flood her consciousness as light seemed to shine down on her like a spotlight. The words actually created a poem of love, or ode, to Jesus. Sharon called this ode *Meadows of Emerald and Lace*. It reads as follows:

As she walks through meadows of emerald and lace
The sun shines upon her radiant face
Her eyes are crystal blue
The color of the sky and her skin so soft and fair
As a soft warm breeze blows golden strands of her hair
She is clothed in purest white as she waits for her groom
The King of Kings will arrive and bring her home very soon
She walks through meadows of emerald and lace
Full of God's love and showered by His grace

Now the skies open wide and her bridegroom appears
The love that she feels brings her to tears
He descends from His throne gathering her gently in His arms
He says, "Well done my beloved, now it is time to come home"
He places a crown of gold upon her head and leads her to her eternal joy
He gently holds her hand as she climbs every stair
For she knows not what waits for her there
For eyes have not seen nor ears have heard the glories of the Lord

~ SHARON MILLIMAN, 2015

The Conversation in the Kitchen

Sharon continued to care for her ailing mother out of a deep love and commitment. Such sacrifice, often meagerly celebrated on earth, has monumental importance to God. Few commitments express a greater personal sacrifice than caring for someone slowly deteriorating from Alzheimer's disease. Yet, Sharon decided to sacrifice for her mother until the conclusion of the disease. Just because she sacrificed everything in love, the grinding work didn't always feel natural or easy. It took an incredible degree of courage to face every morning. Sharon, being human, sometimes doubted that she had enough strength to endure such difficult responsibilities. After all, there was little she could do to improve her mother's slow, steady, mental deterioration. Thus, she felt utterly helpless, watching her mother change for the worse. Sharon wondered if Jesus had abandoned her to a life of alienation and pain. In other words, she wondered why she was sent back from heaven, her loving home, only to be punished and suffer on earth.

Feeling tired and lost, Sharon heard a voice while cleaning her kitchen. It was a familiar, calming voice that made her "heart sing and her soul soar." She turned and saw Jesus leaning against the kitchen counter with His arms and feet crossed. When Jesus spoke, He referred back to Sharon's experience of Him in heaven:

Oh my precious Dove, you cry because you think I cast you away when you were with me. That is so far from the truth. I hold you so dear. It simply wasn't your time. I have a job for you to do.

Jesus wanted Sharon to understand that she was not suffering for the sake of suffering. Nor was she cast out from heaven to be punished. Rather, Jesus conveyed to Sharon that she had an important job, or mission, to complete on earth. Although missions were created out of love and for love, operations in love really represent hard, slogging work. Yet, Jesus saw a higher purpose for Sharon despite the difficulties she endured. Jesus continued his conversation in the kitchen:

> Sharon, you are here because your life has meaning. You have to step aside and take the "you" out of the equation and let me that do the work. You are doing just fine in what you are doing because you do it out of love. So, don't be so hard on yourself. I will handle it. I am capable. You just be. Just be present and at peace. And keep on loving others the way you always do. All that has happened in your life has prepared you for this moment, to make you strong enough for this very important job I have asked you to do for me. Remember, I am always with you to give you strength... Just love. It's that simple. That is the purpose of life, my beautiful Dove.

Jesus encouraged Sharon to let Him take care of her mother. His statement may seem baffling from a "down in the trenches" point of view because Sharon still tended to her mother's many needs. To help clarify this confusion, it is important to differentiate physical work and spiritual work. The latter includes tackling stress, chaotic emotions, lost perspective, and hopelessness. In order for Sharon to succeed in her difficult work, she needed to take herself out of the equation and allow Jesus to do all the worrying. Unfortunately, Sharon had difficulty letting go of her fear. It required her to let go of temporary attachments, to be passerby, and relate to the world much like an infant. To requote the Gospel of Thomas, when the disciples asked Jesus when He would appear, Jesus answered:

> On the day when you are naked as newborn infants who trample their clothing, then you will see the Son of the Living One and you will have no more fear. (Verse 37)[2]

Newborn infants deal with reality in the moment. They don't create earthly empires to grow and protect. Conversely, many adults want to manage events beyond their control; to become their own god. Not to misunderstand this point, pursuing mission-related goals can be a noble endeavor. Yet, there comes a point when we need to let the universe unfold as designed. Living fearlessly requires living in the here and now; to just be. As a psychologist, I know that obsessive worrying rarely helps anyone. Quite the contrary, anxiety and fear only paralyze our life's work. Because Sharon was paralyzed by fear while living in a deteriorating situation, she felt like a failure. She was not a failure, for there was nothing she could have done for her mother except to care for her in love. In the end, that was the whole point.

Meeting Jesus by the Flowers

Everything in life has a season. There is time for birth and a time for death. There is a time for joy and time for sorrow. There are valuable lessons to be learned no matter the season. Jesus appeared to Sharon during a low point in her sorrow. It was a time of rejection, betrayal, and loneliness. Indeed, Sharon was soured by a world that seemed harsh and cruel. Feeling ineffective in an unsympathetic world, she began to lose sight of the lessons she learned during her NDE. Consequently, Sharon began to doubt herself.

Jesus was standing in her backyard flower garden holding a perfect pink rose, her favorite color. He held the rose for Sharon as He spoke these words of both learning and comfort:

> This life is a journey that all must take. Please don't question yourself so much. These messages you are being given are true and valid. You have the answers, and you do know the truth. The answers have always been inside your heart. Stand at your gate and take the rose, my precious Dove. It is time for you to fly. Today is a new and wondrous beginning. You were like a caterpillar all wrapped up tight inside a cocoon but you are now emerging out as a beautiful butterfly. I love you and will always love you. You will never walk alone. I walk right there beside you. So hold your head up high and always spread your joy and love.

Jesus reframed Sharon's sorrow as an opportunity for hope. First, Jesus normalized her pain as part of a journey that we all must take. Since Sharon was born a fallible human being, she could expect to make mistakes and, in some cases, invite catastrophe. Fortunately, falling into a dell was not an unforgivable sin; mistakes are just lessons needed to motivate growth. Sharon was not seeing the "big picture" and thereby became paralyzed in fear and self-doubt. Jesus appeared to Sharon because He did not want her to waste her precious mistakes by becoming mired in shame. So, He handed Sharon a pink rose, an age-old symbol that represents gentleness and admiration, to offer her renewal through grace. Let's revisit the idea of renewal by Christ as discussed in chapter five. Jesus ignited a fire under Sharon to burn dead wood into ash. Seeds sprouted from the ash and now would be roused by the Light and fed by the nutrients of Spirit. Part of the burning required Sharon to discover the truth within, the primal knowledge infused in her soul. Specifically, she needed to see the divine in the mirror. Only then would she be primed to emerge as a new being of beauty, transformed much like a butterfly.

Letting go cannot fully be accomplished on earth. The human ego always gets in the way. Thus, Sharon would no doubt experience more periods of doubt and suffer as a fallible human being. But such lapses would be moderated by walking with Jesus. Sharon explained, "When I struggle, I ask Jesus to be like Him. Jesus responds by giving me a breeze, or a sunrise, or a bird's nest. I don't have to ask for what I need because He already knows. He helps me every single time!" Indeed, Jesus promised Sharon ongoing help while leaning against the kitchen countertop. He continued:

> Listen, quiet your heart, and be at peace for I am always with you. If you don't hear me talking, it's because you are not listening. You have the courage and the strength to do all that your heart desires and all that my Father has called you to do. It has been shouted from the highest mountains and heard in the lowest valleys. Its whisper has been heard throughout all human experience. So you must trust that it is true. Trust and believe with all your being that love is the answer. It is agape love; pure unconditional love that is the answer.

Jesus was quite clear that He would always guide Sharon. I believe that Jesus communicates with all of us in different ways. Unfortunately, we become deaf to His words when we do not listen. Just because Jesus does not always speak to us in a garden doesn't mean that He is not guiding our lives with a gentle nudge. We need only to seek opportunities to act like Christ and listen to His Spirit: to sacrifice for those in need, hear the loving whispers in our mind, search for inner knowledge, respond to calls of service, forgive those that hurt us, take heed to spiritual dreams, search for life's synchronicities, pray for the gifts of the Spirit, read His words. In sum, if we embrace the agape we will be listening to Jesus. In turn, Jesus will always respond to every need by knowing our every thought, need, and prayer. He will never abandon anyone because every mission is vitally important. Examine Sharon's life, for instance. Even though she lacks earthly fame, her life journey is shouted from the highest mountains and heard in the lowest valleys. The same applies to anyone who seeks divine love. Jesus is part of everyone's love journey as an expression of God's creation. If we listen to Jesus, then we will recognize our own magnificence, lose our fear, and replace our angst with repose. In regard to repose, Jesus directed Sharon to:

> Open your heart and don't be afraid. Just cast all your fears aside and accept your new life; just be at peace.

This short message sums up Jesus' purpose for visiting Sharon in her garden. He wanted her to become renewed, discover her true identity, and find repose. Still, Jesus wasn't quite finished. He ended His lesson in the kitchen by imparting some amazing information. Jesus added:

> Remember this: I am in you and all around you. Turn wood and you will find me. Lift a stone, I am there. Like the sun warms your skin, I will touch you. As the rain washes you, I will also. Without you, I am nothing. With you, I am eternity.

I was amazed reading this section of Sharon's account. The first part of her transcription echoed what Jesus taught His disciples in antiquity. In the Gospel of Thomas, Jesus said:

> I am the Light that shines on everyone. I am the All. The all came forth from me and the All came into me. Split the wood, I am there. Turn over the stone, and there you will find me. (Verse 77)[2]

I was also amazed by the last two points of Jesus' message, not because they echoed gospel texts, but because they communicated something new. Let's examine the statements, "Without you I am nothing. With you I am eternity." Jesus boldly speaks to the nature of God. Perhaps this revelation should give us pause. How can God, the Alpha and Omega, be nothing without other living beings? A partial answer may require us to consider God's perspective, even at the risk of presumptuous thinking. Imagine if you were alone in the universe. What would be the meaning of your existence if you were undefined by space and time as the All? There would be no surprises, no challenges, and no sharing. Perhaps God does not wish to experience Godself alone. Perhaps God shattered the Source consciousness, like dropping a pane of glass on pavement, to share experiences with evolving, self-creating beings. If my theory is correct, then we give God, and ourselves, co-creative purpose in seeking love. By existing in unity with God, we give purpose to the infinite universe.

A Rainbow in the Dark

Sharon witnessed an amazing rainbow shining brightly against the dark night sky. Clearly, she witnessed a supernatural event. Perhaps she even saw Jesus again in a new form. In any case, Sharon remembered God's grand revelation of the universe stretching out as a rainbow during her NDE. In similar measure, Sharon's rainbow reminded me of my own vision of Jesus, as described in chapter one. In all three instances, God's rainbow represents all realities and possibilities. Herein rests our hope for an ever-expansive, eternal future.

No loving experience extends beyond the full rainbow of Jesus. As a rainbow in the dark, Jesus shines as a beacon for those who have lost love: the rainbow reveals infinite possibilities for the hopeless. Such a representation of salvation was reinforced by a brief image I saw while lying in bed: my mind captured a rainbow diagonally dividing darkness from light. Blue sky and clouds colored the upper left corner whereas a void blackened the lower right. I knew that the rainbow served as a bridge from one existence to another. In other words, Jesus serves as the portal for the lost to enter the Light. Of even greater wonder is the idea that I emulate Jesus whenever I share in His rainbow.

I hope to be an ember produced by the fire tended by Jesus. In whatever small measure it serves, it is my sincere hope that this book represents some aspects of the rainbow. I did not want simply to rehash the known spectrum, but rather reimagine Jesus so that people can live more connected to God. I believe that humanity desperately needs to reimagine spirituality at this historical juncture. The world still smells like a corpse to me; we have generally failed to emulate Jesus' example to love for the last two thousand years. Although the message of Jesus has been accepted by a large segment of the world, the world rejects

Him in practice. Unfortunately, too many people have reduced Jesus to a plastic action figure defined by rote doctrine; He exists as the ultimate, inflexible abstraction. More people need to be like Sharon in seeking a personal relationship with Jesus through openness, humility, and intimacy. More people also need to be like Sharon by emulating Jesus through acts of unconditional regard, sacrifice, and service. Most of all, more people need to discover the divine within and without. Once we set uncompromising value in the All, perhaps humanity will stop destroying other expressions of God. After all, what we do to others we do to ourselves. Such a worldwide shift requires that more people love God, love other people, love animals, love the earth, and love the person reflected in the mirror.

I hope that this book has inspired you, the reader, to live as God meant you to live on earth. God sent Jesus to show us the way, not only two thousand years ago, but today in this very moment. As an expression of God, as an heir to the Kingdom, I wish you all the success possible in your mission to learn love. Know that you will learn love best by discovering your sacred place within the All.

REFERENCES

PROLOGUE

1. Gallup, G., & Proctor, W. (1982). *Adventures in immortality*. New York: McGraw-Hill Companies, (pp. 198-200).

2. Near-Death Experience Research Foundation. (1998). NDERF home page. Retrieved October 29, 2016, from http://www.nderf.org

3. Long, J. (2002). Another Look at Beings Encountered During the Near Death Experience. Retrieved October 29, 2016, from NDERF, http://www.nderf.org/NDERF/Research/beingsstudy.htm

4. Julian of Norwich (1978). *Julian of Norwich: Showings* (Classics of Western Spirituality ed.). Mahwah, NJ: Paulist Press, (pp. 20, 18, 22, 180).

5. United Nations Educational, Creative, Scientific and Cultural Organization. (2012). Norwich. Retrieved October 29, 2016, from Creative Cities Network, http://en.unesco.org/creative-cities/norwich

6. Carmody, D. L., & Carmody, J. (1983). *Western ways to the center: An introduction to western religions*. United States: Wadsworth Publishing Company.

7. Meyer, M. W., & Pagels, E. (2007). *The Nag Hammadi scriptures: The revised and updated translation of sacred Gnostic texts*. New York: HarperCollins Publishers (pp. 7, 2, 7).

8. Ehrman, B., (2003). *Lost scriptures: Books that did not make it into the new testament*. New York: Oxford University Press.

9. Leloup, J.-Y., (1986). *The gospel of Thomas: The gnostic wisdom of Jesus.* Rochester, VT: Inner Traditions Bear and Company, (pp. 1, vii, 1, 2, 9).

10. Meyer, M. W., & Pagels, E. (2007). *The Nag Hammadi scriptures: The revised and updated translation of sacred Gnostic texts.* New York: HarperCollins Publishers (pp. 158, 157).

11. Leloup, J.-Y., English, J. R., & Needleman, J. (2004). *The gospel of Philip: Jesus, Mary Magdalene, and the gnosis of sacred union.* Rochester, VT: Inner Traditions Bear and Company (p. 5).

12. Venifica, A. (2005). Symbol meaning of feathers. Retrieved October 29, 2016, from Whats-Your-Sign.Com, http://www.whats-your-sign.com/symbol-meaning-of-feathers.html

CHAPTER ONE

1. Pelikan, J. (1999). *Jesus through the centuries: His place in the history of culture.* New Haven, CT: Yale University Press.

2. Kowalska, St. M.F. (2013). *Diary: Divine mercy in my soul.* Stockbridge, MA: Marian Press, 3rd Edition.

CHAPTER TWO

1. Long, J. (2010). *Evidence of the afterlife: The science of near-death experiences.* New York: Harper Collins.

2. Holmes, S. R. (2012). *The quest for the Trinity: The doctrine of god in scripture, history, and modernity.* United States: Inter-Varsity Press, US.

3. Carter, C., (2010). *Science and the near-death experience: How consciousness survives death.* Rochester, NY: Inner Traditions Bear and Company, (p. 45).

4. Julian of Norwich (1978). *Julian of Norwich: Showings* (Classics of Western Spirituality ed.). Mahwah, NJ: Paulist Press, (pp. 190, 284, 342, 233).

5. Leloup, J.Y., (1986). *The gospel of Thomas: The gnostic wisdom of Jesus.* Rochester, VT: Inner Traditions Bear and Company, (pp. 177, 143, 156, 210).

6. Leloup, J.-Y., English, J. R., & Needleman, J. (2004). *The gospel of Philip: Jesus, Mary Magdalene, and the gnosis of sacred union.* Rochester, VT: Inner Traditions Bear and Company (p. 15).

7. Eadie, B. J. (1992). *Embraced by the light.* Placerville, CA: Gold Leaf Press (MI), (p. 41).

**Individual NDE Accounts:

Near-Death Experience Research Foundation. (2016, January 7). Current NDERF near-death experiences. Retrieved October 29, 2016, from NDERF, http://www.nderf.org/NDERF/NDE_Archives/NDERF_NDEs.htm

CHAPTER THREE

1. Leloup, J.-Y., English, J. R., & Needleman, J. (2004). *The gospel of Philip: Jesus, Mary Magdalene, and the gnosis of sacred union.* Rochester, VT: Inner Traditions Bear and Company (p. 83, 12, 59, 103).

2. Storm, H. (2005). *My descent into death: A second chance at life.* New York: The Doubleday Religious Publishing Group, (pp. 75, 76).

3. Leloup, J.-Y., (1986). *The gospel of Thomas: The gnostic wisdom of Jesus.* Rochester, VT: Inner Traditions Bear and Company, (pp. v, 83, 22).

4. Blenkinsopp, J. (1996). *A history of prophecy in Israel.* Louisville, KY: Westminster/John Knox Press, U.S.

5. Casey, S. K. (2015). *Clouds of heaven, beings of light.* United Kingdom: Circle Books.

6. Julian of Norwich (1978). *Julian of Norwich: Showings* (Classics of Western Spirituality ed.). Mahwah, NJ: Paulist Press, (pp. 296, 298, 301, 294, 299, 298, 217).

7. Eadie, B. J. (1992). *Embraced by the light.* Placerville, CA: Gold Leaf Press (MI), (p. 42).

**Individual NDE Accounts:

Near-Death Experience Research Foundation. (2016, January 7). Current NDERF near-death experiences. Retrieved October 29, 2016, from NDERF, http://www.nderf.org/NDERF/NDE_Archives/NDERF_NDEs.htm

CHAPTER FOUR

1. Turner, A. K. (1995). *The history of hell.* San Diego: Houghton Mifflin Harcourt, (pp. 132, 127, 128, 132).

2. Hill, M. & Wallace, S. H. (1999). *Basic catechism: creed, sacraments, morality, prayer.* Boston, MA: Pauline Books & Media, (pp. 116, 70, 65).

3. Kowalska, St. M.F. (2013). *Diary: Divine mercy in my soul.* Stockbridge, MA: Marian Press, 3rd Edition (p. 19).

4. Luther, M. (1961). *Martin Luther: Selections from his writings*. New York: Anchor/Doubleday & Company, (pp. 492-494).

5. Luther, M. (1961). *Martin Luther: Selections from his writings*. New York: Anchor/Doubleday & Company, (pp. 501-502).

6. Beck, A., Rush, J., Shaw, B., & Emery, G., (1979). *Cognitive therapy of depression*. New York: Guilford Press.

7. Julian of Norwich (1978). *Julian of Norwich: Showings* (Classics of Western Spirituality ed.). Mahwah, NJ: Paulist Press, (pp. 266, 267-268, 284, 259, 342).

**Individual NDE Accounts:

Near-Death Experience Research Foundation. (2016, January 7). Current NDERF near-death experiences. Retrieved October 29, 2016, from NDERF, http://www.nderf.org/NDERF/NDE_Archives/NDERF_NDEs.htm

CHAPTER FIVE

1. Hylton, J. Macbeth: Entire play. Retrieved October 29, 2016, from The Complete Works of William Shakespeare, http://shakespeare.mit.edu/macbeth/full.html

2. Leloup, J.-Y., (1986). *The gospel of Thomas: The gnostic wisdom of Jesus*. Rochester, VT: Inner Traditions Bear and Company, (pp. 124, 81, 82, 67, 182, 189, 220).

3. Julian of Norwich (1978). *Julian of Norwich: Showings* (Classics of Western Spirituality ed.). Mahwah, NJ: Paulist Press, (p. 225).

4. Leloup, J.-Y., English, J. R., & Needleman, J. (2004). *The gospel of Philip: Jesus, Mary Magdalene, and the gnosis of sacred union*. Rochester, VT: Inner Traditions Bear and Company (p. 39).

5. Maslow, A. H. (2014). *Toward a psychology of being*. Floyd, VA: Sublime Books, (p. 30).

6. Hill, R. L. (2015). *Psychology and the near-death experience: Searching for God*. United States: White Crow Books.

**Individual NDE Accounts:

Near-Death Experience Research Foundation. (2016, January 7). Current NDERF near-death experiences. Retrieved October 29, 2016, from NDERF, http://www.nderf.org/NDERF/NDE_Archives/NDERF_NDEs.htm

CHAPTER SIX

1. Hill, R. L. (2015). *Psychology and the near-death experience: Searching for God.* United States: White Crow Books.

2. Wothingham, E. L. (2001). *Forgiving and reconciling: Bridges to wholeness and hope.* Madison, WI: InterVarsity Press.

3. Miller, W. R., Rollnick, S., & Conforti, K. (2002). *Motivational interviewing, Second edition: Preparing people for change* (2nd ed.). New York: Guilford Publications.

4. Croft, B. (2016). Ruwach - old testament Hebrew lexicon - new American standard. Retrieved October 29, 2016, from Bible Study Tools, http://www.biblestudytools.com/lexicons/hebrew/nas/ruwach-2.html

5. Leloup, J.-Y., English, J. R., & Needleman, J. (2004). *The gospel of Philip: Jesus, Mary Magdalene, and the gnosis of sacred union.* Rochester, VT: Inner Traditions Bear and Company (pp. 65, 43, 105, 71, 77, 77, 161).

6. Leloup, J.-Y., (1986). *The gospel of Thomas: The gnostic wisdom of Jesus.* Rochester, VT: Inner Traditions Bear and Company, (pp. 110, 143, 129).

7. Julian of Norwich (1978). *Julian of Norwich: Showings* (Classics of Western Spirituality ed.). Mahwah, NJ: Paulist Press, (p. 251).

8. Moorjani, A. (2012). *Dying to be me: My Journey from cancer, to near death, to true healing.* United States: Hay House, (p. 123).

**Individual NDE Accounts:

Near-Death Experience Research Foundation. (2016, January 7). Current NDERF near-death experiences. Retrieved October 29, 2016, from NDERF, http://www.nderf.org/NDERF/NDE_Archives/NDERF_NDEs.htm

CHAPTER SEVEN

1. Leloup, J.-Y., (1986). *The gospel of Thomas: the gnostic wisdom of Jesus.* Rochester, VT: Inner Traditions Bear and Company, (pp. 129, 151, 172, 215, 78).

2. Putnam, R. (2000). *Bowling alone: The collapse and revival of American community.* New York: Simon and Schuster Paperbacks, (p. 222).

3. Statistica, Inc. (2014). Average use of Americans in 2010 | survey. Retrieved October 30, 2015, from The Statistics Portal, http://statista.com/statistics/191552/average-daily-internet-use–of–us–americans-in-2010-by-age-group

4. Leloup, J.-Y., English, J. R., & Needleman, J. (2004). *The gospel of Philip: Jesus, Mary Magdalene, and the gnosis of sacred union.* Rochester, VT: Inner Traditions Bear and Company (pp. 161, 143, 115, 91, 93 123, 75, 173).

5. Eadie, B. J. (1992). *Embraced by the light.* Placerville, CA: Gold Leaf Press (MI), (pp. 56-57).

6. Julian of Norwich (1978). *Julian of Norwich: Showings* (Classics of Western Spirituality ed.). Mahwah, NJ: Paulist Press, (p. 231).

7. Borjigin, J. et al. (2013). Surge of neurophysiological coherence and connectivity in the dying brain. *Proceedings of the National Academy of Sciences, 110*(35), 14432–14437. doi:10.1073/pnas.1308285110

8. Hill, R. L. (2015). *Psychology and the near-death experience: Searching for God.* United States: White Crow Books.

**Individual NDE Accounts:

Near-Death Experience Research Foundation. (2016, January 7). Current NDERF near-death experiences. Retrieved October 29, 2016, from NDERF, http://www.nderf.org/NDERF/NDE_Archives/NDERF_NDEs.htm

CHAPTER EIGHT

1. Long, J. (2010). *Evidence of the afterlife: The science of near-death experiences.* New York: Harper Collins.

2. Kurian, G. T., & Johnson, T. M. (2001). *The world Christian Encyclopedia: A comparative survey of churches and religions in the modern world* (2nd ed.). New York: Oxford University Press, 2001-.

3. Pew Research Center. (2015, May 12). America's changing religious landscape. Retrieved October 30, 2016, from Pew Research Center, http://www.pewforum.org/2015/05/12/americas-changing-religious-landscape/

4. Leloup, J.-Y., (1986). *The gospel of Thomas: The gnostic wisdom of Jesus.* Rochester, VT: Inner Traditions Bear and Company, (pp. 75, 148, 156, 120).

5. Miller, C. (Ed.). (1996). *The book of Jesus: A treasury of the greatest stories and writings about Christ.* New York: Simon & Schuster, (pp. 178-179).

6. Merritt, J. (2012). *A faith of our own: Following Jesus beyond the culture wars.* New York: Grand Central Pub, (p. 126).

7. Putman, R. (2000). *Bowling alone: The collapse and revival of American community.* New York: Simon and Schuster Paperbacks, (p. 67).

8. National Humanities Center. Religion in the civil war: The southern perspective, divining America, TeacherServe©, national humanities center. Retrieved November 11, 2015, from TeacherServe, http://nationalhumanitiescenter.org/tserve/nineteen/nkeyinfo/cwsouth.htm

9. Long, J. (2010). *Evidence of the afterlife: The science of near-death experiences.* New York: Harper Collins.

10. Needleman, J. (2003). *Lost Christianity: A journey of rediscovery.* New York: Jeremy P. Tarcher/Penguin, (pp. 25-26).

11. Storm, H. (2005). *My descent into death: A second chance at life.* New York: The Doubleday Religious Publishing Group, (p. 73).

**Individual NDE Accounts:

Near-Death Experience Research Foundation. (2016, January 7). Current NDERF near-death experiences. Retrieved October 29, 2016, from NDERF, http://www.nderf.org/NDERF/NDE_Archives/NDERF_NDEs.htm

CHAPTER NINE

1. Gulley, P. (2011). *The evolution of faith: How God is creating a better Christianity.* New York: HarperCollins Publishers, (pp. 138, 137, 145, 146).

2. Julian of Norwich (1978). *Julian of Norwich: Showings* (Classics of Western Spirituality ed.). Mahwah, NJ: Paulist Press, (pp. 198, 237, 225, 242, 259, 262, 217, 210, 227).

3. Tolstoy, L. (2006). *Leo Tolstoy: Spiritual writings.* Columbia, SC, United States: Orbis Books (USA), (pp. 60, 58).

4. Leloup, J.-Y., Rowe, J., & Needleman, J. (2002). *The gospel of Mary Magdalene.* Rochester, VT: Inner Traditions Bear and Company, (p. 25).

5. Eadie, B. J. (1992). *Embraced by the light.* Placerville, CA: Gold Leaf Press (MI), (pp. 116, 85).

6. Ehrman, B. D. (2003). *Lost scriptures: Books that did not make it into the new testament.* Oxford: Oxford University Press, (p. 182).

7. Storm, H. (2005). *My descent into death: A second chance at life.* New York: The Doubleday Religious Publishing Group, (pp. 74-75, 76).

8. Hill, R. L. (2015). *Psychology and the near-death experience: Searching for God.* United States: White Crow Books.

9. Richie, G. (1978). *Return from tomorrow.* Grand Rapids, Revel Books, (pp. 65-67).

10. Leloup, J.-Y., English, J. R., & Needleman, J. (2004). *The gospel of Philip: Jesus, Mary Magdalene, and the gnosis of sacred union.* Rochester, VT: Inner Traditions Bear and Company (pp. 85, 79, 109).

**Individual NDE Accounts:

Near-Death Experience Research Foundation. (2016, January 7). Current NDERF near-death experiences. Retrieved October 29, 2016, from NDERF, http://www.nderf.org/NDERF/NDE_Archives/NDERF_NDEs.htm

CHAPTER TEN

1. Leloup, J.-Y., English, J. R., & Needleman, J. (2004). *The gospel of Philip: Jesus, Mary Magdalene, and the gnosis of sacred union.* Rochester, VT: Inner Traditions Bear and Company (pp. 95, 109).

2. Leloup, J.-Y., (1986). *The gospel of Thomas: The gnostic wisdom of Jesus.* Rochester, VT: Inner Traditions Bear and Company, (pp. 174, 120, 177).

3. Milliman, S. (2016). *A Song in the Wind: A Near Death Experience.* Westbow Press.

Paperbacks also available from
White Crow Books

Elsa Barker—*Letters from a Living Dead Man*
ISBN 978-1-907355-83-7

Elsa Barker—*War Letters from the Living Dead Man*
ISBN 978-1-907355-85-1

Elsa Barker—*Last Letters from the Living Dead Man*
ISBN 978-1-907355-87-5

Richard Maurice Bucke—
Cosmic Consciousness
ISBN 978-1-907355-10-3

Stafford Betty—
The Imprisoned Splendor
ISBN 978-1-907661-98-3

Stafford Betty—
Heaven and Hell Unveiled: Updates from the World of Spirit.
ISBN 978-1-910121-30-6

Ineke Koedam—
In the Light of Death: Experiences on the threshold between life and death
ISBN 978-1-910121-48-1

Arthur Conan Doyle with Simon Parke—
Conversations with Arthur Conan Doyle
ISBN 978-1-907355-80-6

Meister Eckhart with Simon Parke—
Conversations with Meister Eckhart
ISBN 978-1-907355-18-9

D. D. Home—*Incidents in my Life Part 1*
ISBN 978-1-907355-15-8

Mme. Dunglas Home; edited, with an Introduction, by Sir Arthur Conan Doyle—*D. D. Home: His Life and Mission*
ISBN 978-1-907355-16-5

Edward C. Randall—
Frontiers of the Afterlife
ISBN 978-1-907355-30-1

Rebecca Ruter Springer—
Intra Muros: My Dream of Heaven
ISBN 978-1-907355-11-0

Leo Tolstoy, edited by Simon Parke—*Forbidden Words*
ISBN 978-1-907355-00-4

Erlendur Haraldsson and Loftur Gissurarson—
Indridi Indridason: The Icelandic Physical Medium
ISBN 978-1-910121-50-4

Goerge E. Moss—
Earth's Cosmic Ascendancy: Spirit and Extraterrestrials Guide us through Times of Change
ISBN 978-1-910121-28-3

Steven T. Parsons and Callum E. Cooper—
Paracoustics: Sound & the Paranormal
ISBN 978-1-910121-32-0

L. C. Danby—
The Certainty of Eternity: The Story of Australia's Greatest Medium
ISBN 978-1-910121-34-4

Madelaine Lawrence —
The Death View Revolution: A Guide to Transpersonal Experiences Surrounding Death
ISBN 978-1-910121-37-5

Zofia Weaver—
Other Realities?: The enigma of Franek Kluski's mediumship
ISBN 978-1-910121-39-9

Roy L. Hill—
Psychology and the Near-Death Experience: Searching for God
ISBN 978-1-910121-42-9

Tricia. J. Robertson —
"Things You Can do When You're Dead!: True Accounts of After Death Communication"
ISBN 978-1-908733-60-3

Tricia. J. Robertson —
More Things you Can do When You're Dead: What Can You Truly Believe?
ISBN 978-1-910121-44-3

Jody Long—
God's Fingerprints: Impressions of Near-Death Experiences
ISBN 978-1-910121-05-4

Leo Tolstoy with Simon Parke—
Conversations with Tolstoy
ISBN 978-1-907355-25-7

Howard Williams with an Introduction by Leo Tolstoy—*The Ethics of Diet: An Anthology of Vegetarian Thought*
ISBN 978-1-907355-21-9

Vincent Van Gogh with Simon Parke—*Conversations with Van Gogh*
ISBN 978-1-907355-95-0

Wolfgang Amadeus Mozart with Simon Parke—*Conversations with Mozart*
ISBN 978-1-907661-38-9

Jesus of Nazareth with Simon Parke—*Conversations with Jesus of Nazareth*
ISBN 978-1-907661-41-9

Thomas à Kempis with Simon Parke—*The Imitation of Christ*
ISBN 978-1-907661-58-7

Julian of Norwich with Simon Parke—*Revelations of Divine Love*
ISBN 978-1-907661-88-4

Allan Kardec—*The Spirits Book*
ISBN 978-1-907355-98-1

Allan Kardec—*The Book on Mediums*
ISBN 978-1-907661-75-4

Emanuel Swedenborg—*Heaven and Hell*
ISBN 978-1-907661-55-6

P.D. Ouspensky—*Tertium Organum: The Third Canon of Thought*
ISBN 978-1-907661-47-1

Dwight Goddard—*A Buddhist Bible*
ISBN 978-1-907661-44-0

Michael Tymn—*The Afterlife Revealed*
ISBN 978-1-970661-90-7

Michael Tymn—*Transcending the Titanic: Beyond Death's Door*
ISBN 978-1-908733-02-3

Guy L. Playfair—*If This Be Magic*
ISBN 978-1-907661-84-6

Guy L. Playfair—*The Flying Cow*
ISBN 978-1-907661-94-5

Guy L. Playfair —*This House is Haunted: The True Story of the Enfield Poltergeist*
ISBN 978-1-907661-78-5

Carl Wickland, M.D.—*Thirty Years Among the Dead*
ISBN 978-1-907661-72-3

John E. Mack—*Passport to the Cosmos*
ISBN 978-1-907661-81-5

Peter & Elizabeth Fenwick—*The Truth in the Light*
ISBN 978-1-908733-08-5

Erlendur Haraldsson— *Modern Miracles*
ISBN 978-1-908733-25-2

Erlendur Haraldsson— *At the Hour of Death*
ISBN 978-1-908733-27-6

Erlendur Haraldsson—*The Departed Among the Living*
ISBN 978-1-908733-29-0

Brian Inglis—*Science and Parascience*
ISBN 978-1-908733-18-4

Brian Inglis—*Natural and Supernatural: A History of the Paranormal*
ISBN 978-1-908733-20-7

Ernest Holmes—*The Science of Mind*
ISBN 978-1-908733-10-8

Victor & Wendy Zammit —*A Lawyer Presents the Evidence For the Afterlife*
ISBN 978-1-908733-22-1

Casper S. Yost—*Patience Worth: A Psychic Mystery*
ISBN 978-1-908733-06-1

William Usborne Moore—*Glimpses of the Next State*
ISBN 978-1-907661-01-3

William Usborne Moore—*The Voices*
ISBN 978-1-908733-04-7

John W. White—*The Highest State of Consciousness*
ISBN 978-1-908733-31-3

Lord Dowding—*Many Mansions*
ISBN 978-1-910121-07-8

Paul Pearsall, Ph.D. —*Super Joy*
ISBN 978-1-908733-16-0

All titles available as eBooks, and selected titles available in Hardback and Audiobook formats from www.whitecrowbooks.com

CPSIA information can be obtained
at www.ICGtesting.com
Printed in the USA
BVHW080652140220
572296BV00003B/268